Faith, Reason, and Economics

For Woody Milroy —
with gratitude & esteem
Anthony Walmans

Faith, Reason, and Economics

Essays in Honour of Anthony Waterman

Edited by Derek Hum

ST. JOHN'S COLLEGE PRESS
UNIVERSITY OF MANITOBA

St. John's College Press
92 Dysart Road
The University of Manitoba
Winnipeg, Manitoba, R3T 2M5

Printed in Canada.

National Library of Canada Cataloguing in Publication Data

Main entry under title:

Faith, reason, and economics : essays in honour of Anthony Waterman / edited by Derek Hum.

  Includes bibliographical references.
  ISBN 0-920291-25-2

  1. Economics. 2. Humanities. I. Hum, Derek, 1944-
II. Waterman, A. M. C. (Anthony Michael Charles), 1931-
HB.F34 2003   330   C2002-911526-4

Contents

Contents

Preface

I distinctly remember the first time I laid eyes on Anthony Waterman. I had accepted a sessional teaching post at the University of Manitoba with the promise that the appointment would be converted to a tenure track one when I completed my doctorate. Upon arrival in Winnipeg, I was informed that the department head who offered me the position had resigned, and that Anthony Waterman was now acting head. Wondering whether my appointment might have occasioned the departure of the former head, I was naturally apprehensive when I first encountered Anthony in the hallway as he was rushing off to some important meeting, undoubtedly to plot some strategy by which my probationary position might be abrogated. Anthony's only words to me on that occasion were something to the effect: "Welcome to the department, Hum." It was only much later that I learned that Anthony addressed most people by their surnames until such time as he believed a relationship was well enough established for informality.

Some thirty years later, I happened to be in conversation with Wayne Simpson, the current department head, about university matters in general, but especially the elimination of mandatory retirement and speculating about which of our colleagues might now decide to stay on, and what effect individual decisions might have on our department. We readily agreed that Anthony's departure would be a great loss, and all were relieved when he decided to continue in the department, albeit on a reduced load basis. But without an official retirement, there would be no occasion to honour Anthony in a customary fashion, such as a *Festschrift*, but Wayne suggested that I undertake such an enterprise anyway. Thus, the idea of this volume was born, and I have enjoyed every minute of this undertaking.

This volume would not have been possible without the kind and enthusiastic response of the many contributors. I owe an immense debt to them for their enthusiasm, encouragement, cooperation, and, it must be added, their forbearance. It is their reflections and scholarship that make this collection of essays so valuable. Not only are the words and phrases unique to the individual essayists but also the style of each contribution, as I tried to respect the conventions of each individual's professional practice and preference. For this reason, the essays in this volume vary somewhat in style and presentation; some have figures, others employ mathematical equations or Greek, or appendices. Despite my general plea to refrain from footnotes or endnotes of any kind, not all contributors felt comfortable with these restrictions. Thus, each essayist was left to shape his or her own contribution according to their own judgement. Consequently, some contributors have used footnotes sparingly and other more liberally, depending upon situation and practice. The sole exception is Lawrence Ritchey, who employed neither footnotes nor endnotes—just some quarter notes and half notes.

I am also extremely grateful for the encouragement and financial support for this project from many quarters, including St. John's College, the Department of Economics, the Institute of Humanities, the Office of the Dean of Arts, and the Office of the Vice-President (Research). Several of Anthony's colleagues and students also contributed financial support and remain anonymous. My task as volume editor was immeasurably lightened by the editorial management of Carol Dahlstrom, who guided me through all the intricacies of publication. The cover design was expertly executed by Karen Armstrong, and line drawings are rendered compliments of Blendmedia Group, Inc. I also owe a debt to David Carr, director of University of Manitoba Press, for his guidance and advice. Finally, I wish to acknowledge the administrative support given me for this editorial project during my sabbatical leave at the Melbourne Institute of Applied Economic and Social Research, and University College, Melbourne University, Australia, and the Zentrum für Kanada-Studien, University of Trier, Germany.

Introduction: A.M.C. Waterman, A Faith Full Economist

Derek Hum

Faith, reason, and economics—three simple words that nicely encapsulate Anthony Waterman's life and aptly describe the basis of his ongoing relationship with his many friends, students, and colleagues.

Anthony Michael Charles Waterman was born on 4 June 1931 in Southampton, England, and received his education from the age of ten at King Edward VI School. He proceeded to Selwyn College at Cambridge and went down with very good results in the Economic Tripos. His tutor was the colourful and strong-minded Joan Robinson. Whilst during this period at Cambridge, Anthony also contributed military service as a lieutenant in the Queen's Own Dorset Yeomanry. Having had just enough of both university and the military for the time being, Anthony next sought his fortune in the real world and, like many Englishmen, made his way to the colonies; for Anthony, it was to be Canada. He found employment as an auditor with a firm of chartered accountants in Sarnia, and then as an economic analyst with Canadian Industries Limited (CIL) in Montreal, becoming fluently unilingual. Five years of business employment was apparently enough to persuade Anthony to enter St. John's College for the next three years, where he took a degree in theology in 1962. He was ordained as a priest in 1963, in the Diocese of Rupert's Land, and served as assistant curate, All Saints' Church in Winnipeg from 1962 to 1964. A second epiphany of sorts must have also occurred during this period, for it was in 1964 that Anthony became a Canadian citizen, just in time, it would appear, to protect him from imagined dangers of venturing "down under" to the Australian National University, where he read economics history and earned his doctorate. His supervisors were Noel Butlin and Trevor Swan.

The year was 1967. Canada celebrated its centenary and was now a country deemed to have a decently long enough history worth considering, and Anthony returned to Canada to teach economics at St. John's College and the University of Manitoba, where he has remained since. He became professor of economics in 1972 and was head of the Department of Economics from 1972 until 1976, a year during which he was also priest-in-charge, St. Michael and All Angels Church, Winnipeg.

Anthony's passages through the academic community and the church, as well as the military and business worlds, are more than slightly tinged with the requirements of either faith or reason, or both. How each individual resolves the matter of faith and reason is an unique personal journey. That Anthony is able to do so, and to combine a life of scholarship with Christian service is exemplary, and his example affords hope and guidance to all his friends, colleagues, and past parishioners. Economists need no reminding that, whatever the complementary nature of differing interests, the scarce resources of energy and effort must be wisely allocated to competing ends. Consequently, no longer able to sustain the mounting demands on his time and attention, Anthony resigned his orders in 1982 to devote full time to academic scholarship. Nonetheless, it is fair to say that, to this day, Anthony Waterman continues to speak to laity and layman alike—often together from a single text—constructing his arguments with military precision, with the right blend of faith and reason, and the necessary grace, rigour, and civility as the occasion exactly demands.

The beginnings of Anthony Waterman's career as an economic scholar is atypical. After his early time at Cambridge, and a brief experience with both the military and the world of commerce, Anthony succeeded in obtaining further degrees, first in theology and then in economics. Having narrowed his life pursuits to these two, Anthony continued to travel both paths simultaneously. He tutored in theology in Canberra in 1965 and lectured in theology at St. John's College in 1975–76 and 1988, even after becoming a full professor in economics at the University of Manitoba in 1972, and head of the Department of Economics.

Interestingly, Anthony's first refereed journal article was not in economics at all. His article in 1965 in the *Canadian Journal of Theology* entitled "The Lord's Day Act in a Secular Society: A Historical Comment on the Canadian Lord's Day Act of 1906" won first prize in a half-centennial essay competition. Here, there is already the hint of a mind eager to blend the concerns of faith with the more secular issues of public policy, and to frame the subject in its proper historical circumstances. This long road travelled over the years is marked in 1992 by another significant signpost when Anthony's *Revolution, Economics and Religion: Christian Political Economy, 1798–1833* was awarded the Morris Forkosch prize for the best book in intellectual history by the *Journal of the History of Ideas*. In the discipline of modern economics, Anthony has apparently found a comfortable home both for affirming faith and for applying reason.

Anthony's career as an academic economist, however, began in a rather conventional fashion. His first major work was *Economic Fluctuations in Australia, 1945–1964,* published in 1972 by the Australian National University Press. He also published research in macroeconomics having to do with inflation, economic growth, and stabilization policy. His choice of topics and writings began to stray from the traditional economic subjects and, by the early 1980s, the blend of economics with the concerns of theological questions was clearly visible. His article in *Canadian Public Policy* in 1983, "The Catholic Bishops and Canadian Public Policy," revealed that Anthony was uniquely qualified and immensely interested in combining scholarship on matters of faith, reason, and economics. And so he has, ever since, but focussing closely on a time in history when scholars and society made much less of any division between religious and secular discourse, just as did Malthus, whose writings and ideas eventually became one of Anthony's enduring scholarly passions.

Anthony's first scholarly piece to mention Malthus directly in its title also appeared in 1983—the year he published his paper on the Catholic bishops and their proclamations on public policy. The article was entitled "Malthus as a Theologian: The *First Essay* and the Relation between Political Economy and Christian Theology." There have since been many other scholarly contributions by Anthony on the subject of Malthus; such is the volume and quality of these pieces that Anthony is now firmly acknowledged as one of the world's leading authorities on Malthus. Again interesting might be the observation that Anthony's 1998 article in the *History of Political Economy* has the title "Reappraisal of 'Malthus the Economist,' 1933–97." Malthus has now been labelled and examined by Anthony both as a theologian and as an economist. Much like his subject of interest, then, Anthony can also be placed as a scholar of faith and reason. And further evidence will undoubtedly be before us, as Anthony finishes his *Reconstruction of Malthusian Political Economy* (in progress) for Cambridge University Press.

The authoritative *Oxford Dictionary* describes a *Festschrift* as a collection of writings forming a volume presented to a scholar or savant on the occasion of his attaining a certain age or period in his career. Despite being Cambridge-educated, Anthony Waterman can have no quarrel with this Oxonian description. Anthony has reached a certain stage in his career (I don't know how I should describe this stage, but certainly not the last of Shakespeare's Seven Ages of Man). Nonetheless, Anthony has reached the point where, at the University of Manitoba, he must accept what is known as "mandatory reduction of load." In Anthony's case, this simply means more time to devote to his research and writing and slightly less to teaching and university administration. It is fitting that so many individual acquaintances of Anthony's—former students, friends, colleagues, and fellow scholars—should be brought together to acknowledge his influence and achievement. The essays collected here are exceptionally erudite, wide ranging, and readable; their quality testifies to Anthony's own high standards, and they are a fitting tribute to an interesting career and unusual person.

A t times, essays in a collection serendipitously centre on a single theme, thereby conveying a sense of coherence and consistency. This fact might either reflect the limited talents of the editor selecting the contributors, or worse, the narrow circle of colleagues of the person in whose honour the *Festschrift* is held. The second of these alternatives may be safely dismissed as nonsense. The range of Anthony's interests, and *a fortiori*, his group of friends, correspondents, and colleagues is truly wide ranging—from church doctrine, music, intellectual history, literature, and, of course, political economy in that nice—meaning exact—sense of the term. The catholicity of Anthony's interests is accordingly reflected in this collection. Therefore, it would be extremely foolhardy on my part to attempt any connecting narrative for the essays that follow. The essays stand on their own individually; yet as a collection, they truly reflect Anthony's tastes, interests and even passions. More delightful as introduction, perhaps, might be some account of the relationship that each individual author enjoys with respect to Anthony, as well as some ferreting out of some lesser known connections among them.

The person with the longest acquaintance with Anthony might be Murdith McLean, former warden of St. John's College, who first met Anthony when they were undergraduates in theology. Murdith was a year behind Anthony, but they both soon found delight in each other with vigorous debate and a shared taste in music. Murdith was a member of a small madrigal group that Anthony formed. Anthony and his wife, Margaret, even played host and chaperon when Murdith's then fiancée, Lynn, came to visit in 1961. The bonds between Anthony and Murdith over the years have been through music and the church rather than economics. Anthony's relationship with Lawrence Ritchey is also through music rather than economics. I am especially grateful for Lawrence's agreeing to my request for a musical contribution, thereby making this (I believe) the first ever volume of essays honouring an economist to include an original madrigal composition. Lawrence is director of music at St. John's Anglican Cathedral as well as a fellow of St. John's College.

Indeed, St. John's College is the hub or centre of gravity for much of Anthony's contacts, intellectual as well as social. Mary Kinnear, a distinguished historian, is a frequent companion to Anthony at lunch, where they often exchange views on Anthony's most recent outlandish opinion of the day. John Wortley, an historian, also shares with Anthony a love of music, a connection to St. John's College, and a similar personal history of being originally from Britain, and also an Anglican cleric who sought sanctuary in the university. Evelyn Forget, also now at St. John's College, was formerly Anthony's colleague in the Department of Economics, specializing in the history of thought and whose economic scholarship most closely aligns with Anthony's interest in Malthus. All of these individuals have a connection to St. John's College in some way, and at some time or another, so it is not surprising to discover close associations among this group of contributors.

Geoff Brennan has known Anthony from their time at the Australian National University, where Anthony earned his doctorate, and they have been close friends and colleagues since, visiting each other often, either in Canada or Australia. The Dows (Sheila and Alexander) were once in Canada, both studying economics in Winnipeg, and Alexander, too, was based for a short time at St. John's College as a junior fellow while studying for his doctorate. Ross Emmett was associated with St. John's College, while completing his doctoral dissertation under Anthony's supervision. Warren Samuels, Samuel Hollander, Walter and Shelagh Eltis, and Paul Samuelson are all acquainted with Anthony, initially through his research writings and correspondence, and then eventually through meeting at conference gatherings and having academic visits with each other. The degree of connection among some is sometimes bewilderingly close as well as complex; for example, Warren Samuels was asked by Anthony to be the outside examiner for Ross Emmett's doctoral dissertation. And who can forget the published intellectual exchanges between Hollander and Samuelson on the classical canonical model? Knud Haakonssen is a dear friend of Anthony's, sharing an intellectual interest in the philosophy of the nineteenth century, as does Jonathan Clark, in the history of this period. Jonathan Clark visited Manitoba at Anthony's invitation, when Anthony was director of the Institute for the Humanities.

If Murdith McLean has the longest standing acquaintance with Anthony, Nancy Folbre's is perhaps the most recent. Nancy Folbre first encountered Anthony when she visited Manitoba (some time in the mid-1990s) to give a lecture about whether or not a feminist perspective has anything unique to offer to the study of economics. (It is my recollection that Anthony was sceptical.) The sharp questioning of her position by Anthony on this occasion, and during subsequent correspondence and conference meetings, led both to a deep mutual appreciation for the quality of each other's mind, and they have become good friends since.

Though not a contributing essayist, I shall invoke editorial prerogative and record my own relationship with Anthony. Set against Anthony's many life-long friends and colleagues, I appear *in medias res* in the Waterman chronicles. My association dates from my arrival in Winnipeg to join the Department of Economics for what was intended to be a brief two-year stint. Clarence Barber was department head when I was hired in spring of 1972, though, when I arrived in the fall of that year, Anthony had just taken on the headship. The next summer, my wife and I visited Anthony and Margaret at their cottage in Sarnia, Ontario, and the four of us attended the Stratford Festival together, picnicking and discussing Shakespeare. But what I recall most vividly is the agreeable conversation that Anthony and I had during one long evening at their cottage, after our wives had retired for the evening. We argued at length about whether the basis for faith was different in kind rather than degree from the basis for reason, and whether propositions in ethics could ever be likened to epistemological ones. (I had not even heard of Thomas Chalmers then.) Perhaps it was because I was too recent an arrival in the department, but I was struck by the fact that we did not discuss anything having to do with economics or departmental business at all. Rather, our discussions were all about—faith and reason. In retrospect, I may have subconsciously decided at that very point that this would be an interesting place to stay and work, and that collegial exchanges would be anything but narrow with Anthony. We have been colleagues in the department and friends at St. John's College ever since. I also enjoy a collegial relationship with Mary Kinnear, Murdith McLean, and Lawrence Ritchey at St. John's. Evelyn Forget is a past departmental and current college colleague. Sheila Dow was briefly my research assistant; Ross Emmett studied microeconomic theory with me during his doctorial course work and I, much, much earlier, read economic theory with Walter Eltis as my tutor at Oxford. I am acquainted with almost all the essayists in the volume, and admire them all for their scholarship and cooperation.

A nthony is a small *c* liberal in the nineteenth-century meaning of that term, but a capital *C* contrarian in most political and economic discussions about modern fashions. Not surprisingly, conversation at daily lunch table in St. John's College with Anthony in attendance is seldom boring. Anthony enjoys invigorating fast-paced walks, challenging arguments, Jane Austen, and singing English madrigals. He is also partial to the taste of roast beef unmasked by condiments, a strong Stilton, Margaret's trifle, and a dry sherry. For Anthony, an ideal evening at home would be one accompanied by fine wine and a hand of bridge while listening to Bach—after a full day's reading and contemplating the wisdom—and necessary amendments, of course, to Thomas Malthus.

Conservatism as a Political Philosophy:
An Economist's Approach

Geoffrey Brennan and Alan Hamlin

Among Anthony Waterman's many distinctive characteristics, his occasional self-identification as a High Tory is one of the more notable. It is notable, first, for its anachronism. Originally, as we understand it, the Tories were those who supported James II against the "glorious revolution." Through the eighteenth and early nineteenth centuries, the term came to refer to those who supported the established church and the political authority of the aristocracy. In Anthony's case, the principal element of the High Tory program seems to revolve around the integration of church and state within a Christian society—an integration that he concedes is now almost certainly infeasible, however desirable it may be in principle and may once have been in practice. Although the contemporary British Conservative Party still sails under the Tory banner, the policy positions of that party do not include anything that remotely connects with the Waterman church-state integrationist ambition. Simply put, to identify as a High Tory is to embrace a category that has no modern equivalent.

The identification is also notable for its disciplinary eccentricity. Those economists (few perhaps) who would see any relevance in such categories at all would, we suspect, be more likely to identify with the Tories' natural enemies, the "Old Whigs," as Friedrich Hayek did in his famous essay, "Why I am Not a Conservative.". It has generally seemed to economists that the Whigs were those who best understood the virtues of the free-market order. And economists since Adam Smith have been inclined to identify more readily with those who understood and supported the market order. Or, if they did not, the opposition was not likely to be along Tory lines.

Now, we are not entirely clear on what grounds Anthony might seek to defend his Tory affections, or even if he would think that any such grounds are

Faith, Reason, and Economics: Essays in Honour of Anthony Waterman. Ed. Derek Hum. Winnipeg: St. John's College Press, 2003.

necessary. Perhaps "affections" are simply to be *declared*. Nor are we convinced that there is any necessary connection between the sorts of considerations that are relevant to Anthony's position and those that we will invoke in the argument about conservatism more generally that follows. There is, however, a traditional association between Toryism and conservatism. And, in bringing to bear what are essentially economist's lines of reasoning in explicating and partially defending one version of conservatism, it may well be that we will create some analytic space in which Anthony himself might be happy to stand.

In any event, we want to take the opportunity that this occasion provides to explore the relation between economics and "conservatism," with the latter term understood in a fairly straightforward—if not necessarily standard—way. We begin by stating what we understand to be the core commitments of conservatism and then briefly defend that understanding against the charge of misrepresentation. We then turn to the question of how conservatism so understood connects with various themes in economics, and how a defence of conservatism as a political philosophy along economistic lines might be developed.

WILL THE REAL CONSERVATISM PLEASE STAND UP?

As everyone who writes on conservatism concedes, defining what precisely is to be discussed is a genuine difficulty. Indeed, at least some self-identifying conservatives seem to think that any attempt to uncover a "definition"—at least a definition that would make conservatism amenable to the kind of analysis that is, say, characteristic of modern political philosophy—would itself be a mistake. The thought is that the very methods of analysis that require clear definitions misunderstand the nature of conservatism. Conservatives in this tradition are inclined to speak of a conservative "sentiment" or a conservative "disposition," but to reject talk of a conservative "political philosophy." They seem to be concerned that such talk is excessively hospitable to a kind of foundationalism that they expressly reject.

The tradition is mixed here. There are some writers in the conservative tradition who have seemed to take this ostensibly anti-analytic line: Edmond Burke most notably, and possibly Michael Oakeshott.[1] But there are others—of which Hume and Hayek are the most notable examples, the latter's protestations to the contrary notwithstanding—whose style of reasoning is wholly hospitable to more systematic, not to say rigorous, treatment.

In any event, it should be clear that to pursue the kind of enterprise that we have in mind—to analyze the intellectual connections, if any, between economics and conservatism—requires a more analytically explicit approach. And this requires in turn that conservatism itself be rendered in broad abstract terms. Quite apart from any other consideration, we are economists, and, for us, intellectual activity is to be understood as the application of logical reasoning to clearly stated premises. If there are problems with this approach, then we assume

8

that they can be exposed in terms of that same method of analysis. (We hint toward the end of this essay why there might be problems of this kind.)

Moreover, even if there *are* "costs" associated with the method, there are also some benefits. In particular, it is striking that conservatism does not seem to receive much treatment within standard political philosophy. Contemporary political philosophy does not seem to take the claims of conservatism very seriously. It is recognized (by friend and foe alike) that conservatism is not like most other political philosophies in that it fails to lay down an end that political institutions are supposed to serve. Hayek, for example, refers to conservatism as involving a different "dimension" in the ideological map, though he does not fully exploit that thought. But, for many scholars, conservatism is seen to be more a "mystique" than a well-defined political philosophy—to be intrinsically inhospitable to systematic treatment—and the comments of some of conservatism's putative defenders often promote exactly that view. That is a loss, in our judgement, and one that in a modest way the present effort may help to remedy.

The problem of defining conservatism is hardly assisted by the fact that the term is so indiscriminately applied in contemporary discourse. This is a fact that almost every commentator on conservatism notes and laments. Hayek did so in his 1960 essay, and the situation can hardly be said to have improved since that time. Jerry Muller, in the excellent introduction to his recent anthology, notes that we live "at a time when the label 'conservative' is promiscuously applied to fundamentalists, populists, libertarians, fascists, and the advocates of one or another orthodoxy." Yet, as he insists that his anthology shows, "there is an identifiable constellation of shared commitments, predispositions, arguments, metaphors, and substantive commitments, which taken together form a distinctive conservative pattern of social and political analysis" (xiii).

Much ideological debate, both in the practice of politics and in press commentary, is irreducibly bipolar. Politics, especially in two-party systems, is often rendered as *basically* a matter of contestation along a simple "left-right" spectrum. Though everyone probably accepts that, in principle, things are more complicated than this, there is often, nevertheless, a remarkable conflation of very different positions so as to accommodate that bipolar view. Thus, the term *conservative* has come to mean *of the right* in most quarters—and that means, in turn, anything that is not *of the left*. Political parties that bear the name *Conservative* are often to be found implementing policies that are extremely radical by any reckoning and defending those policies in terms of a rhetoric that is simply unrecognizable as "conservative" in any plausible sense.[2]

Both the policy choices and the rhetorical slipperiness can, of course, be *explained*. Arguably, policy choices represent the forces of electoral competition, to be analyzed with the aid of modern "public choice" theory (see Mueller, for example). And, for the past century, classical liberals and genuine conservatives have been engaged in a marriage of convenience to combat, as they saw it,

9

the common enemy of collectivism. That marriage involved a lot of papering over the cracks. And the "papering over" had a clear rhetorical dimension. Developing a rhetoric that made little of the differences between classical liberal and conservative—and made much of the evil of the common enemy— had special value. We are the inheritors of that rhetorical tradition. It is therefore hardly to be wondered at if, a century later, the parties to the marriage are not exactly sure where their separate identities lie. So much is clear. However, such *explanation* only serves to alert us to the difficulties. If we want to understand the nature of conservatism, as distinct from, say, classical liberalism or populism or fascism or any of the other "isms" with which conservatism is nowadays often confused, we are not likely to get much help from the politicians!

In the face of that terminological mare's nest, it is perhaps tempting to retreat to anachronistic categories. Hayek does this when he identifies himself as an Old Whig. And we conjecture that Waterman does something of the same, and in similar spirit, when he identifies himself as a High Tory. We do not follow that path. Rather, we retain the term *conservative* both because it has a common descriptive meaning that we think is useful and because we wish to dissociate conservatism as a political philosophy from any particular historical or locational setting. We do not think the term *Tory* would help in this latter respect.

Let us then come to substance. We take it that a defining feature of conservatism is adherence to the proposition that the status quo has normative authority by virtue of being the status quo. We defend that proposition as a definition only as a rough approximation to what many conservatives have thought, and we do not necessarily suppose that they have articulated their position in these terms. The "definition" is, like all the basic premises of economic theory, an abstraction. But we think it comes quite close to capturing what is an essential feature of conservatism as we read it. And it is a feature that connects most readily to a theme in economics: ethics.

TAKING FEASIBILITY SERIOUSLY:
THE ECONOMIST'S APPROACH TO ETHICS

It is a characteristic feature of the "economic" approach to ethical questions that we "take feasibility seriously." In this respect, our approach is borrowed from an analogy with individual consumer choice. Just as the consumer is conceptualized to make his or her choices by confronting her consumption possibilities with her preferences, so the "ethical chooser" is conceptualized as confronting the set of feasible social options with the ethical norms that specify what is ethically desirable. Ethics on this reading is a confrontation of the feasible with the desirable.

The context within which this method is frequently applied within economics involves the "choice" of a particular policy among a set of possible options.

10

The normative framework that is used is usually one in which the consequences of the various policies on offer for various "economic goals" are assessed and policies ranked on that basis. Understanding the consequences of particular policies is clearly a crucial piece of this method—and such understanding depends on the application of economic theorizing to inform the policy chooser how the economic order works. Proper normative theorizing, on this view, necessarily incorporates prior "positive" theorizing. In fact, most economists are inclined to side with Milton Friedman when he conjectures that most disagreements over policy issues reflect not so much differences in fundamental values as differences in beliefs about how the world works.[3]

There are lots of special features of this particular formulation of ethical deliberation: the idea that policies, rather than, say, individual actions or more abstract institutions, that are the objects of normative evaluation; the assumption that evaluation is exclusively consequential in character; the particular quasi-utilitarian conception of desirability; and so on. All of these aspects can be questioned and possibly modified. But the essential *scarcity* that reality imposes on ethical choice cannot. That scarcity is for economists a brutal fact about the world. And we think it to be an unexceptional fact. If there is anything at all to the idea of social science, it is the idea that not everything is possible. Every action always implies some alternative action foregone. And every action will have implications for (some) other actions, rendering some impossible perhaps, and some others more or less likely. Understanding those implications—understanding the ethical value of the actions/options not chosen, what we would call the "ethical opportunity cost"—is, the economist insists, a necessary part of proper normative theorizing.

Accordingly, within the domain of political philosophy, economists naturally seek an application of this feasibility-grounded normative structure in the political domain. In saying this, we are taking it that the ultimate role of "political philosophy" is to assess the normative properties of alternative political institutions, and of alternative actions taken within various possible institutional settings. The object is to help provide answers to questions like How should I vote? Is democracy better than autocracy? What policies should be introduced? Is bicameralism better than unicameralism? And so on. In answering those questions, one needs a clear sense of the content of "desirability." But it is by no means sufficient. It is not enough to know, for example, what justice requires. We need to know also whether justice is feasible, for if justice, under the stipulated definition, is *not* feasibe—perhaps because there are no known institutional arrangements that will ensure that justice so defined is achieved—then telling us what justice requires tells us nothing that is of any use! It is a little like saying that we would all be better off if food cost nothing to produce—which may be true but is not particularly helpful.

In case this is thought to be a specious objection, a simple example might help. Normative tax theory lays down the stipulation that taxes should be "horizontally equitable," that is, understood to require that equals should be treated equally under the tax law. A lot of energy in the literature has been expended in trying to define the basis on which equals are to be understood: on the basis of equal consumption, or income, or wealth; whether annual or lifetime magnitudes; and so on. And plenty of attention, too, has been lavished on the question of how "equal treatment" is to be understood, whether by imposing: identical tax payments; identical payments inclusive of compliance costs; or identical tax payments plus "excess burdens." But suppose all these questions were answered. One thing we know is that no known tax system could ever achieve that equal-treatment norm, however exactly equal treatment is defined. The real problem is to choose among competing tax systems all of which fail to achieve complete horizontal equity. What we need, therefore, if the idea of horizontal equity is to play any role at all in tax choice, is a measure of the *degree* of horizontal inequity, which we should aim to minimize. One might imagine that such a measure will fall more or less automatically out of the specification of the ideal, but that is not so. Is the degree of horizontal inequity given by the number of persons who are treated unequally, or the sum of the absolute value of the deviation of individual tax payments from the average within the set of "equals," or the variance? In fact, the ranking of tax systems is quite sensitive to which of these options is chosen. And of course we need to know just how much evasion and avoidance are undertaken by different individuals under the different tax options and how much it costs different individuals to comply (to the extent that they do) before any final judgement on this matter can be made.

Even then, of course, there remains the question of whether, once a final determination on this matter were made, the most horizontally equitable tax system would prove politically feasible under prevailing democratic institutions. Perhaps no party will pick it up. Perhaps the party that does is likely to get defeated on that account. If, then, democratic institutions cannot give us the best tax systems, is that a reason to give up on democratic processes?[4] And, if we did, can we really be confident that the dictator empowered to implement the system would do so? Or would not do other things as well that would be highly undesirable?

The force of all these questions is just to emphasize how extensive the "feasibility" aspects of normative analysis extend. And to point out that a feasibility-oriented approach has implications for how we formulate our conception of the "desirable." In particular, we need a formulation that allows us to assess which of various alternatives is best or least bad. Desirability has to be formulated in terms of a ranking or as a function of relevant properties. As John Broome might put it, "goodness" has to be formulated in terms of "betterness."

What economists understand about the world is that life is a matter of making choices among imperfect alternatives. Trade-offs between alternative desirable "goods" are almost invariably required. Something almost invariably needs to be given up to get something else. *And this fact is no less true when the "goods" in question are objects of ethical desirability than when they are goods of a more conventional "economic" kind.*

Economists are inclined to think not just that trade-offs between various desired ends are necessary but also that the implicit value function in terms of which such trade-offs are made is likely to be "convex." By this, we mean that the terms of trade between various desired ends are such that the marginal value of any one end, given that all others are achieved at their current levels, is diminishing. In other words, the "ethical demand curve," which shows the value of any one element of desirability in terms of others foregone, is downward sloping. Consider an example familiar to economists. Suppose a trade-off between full employment and inflation has to be made.[5] Then the thought is that you will be prepared to sacrifice more employment to get a 1-percent reduction in the inflation rate the higher the employment level is, and that this will be the case whatever the precise relative value you place on employment vis-à-vis inflation. Or, to take another example, you will be prepared to trade off more "efficiency" to acquire a given improvement in "equity" the more "efficiency" you have.

Economists think that values are likely to be convex in this sense without much more than instinct as justification. We are just used to thinking that values must be convex because preferences seem to be. We extrapolate, from the kinds of market behaviour that we routinely observe to the domain of ethical desirability, without much further argument. But we could, if we chose, appeal to higher authority. One possible line would be to mobilize the Aristotelian conception of balance between the various "goods," to invoke, that is, the notion of the Aristotelian mean. Another line would be to emphasize that the desirability of social states is not entirely independent of the amount of individual preference-satisfaction those states involve. One does not have to be a simple utilitarian to endorse this claim. Other things may be normatively relevant as well. Nevertheless, to the extent that aggregate preference satisfaction (or weighted preference satisfaction) is a "good," then the overall value function will borrow some of its properties from the preference satisfaction ingredient. If, as economists believe, preference satisfaction is itself convex,[6] then any evaluative scheme that has significant reliance on preference satisfaction will tend to be convex also.

CONSERVATISM AS ANTI-IDEALISM

We want to draw out of the foregoing discussion two particular features of the economist's approach to normative analysis. The first is its anti-idealism. The second is the presumption of convexity in the overall value function. Both of these features, we argue, connect with conservatism. The first connection is fairly direct. The second is more oblique.

13

One familiar form of thinking about "desirability" is in terms of the specification of an ideal. In some cases, the very goal to be pursued implies the ideal form. Egalitarians, for example, are committed to equality. Debates may arise about what exactly it is that should be equalized, but, for any specification of the relevant domain, what is required is clear enough. The relevant magnitudes have to be equal. Now, equality is in itself an on/off matter. A particular case is either an instance of equality—or it is not. And this is how things are with any specification of "desirability" that is constructed from an ideal. The ideal is either achieved or it is not. In lots of cases, achieving the ideal perfectly is not feasible. Or it will turn out on reflection not to have been desirable, because achieving the ideal in one domain will mean too great a sacrifice in some other domain. As the horizontal-equity example shows, what we need is some measure of the objective in question that will enable us to say which of two non-ideal situations is the closer to the ideal in a normatively relevant sense. In some cases, closeness to the ideal will be the natural way to think of the relevant measure. But, in fact, specification of the ideal is neither necessary nor sufficient for such purposes. The lack of sufficiency is obvious. In the egalitarian case, for example, there are many measures of *in*equality, and in a surprising range of cases they will give different answers to policy/institutional design questions. Just specifying the nature of the ideal is not enough.[7]

But neither is the specification of the ideal logically necessary. We might well be able to tell which of two situations is the more desirable in some dimension without any notion of what would be ideal in that dimension. In at least some cases, desirability might be rather like tallness, in the sense that it is possible, perhaps with some difficulty, to determine which of any two persons is the taller without ever having any notion of what it would mean to be "ideally tall."

The general message here is that the economist's approach insists that ideal specification is a logically unnecessary step in the specification of the desirable. And, even where attention to the ideal is psychologically useful, because that is the form in which our ethical intuitions come, it is not enough. In that sense, too much attention to the nature of the ideal may be a snare and a delusion—at least for the kinds of ethical reflection required in political theorizing. In that weak sense, the economic approach is anti-idealist.

This anti-idealism has strong redolence with conservative political philosophy. Conservatives are typically extremely sceptical of all forms of political idealism. They are mistrustful of grand schemes. Many conservatives will claim that their position is precisely *not* an ideological position—that they are committed to no political ends at all. This claim should not be read as the argument that conservatives have no substantive normative commitments. No political philosophy can do entirely without them. But the claim might be read as embodying either (or both) of two other propositions:

A: That what conservatives have in common relates not to common ends but to a common posture toward the various ends that they may have;

B: That the normative commitments that conservatives share are not best thought of as "ends" (or ideal states of the world) but rather as metrics that tell us whether particular changes represent improvement.

Certainly the second of these propositions gives conservatives a common cause with what we have called the "economic approach" to normative analysis. And we later in this essay turn to a further argument that gives the economic approach a conservative cast. But it is useful now in locating conservatism to pursue Proposition A, above, briefly.

In his essay "Why I Am Not a Conservative," Hayek remarks that conservatism occupies a different "dimension" from the standard left/right spectrum. Huntington asserts that conservatism is best thought of as a "positional ideology" or a matter less of the ends to be served and more as a matter of the posture to be taken toward those ends. Suppose we take Hayek's offhand remark about dimensions seriously. Suppose we construct a second "dimension" to the standard ideological map, based not on the end that is to be pursued but on the posture to be taken toward that end. The first dimension in this map indicates the primary goal or aspect with respect to which political institutions or policies are to be assessed. This is standard. So, a libertarian is concerned to promote liberty; an egalitarian to promote equality; a communitarian to promote community (or "fraternity" as it might once have been described); a utilitarian to promote aggregate utility; an economic consequentialist to promote weighted aggregate preference satisfaction; and so on. Some political philosophies might seek to promote some combination of all these goals. In these cases, we would need to know something about the weights that various goals had in the overall "betterness" function and the terms on which they are to be traded off. Obviously, the range of possibilities in this latter family is considerable. But we can finesse the details here because our interest focusses on the second dimension.

We refer to this second dimension as a matter of posture toward the goal to be sought. At issue is a contrast between conservatism and radicalism, or "idealism." In constructing this contrast, it will be helpful to appeal to a simple diagram. Take some goal—egalitarianism, say—and let there be a well-defined metric over alternative states of the world that shows the overall ethical value of that state. For a strict egalitarian, we suppose, only the degree of inequality matters in assessing states of the world. And by assumption we have a measure of inequality that captures everything that is normatively relevant in the right way. We are interested in the *shape* of the value function in assessing ideal versus non-ideal states of the world. The ideal occurs by definition where the value function has its maximum, if that is known. So, consider alternative states of the world that are very close to the ideal state in normative value.

(These states may be similar to one another descriptively, but they need not be. The mapping from social states to value might have certain discontinuities, or apparent discontinuities.[8]) Here are two general pictures. One picture is of a smoothly increasing function the slope of which gradually declines in absolute value as the ideal is approached, so that the ideal is at the peak of a convex hill. We depict this in Fig. 1a. The alternative is that in which the ideal has special value very much greater than the points surrounding it. Non-ideal points may have differential value, but the differences in nearby non-ideal points are small compared to the difference in value between the ideal point and others. Here, the ideal represents a kind of value cusp. The ideal lies at the top of a hill that becomes much steeper as the ideal is approached. The value function is concave on either side of the ideal. We illustrate this case in Fig. 1b. Recall that the dimensions shown in Figs. 1a and 1b are by hypothesis identical. The social state that corresponds to the ideal is the same in both cases. And the value placed on achieving the ideal is identical. What differs is the value, vis-à-vis the ideal value, that is achieved by outcomes close to the ideal. What is at stake is convexity and concavity in the underlying value function. It seems natural to describe the case in Fig. 1b as representing "idealism" in the sense that the ideal has salience in the value function. And on that basis it is appealing to think of the case shown in Fig. 1a as representing the conservative case.

What is critical about convexity in the value function is that it goes with a risk-averse posture toward one's goal—whatever that happens to be—whereas the concave case goes with a risk-loving posture in relation to the ideal. Consider a case in which there is a policy that from the *status quo* is likely to move us to the ideal with probability 50 percent and to move us an equal distance away from the ideal with probability 50 percent. The idealist will consider such a risk one well worth taking. The value gains to achieving the ideal are considerable, whereas the loss from failure is simply to replace the *status quo* with some other non-ideal point further from the ideal: the value difference in this latter case are small compared with the value gains in the former case where we could achieve the ideal.

The situation is directly the opposite for the "risk-averse" conservative. The expected gains from moving toward the ideal are rather less than the expected losses from moving away. Accordingly, a fifty-fifty chance of moving in the wrong direction as the right will be a very bad bet for the conservative; better to stay put, even though the status quo is imperfect. In other words, the value function that we have represented as "conservative" corresponds to our intuitive notions of what conservatism entails, namely a reluctance to depart from the status quo unless one can be very confident that the move will lead to an improvement. And analogously, the idealist is one who will endure considerable risk in terms of value achieved if there is a chance that the ideal will be achieved. Policy changes or institutional shifts that the idealist will happily entertain will be anathema to the conservative.

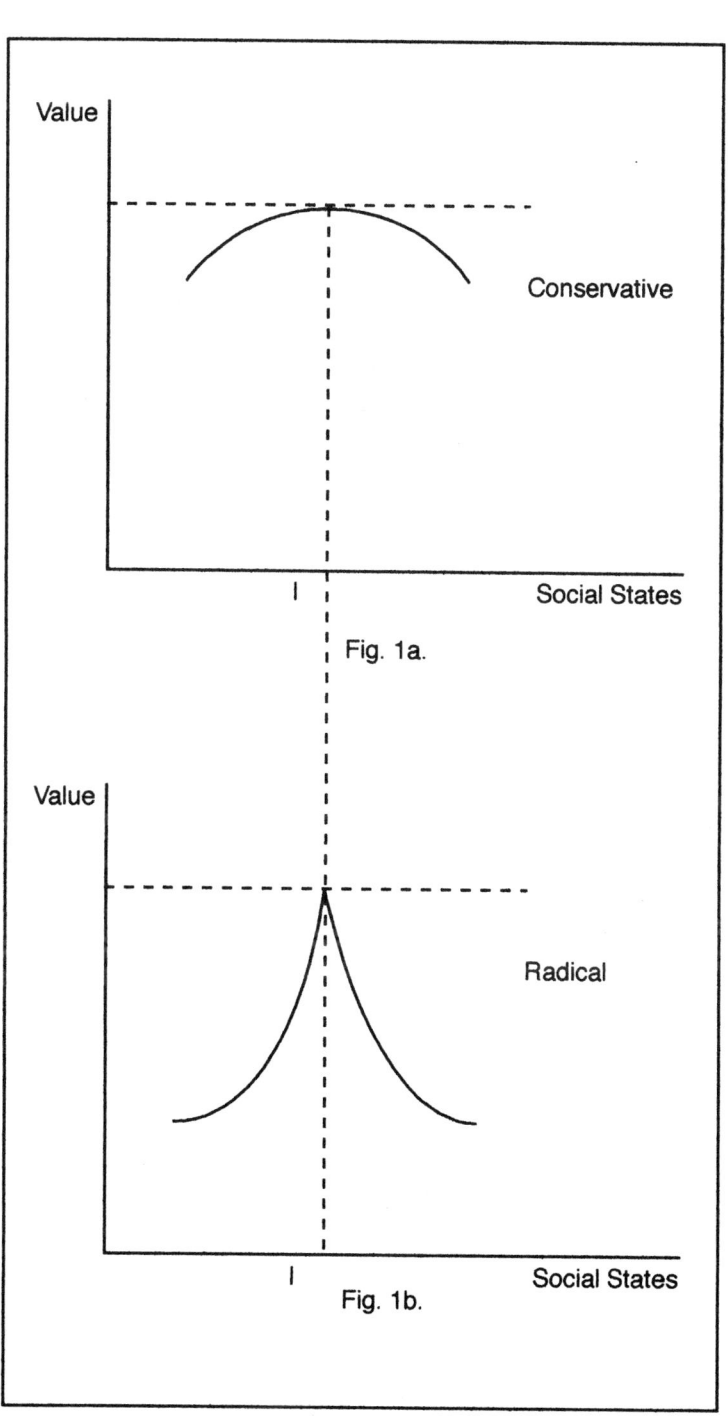

Value

Conservative

Social States

Fig. 1a.

Value

Radical

Social States

Fig. 1b.

It is worth emphasizing here that in this characterization of the conservative position, there need be no particular value placed on the status quo as such. There need be no affection for the familiar incorporated into the value function as such. That is what it means to say that conservatism, and radicalism/idealism equally, operate in a "different dimension." Of course, if there are people who do like the status quo for its own sake, or who have an emotionally grounded fear of the unfamiliar in itself, then such people will be attracted to the conservative posture, though out of different motives from those we have isolated. And, if one can cultivate in oneself an intrinsic affection for the status quo, the conservative as described here might well have reason to do so. What is of interest here is less the particular motivational apparatus that goes with conservatism and more the normative justification that might be seen to underlie it. We are less interested in that sense in describing the "conservative disposition" than in justifying a "conservative political philosophy."

If this account of conservatism/radicalism as engaging a distinct dimension within the ideological landscape is accepted, then there are two obvious points to be made about it. First, any of the standard descriptions of ideological positions are a partial specification of a more elaborate description in which location in both relevant dimensions is specified. So, one could be a radical egalitarian or a conservative one; a radical libertarian or a conservative one; and so on. It would therefore just be a mistake to see oneself as obliged to reject conservatism on the grounds that one is a libertarian. Hayek could describe himself as a "conservative classical-liberal" without any inconsistency whatsoever. However, the arguments that Hayek uses for rejecting conservatism do not seem to relate at all to the ends to be promoted; Hayek seems concerned mostly with the thought that under conservatism no "progress" at all is possible. That, of course, is a mistake. Conservatives on the definition used here clearly *will* sometimes make changes. However, they will do so only when the grounds for such changes are strong enough. They would not be inclined to make very large shifts in a "free-market direction," for example, if there were significant risks of unintended or unforeseen consequences that might be harmful to liberty or to general prosperity.

The second point goes somewhat against the first. If declaring oneself to be a classical liberal is a partial specification of location in a necessarily two-dimensional ideological map, the same is true of conservatism. Nevertheless, within the two-dimensional space, various clusters are possible. It is certainly not meaningless for persons to describe themselves as conservatives *simpliciter*. Conservatives, on the reading offered here, will be those who are especially risk-averse in the domain of policy/institution change. Conservatives may differ quite significantly on the ends that policy should serve. The unintended consequences that the libertarian might fear will be quite different from the unintended consequences that the egalitarian might fear. But it is in the nature of unintended consequences that they are unpredictable. Consider

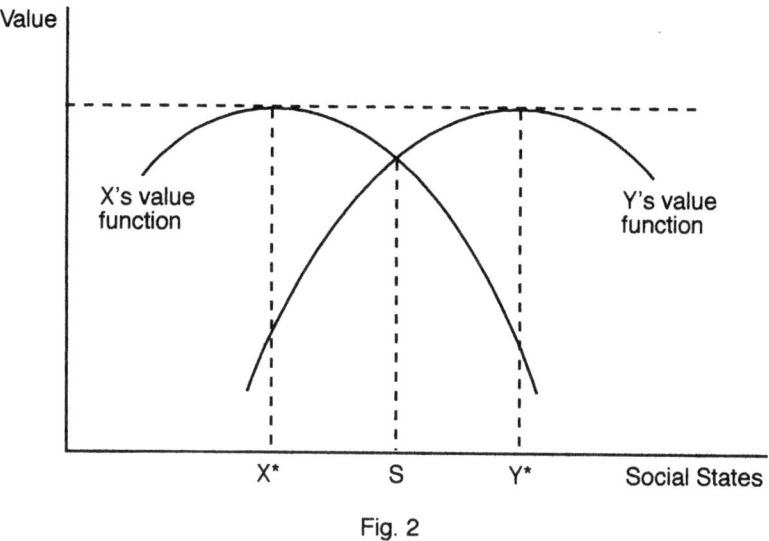

Fig. 2

in Fig. 2 the case of two "conservatives," X and Y, who would like totally opposed moves in social states. For X, the ideal is at X*, and the risk that concerns him is that of moving to Y*. For Y, the ideal is at Y*, and he is worried about the prospect of a move to X*. A policy that involves a fifty-fifty chance of moving from the status quo S to X* or Y* would be opposed by both X and Y, even though their value objectives are utterly at variance. In this sense, conservatism can transcend value differences. It is in that sense that conservatives might rightly say that conservatism is not an ideology of the normal kind, that it propounds no end that should be pursued. It is not that conservatives have no such ends. But the ends might be highly various, and could, as the example shows, play a negligible role in isolating the important things they share.

CONSERVATISM AND INFORMATIONAL SCARCITY

There is one additional piece that is useful in making the case for a family similarity between the economic approach to normative analysis and conservatism. This is the emphasis within the conservative tradition on human ignorance. Much of the opposition to grand schemes in the conservative tradition seems to be grounded in an anxiety about lack of information about the likely consequences of action. An ignorance of possible effects, the complexity of the order that reformers seek to change, the likelihood of unintended consequences—these are repeated themes in conservative literature. As Muller puts it, "Whether termed the 'abuse of reason' (by Burke), 'rationalism in politics' (by Oakeshott) or 'constructivism' (by Hayek), the conservative accusation

19

against liberal and radical thought is fundamentally the same: liberals and radicals are said to depend upon a systematic, deductivist, universalist form of reasoning which fails to account for the complexity and peculiarity of the actual institutions they seek to transform" (14).

Now, economists are no enemies of systematic, abstract, deductivist reasoning; that is our meat and drink! And this fact may obscure the common elements in economic and conservative reasoning involved here. After all, economists are certainly familiar with the idea of "unintended consequences." In fact, the standard defence of markets largely depends on such unintended consequences. Adam Smith states clearly that the good features of market outcomes do not (normally) reflect the intentions of the participants in the market process themselves. And economists ought to be sympathetic to the idea of pervasive ignorance; that is simply one further manifestation of prevailing scarcity. Information is not cheap, even where it is available. Moreover, according to the Austrian tradition, there are certain kinds of information revealed in markets that simply could not be obtained in any other way.

There are other points that the economist might refer to here to buttress the conservative anxiety. Most of the information about the working of complex social processes is information that individuals have a very low incentive to acquire. Institutions are normally changed by political processes; and information about the general consequences of political action is a "public good" to participants in those political processes. As Anthony Downs has noted, the fact that no individual voter can reasonably expect to be decisive in any large-scale electoral decision process means that all voters tend to be "rationally ignorant." Economists know that the chief reason for studying economics is *not* that doing so helps make you rich, whatever some undergraduates (or MBA students) might imagine. Part of the reason that we need market mechanisms to process information is that the market provides individuals with the incentive to acquire and reveal the information that it is necessary to aggregate. The long-standing critique of "socialist calculation" depends, in one influential strand, on an argument of this kind supporting human ignorance.

We might, however, also note that the institutions of public life are not such as to encourage people to confess their ignorance. Politicians do not get brownie points (or votes) by making public statements about their own ignorance. They do routinely go public about the ignorance of their electoral rivals, and that fact could well be one of the chief arguments for adversarial political arrangements. But, when government spokespersons seek to defend the "important policy initiatives" that they are always looking to introduce, they do not begin—or end—with a confession that they are not all that sure of what the consequences of these initiatives will be.

And economists themselves, appearing on television to inform the public about what is going on, are disinclined to just remark that "it's hard to be sure!" Speaking purely personally, we have to say that we are surprised at how often professional colleagues appear on television discoursing with great confidence about matters that we know (and they know) the profession considers highly contested. We are more often impressed with their self-confidence than with their professional integrity. Even where there appears to be substantial professional consensus on particular issues, a little objectivity and temporal reflection indicates that, in many important cases, only a few years ago there appeared to be a fair consensus about a quite different view. Of course, the media select for the opinionated; they are more interesting! But, being reasonably honest, we think that economists know rather less about most things than they pretend to know in public, and that there are really very few claims about policy matters that any of us could reasonably hold with total confidence. That fact is, however, not one that is readily apparent. Nor is it unique to economists. If conservatives are sceptical about relying on the knowledge and wisdom of the putative experts, they are probably right to do so.

This ignorance would not be of great consequence if one were a risk-lover. Unintended consequences hold less fear for those whose informational requirements are less demanding. A "radical" on our account will rationally be prepared to take a risk on moving in the wrong direction if there is a prospect of moving in the right. By definition, the radical needs much less good odds to implement changes. And, for that reason, the radical may be less concerned to acquire relevant information before making a policy move. Put another way, the radical will not be so concerned about the extent of human ignorance. The conservative by contrast will take the issue of ignorance very seriously indeed; he is much more concerned about downside risks. And much more concerned to expose just how much ignorance there is abroad.

CONCLUSION

What we have attempted to do in this essay is defend conservatism as a general political philosophy along essentially economistic lines. To some extent, this is a matter of taking ideas and values that are familiar in the conservative literature—especially that in the English language tradition (Hume, Burke, Hayek, Oakeshott)—and rendering those ideas and values in economic terms. There is, however, a substantive argument at stake here. The argument involves putting together three separate elements—one of them borrowed directly from economics and two borrowed from conservatism. The explicitly conservative elements are:

First, the claim that the social order is extremely complex and that human agents are substantially ignorant of the likely consequences of various attempts to "control" it.

Second, the common-sense understanding of conservatism as involving a presumption in favour of the *status quo*—both in the sense of preferring small changes to large, and in the sense of claiming an onus of proof against any change at all.

The economic element is the claim that the value function by which alternative (feasible) social states are assessed is likely to be "convex." This latter claim is partly a value claim and partly a claim about the nature of preferences. But economists do not believe in convexity because of its conservative implications; the conservative implications, if any, emerge essentially as incidental attributes of the economist's beliefs about the world.

The fact that convexity does, under plausible conditions of ignorance, have such conservative implications may well be a reason for re-examining it. And perhaps conservatives are wrong to think that human ignorance about the consequences of policy/institutional change is as extensive as they apparently do. Perhaps further, the argument that we have presented here has implications for optimal response to certain kinds of shocks that conservatives would find uncongenial. Perhaps. But those possibilities are ones that deserve explicit treatment. The virtue of the "analytic approach" is that it permits, even encourages, such explicit treatment. And, as economists, we think that such encouragement *is* a virtue, however alien it may be to traditionally conservative modes of exposition and argument.

NOTES

1. Though there is textual evidence to suggest that Oakeshott was not inhospitable to a "principled" treatment of conservatism, he was sceptical as to its value. Contrast Oakeshott ch. 1 with, say, p. 407.

2. Hayek makes precisely the same observation. Things can scarcely have been said to have improved in the intervening four decades.

3. That is, of course, a professionally self-serving remark, since it shifts the comparative advantage in ethical debates toward experts in feasibility (the economists?) and away from experts in desirability (the moral philosophers?). However, economists, of all people, have learned not to see interests as *prima facie* evidence for error. Moreover, the obvious free-rider problem casts doubt on whether the interests of the entire profession can adequately explain the behaviour—still less the beliefs—of any individual economist.

4. Again, this is not an idle speculation. Some public finance experts seem to want tax design to be assigned to bodies of "experts" exempt from political influence.

5. The necessity of such a trade-off is somewhat contested. We do not mean here to defend the idea of a non-vertical Phillips curve. We take the example for illustrative purposes only.

6. There are good reasons connected to the observed stability of market outcomes for thinking that aggregate preference satisfaction *is* a convex function.

7. In his paper "If You're an Egalitarian, How Come You're So Rich?," Gerry Cohen raises the question as to whether an egalitarian is committed to acting to reduce inequality unless complete equality will thereby be achieved. Egalitarianism might in principle be totally silent on whether greater inequality is undesirable.

8. We take it that the presence of (apparent) discontinuities is the essence of the familiar "second-best" theorems of welfare economics. The classic reference here is Lipsey and Lancaster.

WORKS CITED

Broome, John. *Ethics Out of Economics.* Cambridge: Cambridge University Press, 1999.

Cohen, G.A. "If You're an Egalitarian, How Come You're So Rich?" *The Journal of Ethics* 4 (2000): 1–26.

Downs, Anthony. *An Economic Theory of Democracy.* New York: Harper and Row, 1957.

Friedman, Milton. "Methodology of Positive Economics." *Essays in Positive Economics* Chicago: University of Chicago Press, 1953. 3–43.

Hayek, Friedrich. "Why I Am Not a Conservative." *The Constitution of Liberty.* London: Routledge and Kegan Paul, 1960.

Huntington, Samuel. "Conservatism as an Ideology." *American Political Science Review* 51 (1957): 454–73.

Muller, Jerry Z. *Conservatism: An Anthology of Social and Political Thought from David Hume to the Present.* Princeton: Princeton University Press, 1997.

Mueller, Dennis. *Public Choice II.* Cambridge: Cambridge University Press, 1989.

Oakeshott, Michael. *Rationalism in Politics and other Essays.* Indianapolis: Liberty Press, 1991.

Edmund Burke's *Reflections on the Revolution in America* (1777): or, how did the American Revolution relate to the French?

J.C.D. Clark

I

Edmund Burke's *Reflections on the Revolution in America* triggered a storm of controversy on its first publication in 1777, but soon acquired the status of a classic of political analysis. It was all the more remarkable in emanating from a man hitherto clearly identified with the reforming wing in Westminster politics and, until then, a friend of reform in the American colonies themselves. Before the outbreak of fighting, Burke had never supported direct British rule in the colonies or endorsed the policies of George III or his ministers. Burke's conversion to the loyalist cause was understandably interpreted as an act of betrayal by his former allies like Paine and Priestley, although Burke himself insisted on the continuity of his principles and the purity of his motives. Yet, despite a torrent of denunciation, it soon became clear that Burke had framed the most insightful and prophetic of all the accounts then written of the violent events that were transforming civil society on the continent of North America and ushering in an age of revolution and totalitarian democracy in the two centuries that were to follow. [1]

Burke had never been to America, but he claimed considerable knowledge of the colonies. [2] He was the Agent for the General Assembly of the Province of New York from 1771; as the crisis developed, he took pains to inform himself in detail about American events. On the basis of knowledge rather than prejudice, he saw that there was something novel, something astonishing, about events in America that his contemporaries in England had failed to appreciate. [3] He began his text with a comparison between the events of 1776 and those of 1688: 'the Revolution', that foundation stone of Whig liberties, was, he argued, a wholly different event from what had just occurred in the Thirteen Colonies.

Faith, Reason, and Economics: Essays in Honour of Anthony Waterman. Ed. Derek Hum. Winnipeg: St. John's College Press, 2003.

The American Revolution was, to Burke, unnecessary: although colonial grievances undoubtedly existed, they were insufficient to explain the scale of what unfolded between 1775 and 1777. Financial problems were only the 'pretexts and instruments' of men who intended to destroy monarchy.[4] As Daniel Leonard had argued, the American Revolution could not be explained by 'such trivial Causes, as those alledged by these unhappy People'.[5] Colonies' established practices of self-government had, Burke considered, recently been eroded by a monarchy that Burke had since the 1760s regarded as arbitrary, but each colony nevertheless had the foundations of an ancient constitution on which a libertarian edifice could again be built.[6] The wealth and dynamically growing population of the colonies before 1776, he now argued, was a simple disproof of the revolutionary rhetoric that merely denounced monarchy as tyranny.[7] Now, wrote Burke ironically, *émigrés* 'have taken refuge in the frozen regions, and under the British despotism, of Canada'.[8] If so, British rule could hardly be so evil.

Burke rightly saw that the American Revolution was not the secular event it appeared to be on the surface: the 'signals' for 'revolutions' had 'so often been given from pulpits', and such was the case here.[9] It was not merely a political revolution: '*It is a Revolution of doctrine and theoretick dogma. It has a much greater resemblance to those changes which have been made upon religious grounds, in which a spirit of proselytism makes an essential part.*'[10] Behind colonists' new language of abstract human rights lay a long history of religious debate in which a right of resistance had been worked out and affirmed, a debate that had long predicted the likely triggers of that asserted right. Nevertheless, natural rights claims could be expected to have the most destructive consequences.[11] American Deists like Jefferson and Franklin were part of an international movement.[12] Burke already knew the aims of such 'political Men of Letters'[13] in Britain, and now saw similar revolutionary implications being put into practice in the colonies.

Burke witnessed with dismay the escalation of events in representative institutions. The Continental Congress was assembled with no mandate to make a revolution, yet by an accelerating logic of its internal politics it was drawn to do just that in the name of 'the nation': 'They have departed from the instructions of the people by whom they were sent.'[14] In so doing, Congress now claimed to be the locus of sovereignty. This need not surprise anyone who seriously considered its composition, argued Burke: the preponderance of mean men, and especially petty lawyers, boded ill.[15] So did the influence of certain reforming members of the landed elite who, from dangerous ambition or intellectual vanity, were willing to risk the social ascendancy of their order.[16]

At the beginning of the parliamentary session of 1774–5, Burke was aware (he claimed on 22 March 1775) that 'anger and violence prevailed every day more and more' in the colonies.[17] By 1777, his black vision of the revolution lamented its 'shocking prodigies', its 'slaughter and captivity', its 'hatred and rage', its corruption of law and manners.[18] The rhetoric of the revolutionaries implicitly condoned violence and the loss of life. Burke was original not least in understanding that violence was intrinsic to the revolution from its outset.[19] Only revolutionary violence on a wide scale could break the bonds of allegiance in every village and farmstead: it was this violence that gave the American revolution its character both as a social transformation and as an episode in which a collective will was forged and brought to bear in countless acts of local coercion to enforce the obedience of the reluctant or the unwilling.

Anticipations of the constitution of the new republic, if a clean break with the old order were to result, equally disturbed Burke. Constitutions were the growth of ages, and could not safely be devised upon first principles.[20] An electoral system might be based on any qualifications, and any choice of qualifications was equally arbitrary.[21] To override ancient territorial divisions would mean reducing real people with natural loyalties and attachments to abstract units, and a logical consequence was the proposal to create representational districts each geometrically square.[22]

Burke already had much experience of public finance, and knew from England's case the massive cost of major wars. He rightly predicted that the colonies could not finance their war against Britain by the orthodox means of taxation and loans, and that paper currency, and inflation, would be the inevitable consequence. Paper currency, he rightly saw, would create a mercantile and 'monied interest'[23] with an interest in the success of the revolution: emancipation from debts contracted in hard currency was their aim. If inflation was not enough, the naked confiscation of property in the name of the nation was already being practised; and 'Revolutions are favourable to confiscation.'[24]

Burke saw that the revolution had unleashed social forces that would make civil society itself, as known to him, impossible to sustain. The monarch had been effectively unseated at the outset, despite the early claim of the revolutionaries to act in his name, and without a strong executive it could be foreseen that government would disintegrate.[25] Justice itself had been politicized.[26] Revolutionary principles could be made the basis for a stable regime only by the rise to political power of a military leader. That outcome duly materialized in the dominance, and finally the presidency, of a hitherto-obscure but burningly ambitious middle-ranking militia officer.[27]

Such a revolution could hardly be contained in North America: these principles, supported by a people in arms, would surely soon be communicated to Britain, and with the same catastrophic consequences.[28]

II

We know, of course, that Burke did not write *Reflections on the Revolution in America*. Yet the outline given above of this hypothetical and unwritten book of 1777 is only a transposition to the American Revolution of the analyses, arguments and concerns that Burke so brilliantly rehearsed for the French in

Reflections on the Revolution in France (1790). Their fit is strangely exact; indeed in some ways Burke's insights into the transformative effects of revolution were more appropriate for America than for France.[29] The number of *émigrés*, in proportion to population, was greater in the American case, as was the value, in proportion to national wealth, of property permanently expropriated.[30] The French constitution did not finally adopt the geometrically square constituencies that were proposed in early discussions; it was the new United States that expanded westwards across the continent by expropriation and genocide, founding new states (divided internally into counties) that were often rectangular, disregarding the ancient and irregular areas of occupancy of native Americans. Despite the havoc of revolution and war in both countries, it was France that experienced a restoration and France in which the principles of hierarchy, heredity and apostolic authority continued to be the more influential; the United States in which those principles were ever more systematically repudiated as the new Republic put into practice its new public doctrine.[31]

No comparison, of course, could yet be made, but English perceptions of the significance of American events were nevertheless strangely muted. In *Common Sense* (1776), Thomas Paine wrote a famously influential tract setting out the revolutionary consequences of Deism: Burke and many of his English contemporaries largely ignored it.[32] In *Rights of Man* (1791) Paine said similar things once more: Burke and many of his contemporaries treated it as a harbinger of the apocalypse. In February 1776, Richard Price published *Observations on the Nature of Civil Liberty, the Principles of Government, and the Justice and Policy of the War with America*,[33] an application to the political world of Price's Arianism. Burke, in his *Letter to the Sheriffs of Bristol*, its Preface dated April 3, 1777, ignored Price.[34] In November 1789, Price published a much slighter piece, *A Discourse on the Love of Our Country*; when Burke read it in January 1790, it was the catalyst for Burke's total rejection of the French Revolution, expressed first in his speech of 9 February and at length in the *Reflections on the Revolution in France*, published on 1 November.

The problem, then, remains: Burke did not write *Reflections on the Revolution in America*. For this unwritten work he was well prepared. His ability to compose substantial pieces of historical analysis was already manifest.[35] His ability to write timely interventions in public debate was also clear, interventions which carried the profundity and depth of analysis of *Thoughts on the Cause of the Present Discontents* (1770). Yet, as the American revolution unfolded, Burke's analysis of it scarcely progressed beyond that fatally limited understanding which he had attained by 1775.

To point out this lacuna in Burke's life and thought is to confront a further dimension of scholarly explanation. The exegesis of texts, and the construction of explanatory narratives of historical events, is on one level an account of what was said and what occurred. But the reassertion of counter-factual analysis[36] has reminded us that explanations of this sort are dependent, overtly or

covertly, on explanations of another sort: explanations of what might plausibly have been written or said, but was not; what might plausibly have been
done, but was not.[37] Seen in this way, the biography of Burke becomes a point
of access to a wider set of problems. Why did men at the time not see the
significance of the American Revolution? Why did they not appreciate the new
phenomena, under their very noses, for which later historians devised such
grandiose names? Why, that is, did men not appreciate the emergence of what
we now call a revolutionary mentality in the late eighteenth century? Why was
it that a counter-revolutionary position was so slow to develop? And what, in
the most general sense, was the connection between the American Revolution
and the French?

III

One answer must be that men did not ignore growing crises but thought about
them in very different, and older, terms.[38] This was in many ways appropriate:
Burke did not fail to notice 'the radicalism of the American Revolution' (or the
French), since no such ideology was coined until the late 1810s and early
1820s, and even then in England: 1776 and 1789 had other causes.[39] Burke's
preoccupations in the years before 1776 were widely shared in English and
colonial American discourse, especially the alleged infringement of legal or
customary rights, the threats posed by executive power, and corruption in public life. From 1767, similar categories were brought to bear in English examina-
tions of the actions of the East India Company.[40] Burke argued that English
ministries' interventions in the affairs of that Company were 'arbitrary' and
violated the right of property—a rule that 'distinguished Law and Freedom
from Violence and Slavery'.[41] The Company's charter 'ought to be held inviola-
ble', he protested against Lord North's threatened reform on 13 April 1772. The
state had no 'right' to the Company's territorial acquisitions, he argued on 5
April 1773, since a 'right' implied 'something settled, and established by certain known rules and maxims; it implied, in short, a *legal decision*'.[42] In the
impeachment of Warren Hastings, which began in 1788, Burke alleged that
Indian maladministration consisted in the arbitrary use of executive power in
disregard of chartered rights and local customs, and the exploitation of local
elites by metropolitan administrators.[43] These positions on Indian affairs were
little different from Burke's initial positions on the controversies between the
American colonies and the home country. Yet no revolution resulted in India
before 1789, despite the strains produced by insensitive administration from a
distance and by a dynamically growing empire. However true this analysis was
for either continent, it denied Burke and his contemporaries a more accurate
insight into the novel elements in the American scene.

The American Revolution, too, had its prominent legal dimension and began as a conflict over jurisdiction. In the development of its legal arguments, it
may be interpreted as, in part, a revolution of natural law against common law.[44]

Burke had had a grounding in the first, via his reading of Samuel Pufendorf at Trinity College Dublin, and in the second when he read for the bar in London in c. 1750–4,[45] yet insisted on seeing the points at issue only in common law terms and did not respond to what was new in American political discourse. Here he may have had some justification, if it is true that natural law arguments did not rise to dominate common law ones in colonial argument before c. 1774.[46] Yet how much did Burke know at the time?

Burke succeeded in being depicted in retrospect as a far-seeing prophet who gave timely warning of the impending American crisis and its consequences. Yet until 1775 he evidently gave a much lower priority to America than this image would suggest. Little in his writings or speeches published before 1775 bore on America. Burke's first recorded parliamentary speech of January or February 1766, on the Stamp Act disturbances, briefly visualised the worst outcome in the colonies as a 'Civil war' rather than any more complex phenomenon.[47] He showed no understanding that the colonies themselves were rapidly changing except in externally quantifiable ways. *A Short Account of a Late Short Administration* (London, 1766) very briefly commended the Rockinghams' repeal of the Stamp Act: 'The Passions and Animosities of the Colonies, by judicious and lenient Measures, were allayed and composed, and the Foundation laid for a lasting Agreement amongst them'.[48] The Rockinghams failed to see trouble approaching in the shape of the Townshend duties, and mounted no systematic opposition to their passage through the Commons in 1767.[49] Writing in *The Public Advertiser* on 24 February 1768, Burke reviewed domestic events of the 1760s in terms both backward-looking and English: the 'People of England' then 'saw the very first Opportunity laid hold on to revive the Doctrines of a dispensing Power, State Necessity, Arcana of Government, and all that clumsy Machinery of exploded Prerogative, which it had cost our Ancestors so much Toil and Treasure, and Blood, to break to Pieces.' America was not mentioned.[50] Burke's pamphlet *Observations on a Late State of the Nation*, published on 8 February 1769, contained criticisms of the Grenvilles' financial policy towards the colonies but little about the colonies' internal state.[51] When Burke predicted 'some extraordinary convulsion in that whole system', he wrote of France, not the American colonies, and traced the source of impending collapse to the state of French public finances.[52] Yet it could easily be argued that no 'extraordinary convulsion' would have occurred in France in 1789 but for France's prior involvement in the American revolutionary war and the additional strains this placed on her: indeed that point was repeatedly made in *The Times* during July 1789.[53] It is the American Revolution rather than the French that is the more necessary to explain if the 'age of revolutions' is to be correctly diagnosed.

Thoughts on the Cause of the Present Discontents (London, April 1770) referred to the colonies in only one clause of one sentence: in this, his most wide-ranging and profound political tract to date, Burke offered insights into the cause of disturbance in England without troubling to enquire into the novel and far more important sources of disturbance in North America.[54] Instead, his priority was to frame an elaborate scenario of recent politics in Britain, in which the growth of Court 'influence' had been the means of the rise of 'arbitrary power'.[55]

In his Commons speech of 9 May 1770 supporting a series of motions censuring the ministry's conduct of American policy, Burke was equivocal on whether the Rockinghams' repeal of the Stamp Act in 1766 could then have been expected to encourage colonists to resist other laws and undertake 'offensive measures' at a later period; evidently (as his recent editor suggests) Burke was now alarmed at the 'violence and extremism' that even the Rockinghams saw in American events by 1770. Instead of entering more deeply into a consideration of the colonies, Burke was drawn into ever more rhetorical denunciations of what he called 'the misconduct, the weakness, the Violence, the duplicity, the inconsistency of administration'.[56] Despite the importance of the occasion in retrospect, Burke did not publish the speech or his motions. Nor did he publish his intervention on the Boston Port Bill on 25 March 1774, when he asked 'Is it right to give the Crown a liberty to Suspend the rights of [the] People', and answered 'No its dangerous.'[57]

Until Burke became a colonial Agent in 1771, his published *Correspondence* contains very little on America; even then, Agency business, dominated as it was by trade and boundary disputes, seldom intruded onto the domestic English political agenda until a turning point in April 1774,[58] and did not give Burke forebodings of approaching catastrophe. His first substantial published pronouncements on American affairs came only on the very eve of armed conflict: *Speech of Edmund Burke, Esq. On American Taxation, April 19, 1774*— not published until 10 January 1775[59]—and *The Speech of Edmund Burke Esq; on moving his Resolutions for Conciliation with the Colonies, March 22, 1775*, published on 22 May 1775.[60] The principles embodied in these two pamphlets of 1775 were indeed present in speeches of 1766–7, but these he had presumably then thought not worth publishing.[61] Although Burke explored in detail his objections to the policies of successive ministries, none of his writings offered any account of what was going on in the colonies to turn political negotiations over taxation into triggers of revolution. The *Speech on American Taxation* now focused on the Townshend duties (as Burke had seemingly not done when they were passed); it essentially called for a repeal of the Townshend tea duty on the same principles that underlay the Rockinghams' repeal of the Stamp Act, a reversion to what Burke grandly termed 'the system of 1766'. It was only taxation imposed after the fall of the Rockingham ministry in 1766, Burke now claimed, that had 'filled the minds of the Colonists with new jealousy, and all sorts of apprehensions, then it was that they quarreled with the old taxes, as well as the new; then it was, and not till then, that they questioned all the parts of your legislative power'. 'Leave the Americans as they antiently stood', argued Burke, and all would be well.[62] It was a shallow understanding of the colonies, and indebted instead to his belief that 'The most ardent lover of his country cannot wish for Great Britain an happier fate than to continue as she was [. . .] left' at the death of George II in 1760.[63]

In his speeches at the Bristol election of October-November 1774, Burke inadequately confessed that the American problem made him feel at the edge of a 'precipice'; that perhaps not even 'any wisdom can preserve us'; that 'The means of recovering our affairs are not obvious.' His dilemma was entailed by the 'system of 1766', namely the combination of the Rockinghams' Declaratory Act, which had asserted Parliament's supreme authority over the colonies, with a profession that the Rockinghams were seeking also to guarantee to the Americans 'liberty' by rescinding taxes imposed by Westminster.[64] The best he could do at the opening of the parliamentary session on 30 November 1774 was to draft a Lords' Protest complaining that 'No proper materials' for an understanding of the American problem had been laid before them,[65] although this conflicted with Burke's prior claims that the nature of the problem was obvious and that the 'system of 1766' was a complete solution. One newspaper report of the Commons' debate of 20 December 1774 had Burke willing to abandon the key component of that 'system', the Declaratory Act.[66] But this was evidently the paper's mistake, for on 6 February 1775 he was still insisting bravely that the colonists 'do not attack the *Sovereignty itself*, but *a certain exercise and use of that Sovereignty*', a use that constituted, to Burke, 'an insufferable Tyranny'.[67] Having framed the issue in this way, Burke was increasingly preoccupied by the 'arbitrary' and 'cruel' nature of British coercive measures.[68]

Not until his Commons speech on conciliation of 22 March 1775 did Burke set out a substantive scheme for ending the American dispute. Yet even this was based on mainly external knowledge.[69] Burke rehearsed statistics of population, trade and agriculture, but when it came to describing the colonists themselves he could only offer generalities: that 'a love of Freedom is the predominating feature', that this was so because they were descendants of Englishmen, and that 'the great contests for freedom in this country were from the earliest times chiefly upon the question of Taxing'. This point, plausible although insufficient, Burke never worked out in detail.

He then turned to another theme of greater import. This disposition to liberty was strengthened by the Americans being 'protestants', but Burke at once showed that his understanding of this matter was limited: 'I do not think, Sir, that that the reason of this averseness in the dissenting churches from all that looks like absolute Government is so much to be sought in their religious tenets, as in their history.' He sought to expand this point:

> All Protestantism, even the most cold and passive, is a sort of dissent. But the
> religion most prevalent in our Northern Colonies is a refinement on the principle

of resistance; it is the dissidence of dissent; and the protestantism of the protestant religion. This religion, under a variety of denominations, agreeing in
nothing but in the communion of the spirit of liberty, is predominant in most
of the Northern provinces; where the Church of England, notwithstanding its
legal rights, is in reality no more than a sort of private sect, not composing
most probably the tenth of the people. The Colonists left England when this
spirit was high; and in the emigrants was the highest of all: and even that
stream of foreigners, which has been constantly flowing into these Colonies,
has, for the greatest part, been composed of dissenters from the establishments
of their several countries, and have brought with them a temper and character
far from alien to that of the people with whom they mixed.

Americans possessed a 'republican Religion'. [70]

That, although prescient, was the limit of Burke's insight; he turned at once in
his *Speech on Conciliation* to the effect of slavery in heightening the rhetoric of
liberty among Anglicans in the southern colonies, where they were numerous.
Having made his point about religion, Burke left it to argue the different point,
unrelated in his account to the first, that many of the colonists were educated in
the law, so producing a litigious culture, and coupled it with the truism that the
distance of the colonies from Britain necessarily made government there weak.
All this was reasonable enough, and eloquently expressed; but it showed no
specific understanding of how any one of these elements, especially the religious, had acted to shape events or arguments. No colonial leader, no colonial
publication, was specifically mentioned in his *Speech on American Taxation* or
Speech on Conciliation; the cast list in both tracts was wholly British. Burke's
only remedy for the crisis was that, since obedience could not be compelled by
force, it had to be elicited by 'affection'; but on how that could be done, given the
legal and religious complexion of the colonial population he had just described,
he had no more to recommend than concessions on taxation.

Tactically, Burke was still bound by the Rockinghamite 'system of 1766' to
argue that 'I do not know, that the Colonies have, in any general way, or in any
cool hour, gone much beyond the demand of immunity in relation to taxes.'[71]
Even in his second speech on conciliation of 16 November 1775, Burke still
'denied that the desire of absolute independency was or could be general in the
colonies'.[72] After the Thirteen Colonies had claimed just that, Burke implausibly
accused the ministry on 6 November 1776: 'you meant to drive them to the
declaration of independency'.[73] On that premise, the revolution was incompre-
hensible; but on that premise, Burke had little need to seek to understand it. His
Letter to the Sheriffs of Bristol, dated 3 April 1777 and his last major published
work on the revolution, was a rhetorically heightened lament at the tragedy now
unfolding, but contributed no new insights into its nature and causes.[74] In his
speech at Bristol in 1780, Burke was more candid: 'the Americans are utter strangers
to me; a nation, among whom I am not sure, that I have a single acquaintance'.[75]

IV

If Burke's categories and analyses of major convulsion were still those of the old world, he nevertheless showed prefigurings and anticipations of the later shift of categories.

It may be that Burke's remark in 1769 about a 'dangerous spirit' evident in the American colonies in opposition to the Stamp Act was one such anticipation. He was explicit that the fast-growing American empire was a phenomenon 'wholly new in the world', and that it could not be dealt with on the basis either of abstract principle or of the ancient constitution. 'All the reasonings about it, that are likely to be at all solid, must be drawn from its actual circumstances.' Yet Burke's reasonings were only about 'commerce', and in 1769 he repeated the Rockingham line that the 'general fury and confusion, which attended their [the colonists'] resistance to the stamp act' was no longer seen.[76] He contradicted this on 19 April 1769 when Thomas Pownall moved for a committee to reconsider, and so presumably repeal, the Townshend duties: Burke's speech in reply was equivocal, held out the prospect that the colonists 'intend to rise in rebellion',[77] and Pownall's motion failed without a division.

Burke never expanded his remark of 1775 about Americans' 'republican Religion', but two Commons speeches in 1772–3 disclosed his position on matters of religion in the British Isles. On 6 February 1772 the Commons debated the so-called Feathers Tavern petition to release Anglican clergy from the obligation to subscribe the Thirty Nine Articles. Burke took the view, which later had greater resonance, that 'If you make this a season for religious alterations, depend upon it you will soon find it a season of religious tumults and religious wars.'[78] His speech also provides evidence of Burke's attachment to 'rational Christianity', which we may term Anglican latitudinarianism: the Scriptures 'certainly furnish every thing necessary to salvation'; if allowed to interpret Scripture merely figuratively, 'I will undertake to prove the orthodoxy of transubstantiation, or any other Romish doctrine equally absurd'; Burke 'would have heartily concurred in the alteration' made at the Reformation.[79] He repeated his support when a similar motion was made on 17 March 1773: in his speech on that occasion, reported at length, he revealed his position that a restraint on religious freedom could only be justified when 'the person dissenting, does not dissent from the scruples of ill informed conscience but from a party ground of dissention in order to raise a faction in the state. But this I am not bound to presume merely on a Doctrinal difference.'[80]

Burke was on close terms with a number of Protestant Dissenters. Yet it was not English Trinitarian Dissent in general that possessed a strong correlation with English support for the American cause before and during the Revolution, but rather the smaller coteries of heterodox Dissenters.[81] With these, Burke (like most of his contemporaries) had nothing to do. By 1777, Burke still showed no awareness of a possible link between doctrinal commitments and political consequences, and it was just this awareness which evidently dawned on him in the 1780s.[82] It was not of Protestant Dissenters in general that he spoke in this second speech of 17 March 1773, announcing his abhorrence of 'the wicked dissenters', men whom he called 'atheists' or 'infidels' and the Dissenter Dr. Leland had called Deists, men 'who by attacking the possibility of all revelation arraign all the dispensations of providence to man'. They, argued Burke, not pious Dissenters in general, ought to be the subject of civil penalties, 'the just object of vengeance': they were rightly to be feared as 'factious men'; they were 'outlaws of the constitution not of this country but of the human Race'.[83] For a tolerant man, the virulence of Burke's language at this point was remarkable.

Why was Burke unaware of the challenge posed by theological hetero-doxy? By what we now see as international Deism, in England represented by John Wilkes, in the Thirteen Colonies by Thomas Paine, Benjamin Franklin, Thomas Jefferson, and George Washington? Or by Arianism, the creed of Rich-ard Price in England, John Adams and others in the colonies? Burke's earliest intellectual adversary, in the 1750s, had been the Deist Lord Bolingbroke. Burke had also differed fundamentally from Price in that decade, a philosophi-cal difference that eventually found political expression in 1789–90.[84] Burke was already aware of the issues; his silence on the American Revolution calls for better explanations than mere oversight.

These two speeches of 1772–3 offer an important clue to Burke's lack of sensitivity to the religious dimension of political dynamics in the Thirteen Colonies, for it was High Churchmen who were most aware of the proclivity of colonial Dissent to invoke a right of resistance,[85] and latitudinarians who were most sympathetic to the colonial cause.[86] Burke presumably regarded colonial Presbyterians and Congregationalists as no essential threat; indeed on 17 March 1773 he spoke passionately of denominations outside the Church of England as part of 'an alliance offensive and defensive [. . .] a front against the Common Enemy', atheism.[87] He presumably would not have been sensitive to the politi-cal problems posed by the Arianism of, for example, John Adams, but there is no evidence that he enquired into it. So undiscriminating was Burke's viewpoint that he evidently failed to respond to the bigoted anti-Catholicism of the Con-tinental Congress's 'Address to the People of Great Britain', dated 21 October 1774.[88] Burke had once let slip, to John Cruger in New York, his knowledge that there was a 'spirit of intolerance [...] both on our side of the water and on yours' in religious matters,[89] but his position on American constitutional griev-ances prompted him to adopt in public a euphemistic view of American reli-gion; as he explained in a Commons debate on Irish trade on 2 April 1778, 'While the narrow and confined policy of Europe [...] had established partial opinions and particular sects, the expanded policy of America had established the *Christian* religion on the broad basis of universal toleration', evidently an outcome he desired for his native Ireland also.[90]

A related reason for Burke's blind spot may have been that his attention on religious matters in the public arena was dominated until the 1780s by the plight of Roman Catholics in Ireland, and that Burke thought about this issue in legal rather than doctrinal terms. Of English Roman Catholics it might indeed be said, in the words of Burke's draft petition in their favour of April 1778, that 'their dissent from the established church is purely conscientious, wholly unmixed with faction, or with any political consideration whatsoever'.[91] It was not what Burke called 'a Doctrinal difference', but a jurisdictional one. After the Catholic Relief Act of 1778 and the Gordon riots of 1780, Burke condemned '*proscribing the citizens by denominations and general descriptions.* [. . .] Crimes are the acts of individuals, and not of denominations.'[92] Although this was a period of the reassertion of Trinitarian teaching within the Church, this reassertion was not accompanied by any repressive acts by Lord North's ministry towards heterodoxy within the ranks of churchmen.[93] Theological heterodoxy was not yet under a spotlight of public attention.

Deism and its social expression were different matters, and here Burke evidently suppressed his suspicions. In the case of Wilkes, the reasons may be found in the chances of parliamentary alliances. The crises that Wilkes triggered were vital to the Rockinghams in their attempts to construct a scenario of domestic politics in which they emerged as the champions of English liberties against a Court party bent on the pursuit of 'arbitrary power', beginning with the Commons' motion on 25 April 1766 condemning general warrants but most urgently from Wilkes's election for Middlesex in the general election of 1768:[94] already this world view was fully formed, and had entirely filled Burke's mental horizon by 1770. He refrained from public criticism of Wilkes, whose conviction for blasphemy and obscenity in 1764 ought to have earned Burke's condemnation, and Burke kept his growing doubts about his ally to private correspondence.[95] In *Thoughts on the Cause*, Burke revealed his distrust of the 'sinister piety' with which some men (by implication, Wilkes) cherished disorders.[96] Yet Burke did not allow his distrust to go further.

On one issue, and that a domestic one, Burke began to part company from his strange bedfellows. John Wilkes backed parliamentary reform in the Commons on 21 March 1776.[97] Burke's antipathy to schemes of parliamentary reform premised on ideas of annual general elections, equal electoral areas and universal manhood suffrage dated from at least as early as 1780–2, and was then expressed by him (although in a draft of a speech never given) in terms that closely matched those of the *Reflections* in 1790; moreover, Burke even then saw that such natural rights claims logically entailed the destruction of the monarchy and the House of Lords, and the popular election of judges, military officers and priests.[98] These were English ideas and English challenges: they played no role in causing the American Revolution, and not until September 1789 did Burke reflect on the role of democracy in the French.[99] Yet these issues informed Burke's thinking in 1780–2, and it is possible that he held the same or similar views in 1776–7 also. Such a change in the English constitution would certainly have been termed a 'revolution', in the sense in which that term was then widely used.

Burke was familiar with the concept of 'public revolutions' or 'general revolutions' and employed it in 1770, quoting a use of the term by the Duc de Sully (1559–1641), meaning great and sudden changes in state affairs.[100] Burke similarly referred to 'the revolutions of America' in his *Speech on American Taxation* of 1774, referring to changes in the policies of successive British ministries on colonial taxation since the 1760s. On 16 November 1775 he spoke of 'the great revolution which within our own Memory has happened in France' to reduce her from first to fourth place among European powers.[101] Burke's conception of a revolution stood in a late humanist tradition. It drew its dramatic force from the turn in Fortune's wheel that dragged down the great from triumph to debasement: kings, queens, venerable prelates, honourable noblemen.[102] But there were no such figures in the American colonies, and Burke's imagination was never engaged as it was in India and then in France. By contrast, his term for what we call the American Revolution, in 1776 and 1777, was a 'war' or a 'civil war'.[103] He was never drawn to reflect on the nature of social change in the colonies; and with the outbreak of fighting, the physical facts of war came to dominate British perceptions and discussions of the American issue. It is also a question how far colonists, who similarly employed the older and limited meaning of 'revolution', were thereby denied a fuller appreciation of what was going on in the Thirteen Colonies; but that is a subject demanding its own study. Thomas Jefferson was evidently not confined in this way,[104] and the wide implications of the American Revolution for the rest of the world were quickly appreciated by others. Burke, and many of his English contemporaries, were not among them.

It was this usage that metamorphosed in the early 1790s, as men first in France and then elsewhere began to reify 'revolution', to turn it from an event to a process, an historical actor in its own right, awe-inspiring, dynamic, good or evil according to preference. Burke soon came to do the same, and with more rhetorical force than any of his English contemporaries.[105] Even here, there may have been anticipations in Burke's earlier language. In his speech of 17 March 1773, supporting a Dissenters' Toleration Bill, Burke said: 'I wish to see the established church of England great and powerful, I wish to see her foundations laid low and deep that she may crush the giant powers of rebellious darkness.'[106] These giant powers might ultimately be in rebellion against God himself, and Burke's speeches of the 1760s and 70s were littered with quotations from Milton's *Paradise Lost*. Burke was disposed to see contemporary political events *sub specie aeternitatis*, but his latitudinarian sympathies blocked any extensive appreciation of the significance of Dissenting Protestantism in arms in the Thirteen Colonies. Only fully mobilized atheism, known to him in the 1790s as Jacobinism, engaged Burke's sense of the diabolically possible.

In 1790 the publication of Burke's *Reflections on the Revolution in France* drew down on him charges of inconsistency: he had behaved in opposite ways over the American Revolution and the French, two episodes, his critics believed, that were essentially related.[107] In 1791, writing in the third person, Burke defended himself in terms that showed he had apparently learned nothing from the earlier episode. Fox had argued that the Americans had rebelled 'because they thought they had not enjoyed liberty enough'; Burke disagreed, and reaffirmed the views expressed in his second speech on conciliation of 1776. He still denied that 'the Americans had from the beginning aimed at independence', yet he produced only one witness in his favour. 'As far as a man, so locked up as Dr. Franklin, could be expected to communicate his ideas, I believe he opened them to Mr. Burke' the day before Franklin left England (an interview for which Burke left no surviving evidence from 1775). Franklin, he wrote, had told him that America sought only 'a security to its *ancient* constitution'. Burke still accepted this minimalist interpretation. He claimed that his 'conversation with other Americans was large indeed': we have seen that this is in doubt. On that basis, Burke insisted he had 'always firmly believed' that Americans were 'purely on the defensive in that rebellion. He considered the Americans as standing at that time, and in that controversy, in the same relation to England, as England did to king James the Second, in 1688. He believed, that they had taken up arms from one motive only; that is our attempting to tax them without their consent.'[108] Yet the early-Stuart royal prerogative in taxation had not been an issue since 1660, and Burke's attempt to equate 1776 with 1688 was as unsatisfactory as the attempt of English Francophiles to equate 1789 with 1688—an attempt that Burke had just repudiated in his *Reflections*. Burke wrote as a man who realized that the consistency of his conduct was in doubt, but who was also aware that to vindicate it he still had to take what Franklin had said at face value. Yet did it not now seem that Franklin may have misled him? Could it still plausibly be argued, after the immensity of the events of 1789 and after the profound insights embodied in Burke's *Reflections* in 1790, that all that had been at issue in 1776 were the 'ostensible causes'?

From a later perspective, we can appreciate that many of the larger issues in the interpretation of the American and French Revolutions depend on how the two episodes were related. Was the American Revolution politically conservative but socially radical (in our sense of those terms), a clarion call to the emancipation of mankind everywhere, the lighting of a flame soon communicated to France? So believed Jefferson, Paine, Price and many of their contemporaries. Or was the American Revolution a politically radical but socially conservative episode, a transfer of power from a metropolitan to a colonial elite that then had few implications for American society and fewer still for the rest of the world? So believed many of the American Federalists. On this great question[109] Burke was silent or ambiguous. Among his political associates Burke indeed founded an historical tradition which insisted on seeing the

American Revolution and the French as essentially different,[110] and it is the extensive consequences of the intellectual bankruptcy of that interpretive tradition that must now be faced.

It seems likely that what is thereby revealed is not Burke's self-deception but his belatedly developing appreciation of the nature of the revolutionary events through which he lived, and an attempt has been made here to trace that growing understanding. In this process, religion was of central importance. Burke has been presented as an Anglican, Trinitarian in his theology but latitudinarian in his views of ecclesiastical polity.[111] In this identity he offers an important insight into that late eighteenth-century mentality in England that first failed so crassly to see the revolutionary phenomenon coming, but, when it was unavoidable, finally pictured it in Manichean, even apocalyptic, terms. England, as has been recently argued, may be a profoundly unrevolutionary culture;[112] if so, what is most at issue since the seventeenth century has been its capacity to conceive, and survive, apocalypse.

NOTES

1. Edmund Burke, *Reflections on the Revolution in France* (London, 1790), ed. J.C.D. Clark (Stanford, 2001), Introduction, pp. 43–53; hereafter cited as Burke, *Reflections*. Page numbers in square brackets are those of the first edition, reproduced in the Stanford edition. Comparisons are invited in these references between the events of the American Revolution to the end of 1777 and Burke's later comments on the first two years of the French Revolution. Burke, *Writings*, refers to Paul Langford (general editor), *The Writings and Speeches of Edmund Burke* (Oxford, 1981–); Burke, *Correspondence* to T. W. Copeland et al. (eds.), *The Correspondence of Edmund Burke*, 10 vols. (Cambridge, 1958–78).

2. 'I think I know America. If I do not, my ignorance is incurable, for I have spared no pains to understand it': *Letter to the Sheriffs of Bristol* (1777), in Burke, *Writings*, III, p. 304; Burke, *Reflections*, pp. 43–53, Introduction.

3. Burke, *Reflections*, [p. 11].

4. Burke, *Reflections*, Introduction, pp. 72–3.

5. Quoted in Gordon Wood, *The Creation of the American Republic 1776–1787* (Chapel Hill, 1969), p. 4.

6. Burke, *Reflections*, [p. 50]. For his view of the strength of colonial legislative assembles see Burke, *Writings*, III, pp. 120–1.

7. Burke, *Reflections*, [pp. 189–92]. For his positive view of colonial population and wealth see Burke, *Writings*, III, pp. 111–18.

8. Burke, *Reflections*, [p. 197].

9. Burke, *Reflections*, [p. 35].

10. Burke, *Writings*, VIII, p. 341.

11. Burke, *Reflections*, p. 95, Introduction; [pp. 85–92].

12. Burke, *Reflections*, pp. 44, 82, Introduction; [p. 132].

13. Burke, *Reflections*, pp. 92–3, Introduction; [pp. 135, 165].

14. Burke, *Reflections*, [pp. 242–3].

15. Burke, *Reflections*, [pp. 59, 62]. For Burke on the salient role of law and lawyers in colonial America and in triggering resistance see *Writings*, III, pp. 123–4: 'The greater number of the Deputies sent to the Congress were Lawyers.'

16. Burke, *Reflections*, [p. 68].

17. Burke, *Writings*, III, p. 107.

18. *Letter to the Sheriffs of Bristol*, in Burke, *Writings*, III, pp. 300–1; *Reflections*, p. 51, Introduction; [p. 219].

19. Burke, *Reflections*, pp. 76–7, Introduction; [p. 96].

20. Burke, *Reflections*, [p. 253].

21. Burke, *Reflections*, [p. 259]. In 1777, Burke courteously distanced himself from the schemes of the parliamentary reformer (and friend of Price) Major John Cartwright: 'It is natural that great variety of opinions should be entertained upon all speculative ideas for the improvement of the constitution': Burke to Cartwright, [post 18 February 1777]: Burke, *Correspondence*, III, p. 329. Cartwright had already published, although anonymously, *American Independence The Interest and Glory of Great-Britain* (London, 1774); *A Letter to Edmund Burke, Esq; Controverting the Principles of American Government, Laid down in his lately published Speech on American Taxation* (London, 1775); and *Take Your Choice* (London, 1776).

22. Burke, *Reflections*, [pp. 244–5].

23. Burke, *Reflections*, p. 80, Introduction; [pp. 163, 277, 338]. On the Act of 1764 extending the prohibition of paper currency in New England to the rest of the colonies, and Burke's knowledge of it, see *Writings*, II, p. 187 n.

24. Burke, *Reflections*, [pp. 156, 229–30, 235, 276].

25. Burke, *Reflections*, p. 51, Introduction; [pp. 288–91].

26. Burke, *Reflections*, [pp. 298–301].

27. Burke, *Reflections*, [p. 318].

28. Burke, *Reflections*, pp. 62, 65–6, 84, Introduction; [pp. 10, 79].

29. Cataclysmic episodes which become the starting points of national myths of origin are often retrospectively sanitized and their transformative qualities explained in safely modern terms. This process was clearly evident in such texts as *The Development of a Revolutionary Mentality*, Library of Congress Symposia on the American Revolution (Washington, 1972), which scarcely addressed its title, and is only slightly modified (by acknowledgement of the role of minorities) in, for example, Harry M. Ward, *The War for Independence and the Transformation of American Society* (London, 1999). The account assumed here is that offered in, for example, Gordon S. Wood, *The Radicalism of the American Revolution* (New York, 1991)—for which see, however, n. 39 below—and

J.C.D. Clark, *The Language of Liberty 1660–1832: Political discourse and social dynamics in the Anglo-American world* (Cambridge, 1994).

30. R. R. Palmer, *The Age of the Democratic Revolution*, 2 vols. (Princeton, 1959-64), I, pp. 188–90.

31. There were, of course, other ways in which France went further, for example in adopting a unicameral National Assembly where the USA adopted a bicameral Congress in 1787. In the French case, the absence of effective military intervention from abroad on French soil (as occurred in the American colonies from 1776) meant that internal conflict in the 1790s often took the form of massacre rather than civil war.

32. In his *Letter to the Sheriffs of Bristol*, Burke made a brief allusion to Paine's *Common Sense*, but a complimentary one: Burke, *Writings*, III, p. 306. Paine does not appear in Burke's published *Correspondence* to 1777. For the Deism of *Common Sense* see J. C. D. Clark, *English Society 1660-1832: religion, ideology and politics during the ancien regime* (Cambridge, 2000), pp. 385–90.

33. In early 1777, Price followed it with *Additional Observations on the Nature and Value of Civil Liberty and the War with America*, and republished the two with a substantial introduction in 1778 as *Two Tracts on Civil Liberty, the War with America, and the Finances of the Kingdom*. For Price's Arianism see Clark, *English Society 1660–1832*, pp. 396–9.

34. Burke, *Writings*, III, pp. 288–330; *Reflections*, p. 65, Introduction. Price is conspicuous by his absence from volume III of Burke's *Writings*, which covers the years 1774 to 1780. Burke's response to Price was in private correspondence, and then only on a Rockinghamite shibboleth: 'Let Dr Price rail at the declaratory act of 1766 [. . .] Let him rail at this declaration, as those rail at freewill who have sinned in consequence of it'. The Declaratory Act went with a generous concession, repeal of the Stamp Act; but 'Others [by implication Price] thought they ought rather to have convicted their Country of Robbery; and to have given up the Object, not as a Liberal donation, but as a restitution of stolen goods. They thought that there were *speculative* bounds with regard to Legislative power': Burke to Richard Champion, [19 March 1776]: Burke, *Correspondence*, III, p. 254. Later, Richard Burke referred to Price's 'combustible piece', evidently his pamphlet: Richard Burke, sr. to Richard Champion, [c. 22 January 1777]: ibid., III, p. 322.

35. Especially 'An Essay Towards a History of the Laws of England' and 'An Essay towards an Abridgement of the English History' in Burke, *Writings*, I, pp. 321–552.

36. For which, see especially Geoffrey Hawthorn, *Plausible Worlds: Possibility and understanding in history and the social sciences* (Cambridge, 1991), ch. 1, 'Counterfactuals, explanation and understanding', and the Introduction to Niall Ferguson (ed.), *Virtual History: alternatives and counterfactuals* (London, 1997) .

37. 'The meaning of a text is known as much by what it omits as by what it relates': A. M. C. Waterman, '"The Grand Scheme of Subordination": The Intellectual Foundations of Tory Doctrine', *Australian Journal of Politics and History*, 40 (special issue, 1994), pp. 121–33, at 121.

38. For Burke's older patterns of discourse see *Reflections*, pp. 23–43, Introduction; Warren M. Elofson, 'The Rockingham Whigs and the Country Tradition', *Parliamentary History*, 8 (1989), pp. 90–115; Reed Browning, 'The Origin of Burke's Ideas Revisited', *Eighteenth-Century Studies*, 18 (1984), pp. 57–71.

39. 'How ideologies are born: the case of radicalism', in J.C.D. Clark, *Our Shadowed Present: modernism, postmodernism and history* (London, forthcoming).

40. For this see especially P. J. Marshall's edition of Burke, *Writings*, V–VII, and H. V. Bowen, *Revenue and Reform: the Indian Problem in British Politics, 1757–1773* (Cambridge, 1991).

41. Burke, *Writings*, II, p. 65 (speech of 26 May 1767).

42. Burke, *Writings*, II, pp. 372–3 (which contains Burke's excuses for the apparently 'arbitrary conduct' of two Governors of Bengal, Robert Clive and Harry Verelst, evidently inconsistent with his later hounding of Warren Hastings), 391.

43. Burke, *Writings*, V–VII, show an attention on Burke's part to the internal affairs of British India that was soon far in excess of his attention to the internal affairs of British America.

44. J.C.D. Clark, *The Language of Liberty 1660–1832: Political discourse and social dynamics in the Anglo-American world* (Cambridge, 1994), p. 4 and passim.

45. F. P. Lock, *Edmund Burke: Volume I, 1730-1784* (Oxford, 1998), pp. 37, 64–73.

46. As is argued in Clark, *Language of Liberty*, pp. 96–7, 100–1, 105, 108–10.

47. Burke, *Writings*, II, pp. 43–5, at 45.

48. Burke, *Writings*, II, pp. 54–7, at 55–6.

49. Paul Langford, 'The Rockingham Whigs and America, 1767–1773', in Anne Whiteman, J. S. Bromley and P.G.M. Dickson (eds.), *Statesmen, Scholars and Merchants* (Oxford, 1973), pp. 135–52, at 137–8. 'Where Grenville was inclined to raise the American issue on the slightest pretext [. . .] Rockingham and his friends seem positively to have evaded it': ibid., p. 140. Nor did they see coming the crisis produced by the East India Tea Export Act of 1773: ibid., p. 143; P.D.G. Thomas, *The Townshend Duties Crisis* (Oxford, 1987), p. 254. There is room for doubt on whether Burke opposed the Townshend duties on 15 May 1767 and what exactly the words of his draft meant: *Writings*, II, pp. 614; Conor Cruise O'Brien, *The Great Melody: A Thematic Biography and Commented Biography of Edmund Burke* (London, 1992), pp. 119–23; P.D.G. Thomas, *British Politics and the Stamp Act Crisis* (Oxford, 1975), pp. 324–8, 358, 368–9; idem, *Townshend Duties Crisis*, pp. 105, 134, 159.

50. Burke, *Writings*, II, pp. 75–9. at 77. Burke's proof of this scenario was not the Townshend duties (in retrospect, momentous) but the Nullum Tempus controversy (in retrospect, obscure).

51. [Edmund Burke], *Observations on a Late State of the Nation* (London, 1769), in *Writings*, II, pp. 102–219, esp. at 187–99.

52. Burke, *Writings*, II, p. 151. Burke did hypothetically forecast 'calamities' if the American colonies were 'compelled' to pay the taxes that his pamphleteering opponent, William Knox, had recommended. But Burke did not single out the Thirteen Colonies: he wrote rather of the impossibility of Britain's apportioning a tax burden among twenty-six colonies 'from Nova Scotia to Nevis': ibid., pp. 166–7. Burke's longest passages on the colonies were those in which he ridiculed Knox's proposal for American members of parliament as impractical, against 'the order of Providence': ibid., pp. 177–81.

53. Burke, *Reflections*, p. 74, Introduction.

54. Burke, *Writings*, II, pp. 241–323; cf. p. 253.

55. Burke, *Writings*, II, pp. 258–61.

56. Burke, *Writings*, II, pp. 323–34, at 323, 326, 332; Thomas, *Townshend Duties Crisis*, pp. 187–9.

57. Burke, *Writings*, II, pp. 404–6, at 405.

58. Burke to the Committee of Correspondence of the General Assembly of New York, 6 April 1774: Burke, *Correspondence*, II, pp. 526–30. Even then he was not offering his own prediction but reporting Lord North's speech of 14 March, which had raised fears of a colonial bid for independence. See also Ross J.S. Hoffman, *Edmund Burke, New York Agent* (Philadelphia, 1956).

59. Burke, *Writings*, II, pp. 406–63.

60. Burke, *Writings*, III, pp. 102–69.

61. Burke, *Writings*, II, p. 25 (Introduction).

62. Burke, *Writings*, II, pp. 411, 458, 462.

63. *Thoughts on the Cause* (1770), in Burke, *Writings*, II, p. 267.

64. *Mr. Edmund Burke's Speeches at his Arrival at Bristol, and at the Conclusion of the Poll* (London, 1774), in Burke, *Writings*, III, pp. 58–9.

65. Burke, *Writings*, III, p. 73.

66. Burke, *Writings*, III, p. 77.

67. Burke, *Writings*, III, p. 83. His speech on conciliation of 22 March 1775 did not propose a repeal of the Declaratory Act; nor was he willing to dispense with it in his second speech on conciliation of 16 November 1775: Burke, *Writings*, III, pp. 195, 198. Not until the debate of 6 April 1778 did Burke renounce this Rockinghamite shibboleth: ibid., III, pp. 373–4.

68. Burke, *Writings*, III, pp. 97–100.

69. Burke, *Writings*, III, pp. 102–69. His editor has argued (pp. 5, 104) that Burke's speech was well-researched and shows an 'apparently extensive understanding' of American society. This verdict needs reconsideration.

70. Burke, *Writings*, III, pp. 102–69, at 119–24, 130. For the role of religion in the revolution see Clark, *Language of Liberty*, pp. 4–5 and passim; Ronald Hoffman and Peter J. Albert (eds.), *Religion in a Revolutionary Age* (Charlottesville, 1994), and references to earlier work there given.

71. Burke, *Writings*, III, p. 156.

72. Burke, *Writings*, III, p. 196.

73. Burke, *Writings*, III, p. 255.

74. *A Letter from Edmund Burke, Esq; One of the Representatives in Parliament for the City of Bristol, to John Farr and John Harris, Esqrs. Sheriffs of that City, on the Affairs of America* (London, 1777), in Burke, *Writings*, III, pp. 288–330. Peace could only be obtained 'not by deciding the suit, but by compromising the difference': ibid., p. 319. Burke remarkably offered no new grounds for thinking that a compromise was possible.

75. *A Speech of Edmund Burke, Esq. At the Guildhall, in Bristol, Previous to the late Election in that City, upon Certain Points relative to his Parliamentary Conduct* (London, 1780), in Burke, *Writings*, III, p. 648. Burke professed a high opinion of that other colonial Agent in London, Benjamin Franklin (Burke to Count Darcy, 5 October 1775: Burke, *Correspondence*, III, p. 228) and claimed 'an acquaintance' with him (Burke to Rockingham, 6 January 1777: ibid., p. 310). Yet it was evidently a slight acquaintance: Franklin 'had too few friends in either house' of Parliament, and 'had made hardly any contact even with Burke until the last few months of his mission': Esmond Wright, *Franklin of Philadelphia* (Cambridge, Mass., 1986), pp. 233–4. Franklin sailed from England on 20 March 1775.

76. Burke, *Writings*, II, pp. 188, 193–4, 199; cf. 'the insolence of the mutinous spirits in America [. . .] the seditious', p. 190.

77. Burke, *Writings*, II, p. 231; Langford, 'Rockingham Whigs and America', p. 138.

78. [W. King and F. Lawrence, eds.,] *The Works of the Right Honourable Edmund Burke*, 16 vols. (London: F. C. and J. Rivington, 1803–27), X, p. 10. Paul Langford has established that this text was an editorial compilation and so may represent Burke's thoughts rather than the speech as given; the phrase is not included in the latest version printed in Burke, *Writings*, II, pp. 359-64.

79. Burke, *Writings*, pp. 362–4. On 3 April 1772 Burke then supported the Dissenters' petition for exemption from the requirement under the 1689 Toleration Act to subscribe the doctrinal as well as (what they already enjoyed) exemption from the disciplinary of the Thirty-nine Articles: ibid., pp. 368–70. 'I cannot consider our dissenters, of almost any kind, as schismaticks'; Burke would tolerate Jews, Mahometans and Pagans; 'Much more am I inclined to tolerate those, whom I look upon as our brethren; I mean all those who profess our common hope; extending to all the reformed and unreformed Churches, both at home and abroad; in none of whom I find any thing capitally amiss, but their mutual hatred of each other': Burke to William Burgh, 9 February 1775, in Burke, *Correspondence*, III, pp. 111–12.

80. Burke, *Writings*, II, pp. 381–90, at 385. Episcopacy, he added, was not essential to Christianity; the Church of England should be characterised by 'a noble and Liberal comprehension': ibid., II, p. 388. On 20 June 1780, Burke spoke in the Commons of his having been 'educated as a Protestant of the church of England by a Dissenter', of having studied the theological controversies of the seventeenth and eighteenth centuries; 'at last [. . .] he dropped them, embracing and holding fast—[to] the church of England': ibid., III, p. 606. The church of Rome was a 'vast structure of superstition and tyranny', he announced on the hustings in 1780: ibid., p. 639. The old myth of Burke as a crypto-Papist is no more than that.

81. Clark, *Language of Liberty*, pp. 317–35.

82. Burke, *Reflections*, pp. 59–60, Introduction; Clark, *English Society 1660–1832*, pp. 361–422.

83. Ibid., pp. 387–8; John Leland, *A View of the Principal Deistical Writers*, 3 vols. (London, 1754–6); Burke, *Reflections*, [p. 133].

84. Burke, *Reflections*, pp. 29–30, Introduction.

85. For High Churchmen as the authors of the most coherent rationale for the English alliance of Church and State, see A.M.C. Waterman, 'The nexus between theology and

political doctrine in Church and Dissent', in Knud Haakonssen (ed.), *Enlightenment and Religion: Rational Dissent in eighteenth-century Britain* (Cambridge, 1996), pp. 193–218.

86. Henry P. Ippel, 'British Sermons and the American Revolution', *Journal of Religious History*, 12 (1982–3), pp. 191–205; Paul Langford, 'The English Clergy and the American Revolution', in Eckhart Hellmuth (ed.), *The Transformation of Political Culture: England and Germany in the Late Eighteenth Century* (Oxford, 1990), pp. 275–307.

87. Burke, *Writings*, II, p. 389.

88. O'Brien, *Great Melody*, pp. 93–4. O'Brien interprets Burke's 'pregnant silence' differently, as a tactic to secure colonial sympathy for the Quebec Act and the Catholic cause.

89. Burke to Cruger, 30 June 1772, in Burke, *Correspondence*, II, p. 310. Burke wrote of colonial Dissenters' resistance to the proposal to send bishops to the colonies.

90. Burke, *Writings*, IX, p. 505.

91. Burke, *Writings*, III, pp. 376–9, at 378.

92. *Speech ... 1780*, in Burke, *Writings*, III, pp. 659-60.

93. James E. Bradley, 'The Anglican Pulpit, the Social Order and the Resurgence of Toryism during the American Revolution', *Albion*, 21 (1989), pp. 361–88; corrected by Grayson Ditchfield, 'Ecclesiastical Policy under Lord North', in John Walsh, Stephen Taylor and Colin Haydon (eds.), *The Church of England c. 168— c. 1833: From Toleration to Tractarianism* (Cambridge, 1993), pp. 228–46, at 233–5.

94. Burke, *Writings*, II, pp. 55n, 185–6 (Wilkes's arrest in 1763 and general warrants); 100–4, 219, 228–30, 233–6, 242, 295, 301 (Wilkes's expulsion from Parliament after the Middlesex election); 223–8, 334–5 (the 'St. George's Fields Massacre' of Wilkes's rioting supporters); 352–6 (the 'Printers' Case' of 1771 over the right to publish parliamentary debates).

95. For Rockingham as 'willing to do almost any thing for him [Wilkes] from his private Pocket' see Burke to Richard Burke, [ante 14 January 1766]: Burke, *Correspondence*, I, p. 231. Burke was an intermediary in negotiations with Wilkes, and their relations in 1766 were good: ibid., pp. 256–9. By 1768, Burke had realized that Wilkes was 'of no prudence and no principles': Burke to Charles O'Hara, 9 June 1768, ibid., p. 352; cf. II, p. 96. Soon, Burke dismissed Wilkes as 'treacherous': Burke to Rockingham, 18 September 1774: ibid., III, p. 32.

96. Burke, *Writings*, II, p. 286.

97. Clark, *English Society 1660-1832*, p. 408.

98. Burke, *Reflections*, Introduction, pp. 54–6.

99. Burke to William Windham, 27 September 1789: Burke, *Correspondence*, VI, pp. 24–6.

100. In *Thoughts on the Cause*: Burke, *Writings*, II, pp. 255–6, 264.

101. Burke, *Writings*, II, p. 452; III, p. 212. For 'the Revolution of Taste' in garden design and 'the revolution in the [East] India House' see Burke to Rockingham, 6 November 1769: Burke, *Correspondence*, II, pp. 105–6. For a 'silent and insensible revolution' producing Britain's decline in power see Burke to Rockingham, 22 August 1775: ibid.,

III, p. 191. For a 'Nursery revolution', a change in the household of the Prince of Wales, see Burke to Richard Champion, 30 May 1776: ibid., III, p. 269.

102. Burke, *Reflections*, pp. 62, 89-90, Introduction. For an argument that the essential feature of the new conceptualization of 'revolution' in the 1790s was not a transition from regression to transformation, i.e. from circular to linear motion, since the second had long been in wide use, see 'Breaking the grip of the social sciences: the case of revolution', in Clark, *Our Shadowed Present*. For a different approach see John Dinwiddy, 'Conceptions of Revolution in the English Radicalism of the 1790s', in Hellmuth (ed.), *Transformation of Political Culture*, pp. 535–60.

103. Burke to Dr. William Robertson, 9 June 1777: Burke, *Correspondence*, III, p. 351; cf. 'the Rebellious spirit of America', Burke to C. J. Fox, 8 October 1777: ibid., III, p. 385.

104. Conor Cruise O'Brien, *The Long Affair: Thomas Jefferson and the French Revolution* (London, 1996).

105. Burke, *Reflections*, pp. 80–2, Introduction; [pp. 11–12, 95, 104].

106. Burke, *Writings*, II, p. 388.

107. For a defence of Burke's consistency see O'Brien, *Great Melody*, pp. 440–52. What is at issue, I suggest here, is less Burke's principled consistency than the way in which his understanding of major episodes developed or failed to do so.

108. In 1791, Burke was obviously defensive about having believed Franklin: the latter had had 'a greater air of openness [. . .] than Mr. Burke had observed in him before. In this discourse, Dr. Franklin lamented, and with apparent sincerity, the separation which he feared was inevitable between Great Britain and her colonies': [Edmund Burke], *An Appeal from the New to the Old Whigs, in consequence of some late Discussions in Parliament, relative to the Reflections on the French Revolution* (London, 1791), pp. 36–41, not yet published in Burke, *Writings*. For the salience of America at this time see Mark Philp, 'The Role of America in the "Debate on France" 1791–5: Thomas Paine's Insertion', *Utilitas*, 5 (1993), pp. 221–37.

109. Bernard Bailyn, 'Atlantic Dimensions' (the Robbins Lecture at the University of London, 2001), forthcoming in Bailyn, *"To Begin the World Anew": The Genius and Ambiguities of the American Founders*.

110. E.g. [Lord John Russell], *The Causes of the French Revolution* (London, 1832).

111. See also Burke, *Reflections*, pp. 25–9, Introduction.

112. Conrad Russell, *Unrevolutionary England, 1603–1642* (London, 1990). Conrad Russell's approach to the historiography of the 'English' Civil War applies to the American Revolution also: 'if we assume a 'two sides' model, with government and opposition [here, Britain and America] arrayed on opposite sides, and if we assume long-term constitutional objectives instead of short-term political ones, we simply cannot describe what was happening' (p. xiv). Such a conclusion, of course, makes the American Revolution both harder to explain, and more important.

Thomas Chalmers and the
Economics-and-Religion Debate

Alexander C. Dow,
Sheila C. Dow, and Alan Hutton

Anthony Waterman has drawn attention to the contribution made to the development of classical economics in Britain in the nineteenth century by Thomas Chalmers. Waterman suggests that Chalmers provides the "'missing link' [. . .] between Malthus' *Essay* and Ricardo's *Principles*: and that this affords qualified support for Samuelson's [. . .] vision of a single 'canonical classical model of political economy'" ("Canonical" 221).

This generous treatment of Chalmers as an important, yet inadequately recognized, contributor to classical economics focusses on the work of someone who is not primarily known for his economics (see, however, Nisbet). Chalmers (1780–1847) was a Presbyterian clergyman in Scotland who is most widely known as the leader of the Great Disruption in 1843, the separation of a group from the General Assembly of the Church of Scotland to form the Free Church. But, in addition to his pastoral duties, Chalmers wrote and spoke widely on economic subjects and was at various times an academic, in the fields of mathematics, moral philosophy, and divinity. Chalmers was actively engaged in economic and social reform as part of his parish ministry, reflecting his views on the interdependence between his economics and his religion. In particular, he was actively involved in debate on Poor Law reform.

While it was not at all uncommon for major nineteenth-century contributions to economics to be made by clergymen, it did not follow that economics and religion were seen as interdependent. Indeed, there was much debate in England in the first half of the nineteenth century on the subject of the relationship (if any) between religious knowledge and scientific knowledge (see Waterman: *Revolution*; "Whately"). Waterman has contributed significantly to our modern understanding of the issues by organizing, together with his

Faith, Reason, and Economics: Essays in Honour of Anthony Waterman. Ed. Derek Hum. Winnipeg: St. John's College Press, 2003.

co-editors, two volumes on the subject (Brennan and Waterman; Dean and Waterman). More particularly, in his *Revolution, Economics and Religion*, Waterman offers a detailed analysis of Christian political economy in the early nineteenth century and Chalmers's role in this movement. Our purpose here is to offer some further analysis of Chalmers's views as to the relationship between economics and religion. The emphasis is placed on the intellectual environment of Scotland as an influence on Chalmers's thought.

We therefore start by considering the intellectual and cultural tradition from which Chalmers's views emerged. While some have seen the Enlightenment period explicitly in terms of a separation of science from religion, we argue that this would be a misleading characterization of the Scottish Enlightenment. In the following section, we consider Chalmers's own theory of human nature, his natural theology, and his approach to the alleviation of poverty. We then consider how to locate Chalmers in relation to the Scottish political economy tradition that had emanated from such key figures as David Hume and Adam Smith. Hume and Smith were more associated with the moderates in the Church of Scotland, while Chalmers (although difficult to categorize) was ultimately associated with the evangelicals. We therefore consider whether such differences override the commonalities between Chalmers and the Scottish political economy tradition, specifically with respect to the issue of the relationship between economics and religion.

In order to consider Chalmers in relation to the tradition in thought emanating from the Scottish Enlightenment, it is useful first to consider religious thought at the time of the Enlightenment itself. It is not uncommon for the Enlightenment period to be represented as the triumph of reason over dogma and thus of science over religion. The representation of Hume as an atheist has served to create the impression that this dichotomization applies to the Scottish Enlightenment, as to enlightenment movements elsewhere. But Hume's scepticism of a particular argument for the existence of God was misinterpreted as a denial of the existence of God. In fact, Hume expressed a view of the role of religion that was to find a strong echo in the views of Chalmers. In his posthumously published *Dialogues Concerning Natural Religion,* Hume writes: "The proper office of religion is to regulate the heart of men, humanise their conduct, infuse the spirit of temperance, order, and obedience; and as its operation is silent, and only enforces the motives of morality and justice, it is in danger of being overlooked and confounded with these other motives" (qtd. in Tweyman 198).

The notion of a separate Scottish Enlightenment is itself a matter for debate (see further: Dow, Dow, and Hutton, "Scottish"; Dow, Dow, Hutton, and Keaney). The specific argument that there was a distinctly Scottish approach to matters of epistemology, logic, and religion has been most fully presented by S.R. Sutherland. While we can identify in both England and Scotland the influences of Puritanism and natural-law philosophy, the hierarchical structure of the Church of England, with the monarch at the head, differed from the more democratic structure of the Presbyterian Church of Scotland, which, while the Established Church in Scotland, remained separate from the monarchy. Further, the relationship between Church and State, the mechanism for selecting the monarch, and the very idea of Scottish nationhood had been matters for fierce public debate since the sixteenth century. Indeed, it was in the early period of the Reformation in Scotland that the idea was formulated (which Chalmers later pursued) of the godly commonwealth. But the idea had waned in the interim through lack of Church resources to pursue social goals.

Sutherland argues that the debates over the relationship between Church and State in Scotland raised issues that did not apply in England, where there was a hierarchy of authority, established by law and by history, not only in the Church but also in the monarchic succession. *A priori* argument could proceed from an established natural order of society in England. But metaphysical arguments about nationhood and legitimation substituted for *a priori* argument in Scotland. It is in this distinction that much of the difference between Scottish and English traditions in epistemology lies, a difference that became evident in the two traditions in political economy. As Sutherland argues, it was not just a matter of finding answers to questions about nationhood, monarchy, and religion but also of establishing ways of answering these questions. In particular, "historical change, whether religious or not, is a subject inappropriate to *a priori* reason" (Sutherland 137).

It was against this background of over a century of metaphysical debate that the General Assembly of the Church of Scotland, in the 1690s, addressed the threat posed by the tenets of religion being opened up to the new rational enquiry of the Enlightenment. In the 1696 Act Against the Atheistical Opinions of the Deists and for Establishing the Confessions of Faith, the Assembly challenged views based on the premises that "there must be a mathematical evidence for each purpose, before we can be obliged to assent to any proposition thereanent, and that natural light is sufficient to salvation" (qtd. in Cameron 117). This stance allowed the continuation of religious persecution, notably the pivotal case of the execution in 1696 of an eighteen-year-old Edinburgh university student for heresy.

Rather than the emergence of a polarization between religion and science, however, there was, first in academic circles then in the parish, a movement toward reconciling the two. Thus John Simson, the professor of divinity at the University of Glasgow, argued that "the truths of faith remained unalterable, but the way these were expounded and defended should, in an academic setting, be continuously brought under review in the light of increase in knowledge" (qtd. in Cameron 119). By 1729, parish minister Robert Wallace was arguing that, while it was insufficient without revelation, reason is the way in which we arrive at an understanding of the truth; rational examination of beliefs was in the Protestant tradition (Cameron 123).

This articulation of a middle road between "a deluge of skepticism" and "blind obedience" (Wallace 73), in the form of a combination of reason and revelation, was in tune with the tradition of natural theology, as expressed by Archibald Campbell, professor of divinity and ecclesiastical history at the University of St. Andrews. Cameron puts Campbell's argument this way: "If a religion contains articles that are contradictory to the nature of things, to common sense or to the principles of reason [. . .] this is sufficient to demonstrate that such a religion has no pretensions to a divine original" (127).

There is much in common between these views and Hume's "mitigated skepticism." His sceptical argument was that reason was insufficient for knowledge; but this scepticism was mitigated by the foundation provided for knowledge by common-sense belief. The religious argument concerns the source of belief (for many theologians, belief arose from revelation, while Hume, like the natural theologians, saw it as arising from experience, that is, natural belief) where the individual's experience is conditioned by the history of society's experience. There is an important commonality between religious knowledge and scientific knowledge in terms of the necessary combination, rather than opposition, between reason and belief. This, we would argue, is a key characteristic of the Scottish Enlightenment. Indeed, Sutherland has articulated the argument that, because of this background of theological debate in Scotland, there is more in common between Hume and Reid, the common-sense philosopher often seen (by himself and by others) as being in opposition to Hume, than with Bishop Butler, whose natural theology came from a different epistemological tradition.

In order to consider how far he can be seen as belonging to the Scottish political economy tradition, we turn now to consider the thought of Chalmers on the relationship between economics and religion.

Shortly before Chalmers was born, Hume died and Smith's *Wealth of Nations* was published. By the time Chalmers reached adulthood, what eventually became known as classical political economy was being forged in public debate over such issues as free trade and taxation. Key figures for Chalmers in the emerging Classical political economy were Malthus, with his argument for "moral restraint" in order to counter the consequences of the natural law of population, and John Stuart Mill's utilitarian argument for social reform. Chalmers's concern was with the most effective means of reducing poverty, given the ultimate limits to growth of production.

Chalmers achieved fame not only for the power of his preaching but also for his arguments against the Poor Law, which provided the basis for payments to the poor. These arguments drew on his experience as a parish minister, where he encountered the social consequences of industrialization as well as first-hand experience of the English factory system at work. Chalmers's argument against the Poor Law was that it did not provide a sustainable answer to poverty.

Compulsory poor relief went against the "natural" laws of population that Malthus had identified. Rather, Chalmers saw the cure for poverty in education, which would restore the moral sense of the community. In an article in the *Edinburgh Review* comparing poverty relief in Scotland and England, Chalmers argued: "It is by leaving the whole matter to the operation of the mechanisms of nature, and by keeping in their right tone and action the principles which reside, or which may be implanted in the constitution of individual men:— And the use of churches is to foster these principles, and to supersede that system by which they have been checked and overborne" (*Political* XX.321). Chalmers offered his proposal for the church's moral teaching to remove the impediments to "natural" moral sense as paralleling Adam Smith's proposal for the rule of law as removing the impediments to free trade (XX.318–19). But he argued against free trade itself because, in an early statement of a form of dependency theory, he advocated production being directed to domestic, rather than foreign, needs.

It was the erosion of community life that had placed impediments on moral sense. Industrialization and the associated urbanization had eroded the habit of church-going and the moral sense that it nourished within the community. This moral sense, on the one hand, encouraged the wealthier members of the community (generally the landowners) to provide the resources for distribution to the poor. On the other hand, the moral sense of the poor encouraged industry and frugality, and Malthusian "moral restraint," reducing the need for poverty relief. Chalmers argued that an important externality of spiritual teachings was that:

> they liberalize the wealthy, and they dignify the poor; and they call forth the slumbering sympathies of the former, and the slumbering delicacies of the latter; and they, each in his own district of moral superintendence, draw into a closer acquaintanceship the people who live in it; and they give strength to the maxims of prudence, and the habits of economy, and the ties of neighbourhood, and the duties of relationship; and thus, on the one hand, diminish the number of the receivers of charity, and, on the other hand, augment the zeal and inclination of the dispensers." (*Political* XX 320)

Chalmers put his principles into practice most notably in experiments where he had set up new churches to reach an urban population that did not have the small-town habit of church-going with which he had been familiar when growing up in Anstruther. The growing city populations were increasingly inadequately served by a church structure that dated from less populous times. The first of these experiments was the parish of St. John's in Glasgow. Chalmers arranged for the Church to administer poverty relief. The Church collection was to be substituted for central funds as the source of finance for poverty relief. Further, rather than the more automatic Poor Law payments, Chalmers's system was to be based on personal relationships. While elders addressed spiritual needs on a personal basis, deacons were appointed to administer payments according to case-by-case assessment of need. Education was provided for all, both in Sabbath schools and in day schools. The experiment was apparently a great success, not least because pauperism was reduced at lower cost and thus with less redistribution of income than the Poor Law system.

Not all were convinced. It is notable that Chalmers's responses to critics of the St. John's experiment involved detailed statistical analysis, employing data on migration rates in and out of the parish, breakdowns of Church revenues by time of service (and thus by category of giver, local or visitor) and comparisons between the St. John's experience and that of other parishes (*Political* XX, Appendices). Chalmers had in early life been a most enthusiastic mathematician, a pursuit that others had thought inappropriate for a clergyman. The opposition between mathematical argument and theological argument that we had noted in the Church of Scotland's views a century earlier was clearly not evident in Chalmers's thought.

But Chalmers's mathematical bent did not mean he was inclined toward utilitarianism. While this philosophy had been used to justify Poor Law relief in England, Chalmers explicitly distanced himself from it. He made this plain in the preface to the first volume of *On Political Economy*, where he set out his purpose as to establish the means of alleviating poverty, given the eventual limit to economic growth. He concludes with respect to the poor that "there is an inseparable alliance between the two elements of their character and their comfort; and that a thorough education of principle throughout the land, though the only, yet is the sure road to the economic well-being of the community at large" (*Political* XIX, x).

While Chalmers had been taken up by the likes of Senior as an ally in English efforts addressed at Poor Law reform, his rejection of utilitarianism led to his fall from favour (Alborn). Chalmers's rejection of utilitarianism stemmed from his Evangelicalism. For Chalmers, preferences were not to be taken as given. They could change with education in general and moral teaching in particular. Industrialization had changed behaviour that had been forged in rural and small-town communities as a result of the habit of church-going. By creating new parishes in the growing cities, Chalmers aimed to recreate the habit of church-going and thus demand for religious instruction.

Further, the outcome of this instruction would be the fostering again of community-oriented behaviour, whereby the individual achieved fulfillment through serving the community (Brown 37). Poverty relief was not to reflect the goal of maximizing consumption as a way to maximize the utility of self-interested individuals. Rather, it was meant to address the basic needs of those who were unable, through their own efforts, to meet those needs themselves. Religious instruction would serve to diminish the importance to the individual of consumption, since this served the needs of the senses. But Chalmers (*Discourses* VIII) distinguished between the goal of maximizing consumption and maximizing money holdings—it was the latter that posed the greater danger to the soul, since it was the more serious form of idolatry: "He who makes a god of his pleasure, renders to this idol the homage of his senses. He who makes a god of his wealth, renders to this idol the homage of his mind; and he, therefore, of the two, is the more hopeless and determined idolater" (196). Thus, presaging the work of both Marx and Keynes (Winslow), Chalmers implied that the love of money for its own sake was unnatural, going against a person's best interests.

By identifying religious instruction as the means of alleviating poverty, Chalmers was making the most direct connection between religion and economics. His analysis was designed to show that learned moral sense would alter behaviour in such a way as to alleviate the constraints on output. The Established Church therefore had a key economic role:

> Our endeavour is to prove, that, in every direction, there is a limit to the augmentation of our physical resources; [. . .] our object will be gained if we can demonstrate, that, even but for the economic well-being of the people, their moral and religious education is the first and greatest object of national policy; and that, while this is neglected, a government, in its anxious and incessant labours for a well-conditioned state of the commonwealth, will only flounder from one delusive shift or expedient to another, under the double misfortune, of being held responsible for the prosperity of the land, and yet, finding this to be an element most helplessly and hopelessly beyond its control." (Chalmers, *Political* XIX xiv)

But Chalmers lost the attention of Senior and others involved in Poor Law reform in England because of this insistence on combining religion and economics, and in Scotland, too, he became distanced from his own church. Chalmers led the Disruption of the Church of Scotland in 1843, taking with him more than one-third of the clergy and almost one-half of the membership to set up the Free Church of Scotland. In relation to the goals he had pursued earlier in life, this development in fact represented failure. He had been a strong proponent of the notion of an Established Church, integral to society, whereas the Disruption broke up the Establishment. Further, as an Evangelical, he sought to increase demand for the services of the Church, whereas the Free Church soon saw its mission more in terms of its existing membership (Brown).

A key feature of the Scottish Enlightenment is its distinctive epistemology, which, as we argued above, involves a close connection with religion through the central importance of belief. Knowledge is then built on a foundation of belief, drawing on society's collective experience of the real world with the application of reason. The purpose of building up knowledge is to address practical questions. The means of constructing knowledge is deductive knowledge applied to principles induced from detailed experience, explained in terms of experience and expressed in such a way as to be applied then to a particular context. This is distinguished from deductive logic applied to axioms that are true if the axioms are true, the *a priori* approach more prevalent in the English Enlightenment. As Adam Smith argued, theories are tools for elucidating problems, which are more persuasive the more psychologically satisfying they are; they are not to be regarded as yielding "truth," since this is beyond our human capacity.

We have argued elsewhere (Dow, Dow, and Hutton, "Applied") that this approach to knowledge continued in the structure of the education system and in the structure of government in Scotland, such that it was evident still in a distinctive approach to political economy in the twentieth century. Here we consider whether Chalmers in particular can be regarded as a link in the chain by which the tradition was perpetuated in the nineteenth century.

Chalmers's economics differed in content from Smith's, for example. But it is the approach to economics rather than its content that we have identified as the identifying feature of the tradition. Because of his theory of human nature, Chalmers continued the tradition of an approach that was incompatible with utilitarianism. Like Smith and Hume, for example, he saw individuals as being social by nature. But the process of industrialization and urbanization had threatened that nature. Indeed, Chalmers discussed the consequences of selfish behaviour (*Discourses* III). While in normal commerce, individuals may be moved to honesty for selfish reasons; selfishness can also encourage fraudulent behaviour. Indeed, selfish pursuit of unreasonable returns can bring about a general glut: "In opposition to the maxim, that the spirit of enterprise is the soul of commercial prosperity, do we hold, that it is the excess of this spirit beyond the moderation of the New Testament, which, pressing on the natural boundaries of trade, is sure, at length, to visit every country, where it operates with the recoil of all those calamities, which, in the shape of the beggared capitalists, and unemployed operatives, and dreary intervals of bankruptcy and alarm, are observed to follow a season of overdone speculation" (*Discourses* VI.vii).

T.L. Alborn refers to Chalmers's deductivism as yielding what he saw as certainty about the economic process and the role of moral sense. While Dugald Stewart, whose lectures Chalmers attended, is characterized as seeing deductive systems as hypothetical, in the Scottish tradition, Alborn argues (34–35) that Chalmers was more influenced by Beattie's reliance on self-evident truths. It is in this deductive system based on truths that Chalmers may most closely be seen to come to the axiomatic method of the emerging canon of classical political economy.

It is difficult to find direct epistemological statements in Chalmers's work. But the methodology he actually employed reveals a combination of deduction and detailed "experimental" case studies rather than axiomatic deduction. He does not have the historical range of, say, Smith or Hume. But the approach is similar. His ideas emerged from his practical experience as a parish minister. Further, his system relies on education as the means of arousing again the moral sense of individuals in the community through knowledge, and on the personal familiarity between the deacons and the poor. This contrasts with the blanket right to Poor Law payments in England, a principle arrived at within an axiomatic deductive system that, Chalmers argues, conflicts with the actual practice of its application, where the rights of the poor are not in fact met (*Christian* XIV Preface).

Chalmers's reliance on religious truths is not a common characteristic of the Scottish political economy tradition. The "Moderates" in the Church of Scotland, who were less concerned with revealed truth than the Evangelicals, had included many of the key figures of the Enlightenment among their number, or as close friends. But Chalmers's Evangelicalism was combined with a natural theology, so that he saw Christian beliefs as having been absorbed through long experience, enhanced by Christian teaching, in rural and small-town communities. What concerned him was impediments to belief. Smith, too, had been concerned about the effects of the factory system on the human experience and accordingly advocated education as a countervailing force. But the factory system had developed significantly by the nineteenth century so that Chalmers was able to see its effects more fully. We could well imagine that Smith and Hume would have been concerned to see the social aspect of behaviour, which conditioned self-interest and thus allowed the more-or-less successful functioning of the economic system, threatened by urbanization. We have already seen, in fact, that Hume saw the effect of the Church in much the same way as Chalmers did, as tempering the excesses of selfish human behaviour.

We conclude that Chalmers can indeed be seen as following in the tradition of Scottish Political Economy. Just as Sutherland identified the Scottish Presbyterian background of Hume and Reid in their epistemology, so we have found it in Chalmers's epistemology. This introduces a connection between religion and economics at the level of the foundations of science and its connection with the real world, that is, at the level of ontology.

But Chalmers took this connection further, to the level of ontological content. The economic system worked better or worse, depending on the strength of moral sense. The Church was charged with education that would restore the religious beliefs, which in turn allowed the natural order of the economy to be restored. Moral sense encouraged sharing by the rich and prudence and frugality in the poor. As a result, the distribution of income would be more equitable, removing poverty, the poor would be more readily employed, the economy would work more smoothly, and the effects of the limits to growth would be mitigated, given the limitation of demand more closely to needs. Absence of moral sense likewise had real consequences; it was in seeking a remedy for poverty that Chalmers most effectively applied his practical as well as academic efforts.

55

The relative lack of attention to Chalmers is no doubt due in large part to the view taken by many at the time that the foundation for his economics in religious belief set him outside the mainstream of classical political economy. But we have argued that, while that may indeed be the case as far as the classical economic canon is concerned, Chalmers's approach had much in common with the Scottish political economy tradition.

WORKS CITED

Alborn, T.L. "Thomas Chalmers's Theology of Economics." *Perspectives on the History of Economic Thought.* Ed. D.E. Moggridge. Cheltenham: Edward Elgar, 1990. 29–39.

Brennan, H.G., and A.M.C. Waterman, eds. *Economics and Religion: Are They Distinct?* Boston: Kluwer, 1994.

Brown, S.J. *Thomas Chalmers and the Godly Commonwealth.* Oxford: Oxford University Press, 1982.

Cameron, J.K. "Theological Controversy: A Factor in the Origins of the Scottish Enlightenment." *The Origins and Nature of the Scottish Enlightenment.* Ed. R.H. Campbell and A.S. Skinner. Edinburgh: John Donald, 1982. 116–30.

Campbell, Archibald. *The Necessity of Revelation.* London: 1739.

Chalmers, T. *Discourses on the Application of Christianity to the Commercial and Ordinary Affairs of Life.* 1820. Reprinted in *Chalmers' Works,* vol. VI. Glasgow: Collins, 1835–42.

_____ . *On the Christian and Economic Polity of a Nation, More Especially with Reference to its Large Towns.* 1821. Reprinted in *Chalmers' Works,* vol. XIV. Glasgow: Collins, 1835–42.

_____ . *On Political Economy, in Connexion with the Moral State and Moral Prospects of Society,* vols. I and II. 1832. Reprinted in *Chalmers' Works,* vols. XIX and XX. Glasgow: Collins, 1835–42.

Dean, J.M., and A.M.C. Waterman, eds. *Religion and Economics: Normative Social Theory.* Boston: Kluwer, 1999.

Dow, A.C., S.C. Dow, and A. Hutton. "Scottish Political Economy and Modern Economics." *Scottish Journal of Political Economy* 44 (1997): 368–83.

_____ . "Applied Economics in a Political Economy Tradition: The Case of Scotland from the 1890s to the 1950s." *History of Political Economy* 32 (Annual Supplement, 2000): 177–98.

Dow, A.C., S.C. Dow, A. Hutton, and M. Keaney. "Traditions in Economics: The Case of Scottish Political Economy." *New Political Economy* 3 (1998): 45–58.

Nisbet, T.J. "Thomas Chalmers and the Economic Order." *Scottish Journal of Political Economy* 11 (1964): 151–57.

Smith, Adam. "History of Astronomy." 1795. *Essays on Philosophical Subjects.* Ed. W.P.D. Wightman. Oxford: Clarendon, 1976. 33–105.

Sutherland, S.R. "The Presbyterian Inheritance of Hume and Reid." *The Origins and Nature of the Scottish Enlightenment.* Ed. R.H. Campbell and A.S. Skinner. Edinburgh: John Donald, 1982. 131–49.

Tweyman, S., ed. *Hume on Natural Religion.* Bristol: Thoemmes, 1996.

Wallace, R. *A Sermon Preached before the Provincial Synod of Dumfries, October 1729.* London: 1731.

Waterman, A.M.C. *Revolution, Economics and Religion: Christian Political Economy, 1798–1833.* Cambridge: Cambridge University Press, 1991.

_____ . "'The Canonical Classical Model of Political Economy' in 1808, as Viewed from 1825: Thomas Chalmers on the 'Natural Resources.'" *History of Political Economy* 23 (1991): 221–41.

_____ . "Whately, Senior, and the Methodology of Classical Economics." *Economics and Religion: Are They Distinct?* Ed. H.G. Brennan and A.M.C. Waterman. Boston: Kluwer, 1994. 41–60.

Winslow, T. "Uncertainty and Liquidity-Preference." *Keynes, Knowledge and Uncertainty.* Ed. S.C. Dow and J. Hillard, 1995. 221–43.

The French Debate on the Morality and the Political Economy of Luxury

Walter Eltis and Shelagh M. Eltis

There were great inequalities in income and wealth in the seventeenth and eighteenth centuries. All who wrote on economies and societies therefore confronted the question of whether the extraordinary and often ostentatious consumption of the wealthiest undermined or boosted the economies within which they spent so extravagantly.

This was a more acute issue in France than in Great Britain. It was entirely clear that the British economy was outperforming the French, and British writers were therefore more inclined to take a favourable view of the central elements in the evolution of their economies, including the extraordinary inequalities in personal expenditure that accompanied the undiluted right of the wealthy to dispose of their property in whatever way they wished.

France in contrast had suffered periods of famine and a succession of crises in the state's finances. These produced three seventeenth-century defaults, the desperation of John Law's financial experiments, and the subsequent failure of attempts at reform by a succession of controllers-general. Every aspect of France's economy and society therefore became a subject of critical debate.

Economic publication increased enormously in France in the 1750s. The number of books published on the economy doubled in the period between 1745–1749 and 1750–1754, and it doubled again between 1750–1754 and 1755–1759. French political economy was also notable for the social and political distinction of the authors of some of its leading contributions. As in Britain, leading philosophers together with bankers and merchants published on political economy; but the early French writers also included thirty-seven ministers and intendants who published on economics between 1750 and 1789 (Théré 37). The leading economic writers who contributed substantially to the

Faith, Reason, and Economics: Essays in Honour of Anthony Waterman. Ed. Derek Hum. Winnipeg: St. John's College Press, 2003.

luxury debate included Argenson, Boisguilbert, Cantillon, Forbonnais, Melon, Mirabeau, and Quesnay.

Fénelon, Montesquieu, Rousseau, and Voltaire also wrote extensively and influentially on luxury. They were deeply concerned with every aspect of French society, and philosophers and theologians no less than ministers and intendants were interested in the effect of luxury on the economy and society.

The various authors attached very different meanings to luxury. It normally denoted inequality; but, in addition, did it divert money from essential expenditure elsewhere, or lock it up unproductively? The debate pitted town against countryside and the old nobility against nouveau riche financiers and tax farmers. Sumptuary laws that laid down the clothing that each social rank was permitted to wear had been designed to contain the consumption of social inferiors within their station, but few survived into the eighteenth century. It is interesting how, late in the century, dress codes were still being advocated by social conservatives.

A few economic writers understood that a successful economy needed industry, agriculture, and commerce and therefore hesitated to categorize swathes of their fellow citizens as members of a potentially redundant luxurious class.

In this essay we present a broad outline of the luxury debate until François Quesnay created what Philippe Steiner has described as "the new science of political economy" (Steiner 5). Quesnay abandoned the social and political issues that had preoccupied his predecessors, and he presented the influence of luxury within the constraints of the economic model he had invented: his celebrated *Tableau économique*.

THE LUXURY DEBATE BEFORE THE PHYSIOCRATS

Pierre de Boisguilbert is sometimes regarded as the founder of French political economy, and he opened the economic dimension of the luxury debate in the final decades of the reign of Louis XIV. Heavy war taxation had brought concern that France's taxable base was being eroded, as impossible burdens on the peasantry caused crops to be abandoned and land to be withdrawn from cultivation. Boisguilbert expressed this in his published works and in impassioned communications to successive controllers-general of finance. He had the profound insight that, despite their individual lowly status, the spending of peasants, given their preponderance in the population, had a huge effect on the economy, bringing a downward spiral to wealth and population if it was damaged (619–21). Boisguilbert's attacks on the unjust nature of the main land tax, the *taille*, and its inefficiencies as a revenue producer, together with his views on how indirect taxes prevented goods coming to market—his striking example was of Norman peasants being obliged to drink water rather than cider (279)—were not matters for dispute. Concern that France's population had fallen lay behind much subsequent debate on luxury.

Boisguilbert cited Henri IV's minister, Maximilien de Béthune, duc de Sully, as setting a precedent in support of his belief in the need to restore the consumption of the peasant class. Sully, he said, supported the grain market through free trade at a price that allowed the exploitation of land of every condition and left the roads free for the transport of grain, which he called the greatest source of revenue for the king and the people. He claimed that Sully saw that taxes were fairly spread on people as well as goods; that customs and the *gabelle* (the tax on salt) were not too high and that fixed capital was sacred (432).

In the eighteenth century, those who thought that the agricultural sector was starved of workers or investment praised Sully, but it was often to attack Jean Baptiste Colbert, minister under Louis XIV, who was seen as having diverted government support to industry to the detriment of agriculture. Since luxury goods were largely imported or the product of protected new industries such as the manufacture of silks and porcelain to substitute for such imports, it was a temptation to declare them unnecessary and harmful.

The Court of Louis XIV used ostentation in dress, jewels, theatrical displays, fountains, statues, etc., as a deliberate statement of the splendour of royalty. This luxury and Louis XIV's wars were financed through the sale of offices and recourse to tax farmers, who bought the right to raise taxes on behalf of the king. Revenues were anticipated for several years.

An aristocratic view of what was needed to place society on its proper path is seen in the Plan de Gouvernement proposed in 1711 to the duc de Bourgogne, then heir to the throne. Known from its place of drafting as the *Tables de Chaulnes*, it blamed luxury for corrupting the behaviour of the whole nation and declared that it made merchants wealthy at the expense of the nobility. At court, the reformers required moderation in furniture, clothing, horses and food, while they insisted on sumptuary laws on the Roman model. They also had measures to restrict positions to nobles alone, attacked marriages where social standing was unequal, and sought to deny noble titles to commoners who bought noble lands. The program was not wholly backward-looking, since it proposed that nobles be permitted to engage in the wholesale trade and be able to join the magistrature without loss of noble status (Galliani 144).

The prospective heir to the throne on whom these plans depended actually died before Louis XIV, and the proposals died with him. But one of their authors, his former tutor, the aristocratic archbishop of Cambrai, François de Salignac de la Mothe Fénelon, had written a book in the 1690s, *Les aventures de Télémaque*, to impart lessons in kingship in a palatable form, and this contained the same ideas. The book proved immensely popular, and Fénelon's attacks on luxury were influential, not least on Rousseau. He set his story in Greek mythology. Subsequent debate cites classical models—praising Sparta if hostile to commerce and luxury; and Athens, if generally favourable to the arts, commerce and technical progress. The study of history was expected to teach practical lessons, and most argument began with an historical survey.

Though Fénelon chose a pagan setting, his ethos is Christian and looks to an after-life. Fénelon regarded wars as the greatest evil inflicted on humankind and said that good kings, far from attacking their neighbours, should act as mediators to prevent wars. Settled peace is needed before population can expand. His ideal monarch encourages agriculture and, to supply workers for it, transports idle artisans from the towns to the countryside (222). Fénelon links excessive taxation with the peasant's unwillingness to marry and raise a family. Though not wholly hostile to trade (72), he wants to reduce the "prodigious number of merchants" who are blamed for importing luxuries from abroad. Undesirable luxury is also seen as home-grown and as bringing *la mollesse* (soft living) and corrupt behaviour in its wake. Since Fénelon's recognition of human imperfections did not allow him to suppose that war could be eliminated, the effect of *la mollesse* on a nation's fighting capacity worried him, and he expressly linked a simple agricultural life with the toughness needed to campaign (109). He praised the Spartan model that his state Salente adopted, and there is a dress code to distinguish ranks.

In the final years of Louis XIV's reign, war debt mounted and focussed attention on paper credit and the money market. The collapse of John Law's Mississippi Company was a searing experience for French investors, whereas the Bank of England fought off rival banks and became invaluable to successive British governments. Since France seemed self-evidently a richer country in natural endowment and her rival's wealth appeared to depend much on trade and colonial expansion, pro-industrial policies that favoured luxury were increasingly defended in France as potentially productive of wealth and employment. It is probably no coincidence that French writers such as Melon, Montesquieu, and Voltaire, who defended luxury, had spent long periods in England. They were familiar with the provocative arguments of Mandeville's *Fable of the Bees*.

Jean-François Melon, former secretary to John Law, produced arguments in favour of luxury in his *Essai politique sur le commerce*. This went through some twenty editions, and it was substantially enlarged in 1736. His views on war, population, and agriculture are similar to Fénelon's. He defined luxury as "an extraordinary sumptuousness which is bestowed by the wealth and security of a government; it is the necessary consequence of every well-administered society. The man who finds himself with plenty wishes to enjoy it; he has there refinements which the less well-off cannot afford, and this refinement is always relative to the age and to the individual. What was luxury for our fathers is now taken for granted; and what is luxury for us will not be for our nephews" (106). This echoed the British mercantilist writers who argued that the acquisition by the mass of the population of what one generation regarded as luxuries would act as a spur to ambition and effort (Perrotta; Eltis)

Melon also noted that at a particular time people would view luxury according to their own circumstances; to the village-dweller it would be evident in the town, and to the town-dweller the capital would be its glaring example

(107). Since luxury was relative to the individual in a hierarchical society that had great disparities of wealth, Melon's luxury is sometimes no more than economic activity that raises the living standard of the poorest.

Melon saw limitless technical progress as creating new employment, and he mocked those who wished to preserve outmoded jobs (89–90). In his eyes, it was always desirable that what had been made by two men should be made by one. He was, however, concerned that domestic rather than foreign workers should produce the added value in turning flax into fabric, or, more profitably, lace. So he concluded, "What must be allowed as luxury must often be forbidden as importation" (144–45).

The theatre, largely court-based, had often been attacked as a prime example of luxury and extravagance: this had been Boisguilbert's opinion (988). Melon dealt with it in a sentence: "Displays cannot be too grand, too splendid, nor can there be too many of them; it is a commerce where France always receives without giving" (125). For him, the highest and even the most absurd form of luxury was costly foodstuffs. Yet he defends these as providing an income for the market gardener, bringing happiness and hope into his family's life (123–24). He claimed that the farmer or winegrower was his prime concern and he praised Henri IV, who wanted the peasant to afford a chicken in his pot. But he believed that if the peasant were over-taxed, a downward spiral of the kind Boisguilbert had discussed (298–99) would result, affecting the whole society.

Melon knew that the main critics of luxury were churchmen. In Catholic France, the church was opposed to much that was readily accepted in Protestant England as normal for the functioning of commerce. The different influences of Catholic and Protestant theology and practice on economic development has been a particular concern of Anthony Waterman. Catholic theology on the evil of usury had hardly changed since mediaeval times, though financial instruments and networks had become highly developed. Indeed, it was not until the Revolution that it became legal to take interest on loans; although the casuists had softened outright prohibition to the faithful, and in practice interest was paid, an individual would be dependent for absolution upon his confessor's attitude. The Crown had exemption from these laws (McManners II.264–65).

While making some emollient remarks about charitable institutions, Melon attacked the Church on many fronts. He believed that clerical and monastic celibacy reduced the population, excessive religious holidays cut production, and that attacks on usury and new forms of dealing in paper financial instruments upset the necessary circulation of wealth. Melon strongly defended *agiotage* (stock-jobbing) against religious objections (260–64). He pointed out that certain market activities had become acceptable, such as dealing in contracts on the City of Paris and in the main land tax, the *taille*. As for other forms of *agiotage*, he accused the Church of hypocrisy, since a famous *agioteur* had named bishops, great lords, and magistrates among those with whom he dealt.

Melon provocatively praised Lucullus, a by-word for luxury in the ancient world, attacked Lycurgus's Spartan sumptuary laws, and insisted that austere Sparta was not more conquering or better governed than "voluptuous" Athens (114). He said that the reformer who through the harshness of his personality wants to make life harsher may sometimes be admired by the populace, but that he is always scorned by the sage whose yardstick is the sweetness of society (114–15).

For Melon, idleness was the greatest vice, and he was ready to blame it for sedition, civil war, and the fall of the Roman Republic (99–100). He referred to the occupation of begging being passed on from father to son, and this will have been seen as an attack on preachers encouraging alms-giving (33). Luxury on the contrary he called the destroyer of laziness and idleness. He maintained that the rich would soon see their wealth disappear if they did not work to keep it and to acquire new riches (109).

Melon met the fear that luxury created *la mollesse* by claiming that it was far removed from the ordinary soldier or junior officer, while no army had been beaten because of the grand style of the General Corps. Indeed, he claimed that ambition to emulate senior officers was a spur to action (108–09).

Published in the same year as Melon's first edition, Voltaire's poem *Le Mondain* celebrates luxury in the most provocative fashion. Voltaire had read and admired Melon's book (Morize 113), and he was in London in 1728 when the fifth edition of Mandeville's *The Fable of the Bees* was much discussed. Voltaire is confrontational in tone: "I thank wise Nature who, for my good, caused me to be born in this age that is so decried by our poor Doctors: this profane time is just right for my conduct. I love luxury, and even soft living [*la mollesse*], all the pleasures, each branch of the Arts, cleanliness, good taste, adornments" (lines 4–11). He calls excess a very necessary thing and praises foreign trade, which brings new goods. He insults Adam, the first man, describing him as having filthy, black, hooked long nails. In a state of nature, neither the food nor hard ground as a bed appeals to him. Rather, he delights in paintings, silverware, tapestries, and mirrors reflecting fountains. In case anyone should doubt his targets, he makes a dig at Fénelon, addressing him as Monsieur du *Télémaque*. Voltaire challenged: "Praise away your little Ithaca, your Salente and its wretched walls where your Cretans, sadly virtuous, poor in belongings and rich in abstinence, lack everything to have plenty" (lines 113–17). In the *Défense du Mondain* of 1739, Voltaire claimed that luxury made a large state wealthy even if it ruined a small one. The rich were born to spend generously. Melon supported this in a letter to the countess de Verne, in which he alluded to the number of families supported by her expenditures on the arts. He maintained that, if people ceased to love paintings, engravings, and every type of curiosity, at least twenty thousand men would be ruined in Paris and forced to look for work abroad. He allowed that sumptuary laws might suit a Swiss canton or have been right for the early development of the Dutch Republic, but now that that state was wealthy, it needed luxury (Morize 152).

The argument was widely used that, whereas equality and a modest style of living was right for a small republic, it was out of the question for a large state such as France and incompatible with monarchical government. Montesquieu's *De l'esprit des lois*, published in 1748, became the starting point of much discussion. He had already touched on luxury in 1721 in his *Lettres persanes*, where he confronted the argument that luxury led to *la mollesse*. As a leading member of the nobility and a wealthy landowner, he was imbued with a sense of the importance and the duties of noble rank. He saw the nobility as the natural military defenders of France. *La Mollesse* would be serious if it were the natural consequence of luxury. His fictional Persian calls Paris the most sensual city in the world. Disparities in wealth are vividly suggested, yet he observes, "In Paris you can see a man with enough to live off till the day of judgement, who works incessantly and runs the risk of shortening his life in order to accumulate, as he says, enough to subsist. [. . .] The same spirit seizes the nation: one only sees work and industry. Where then is this effeminate people of whom you speak?" (letter 107). Though contemporary Britain was manifestly not a republic, it was a trading and maritime nation, and as such it was treated as apart from other monarchies. It is interesting that Montesquieu appended an optimistic view of England's future to his summary of the causes of the fall of the Athenian republic and what he saw as the corruption of the Italian republics of his time. The argument that luxury led to the collapse of states was implicitly met when he wrote in the *Considérations sur les causes de la grandeur des Romains et de leur décadence* that a free government could reform itself through its own laws (396).

Montesquieu held certain opinions that were socially conservative. He showed his dislike of parvenu tax collectors in *Lettres persanes* (letter 48), and he voiced it even more strongly in *De l'esprit des lois,* where he said that they had destroyed the Roman Republic. He held that it would be destructive of a monarchy if theirs became an honoured profession (Bk. XIII, Ch. 20). He maintained that the nobility should not be involved in commerce (Bk. XX, Ch. 21.) Though hostile to financiers, Montesquieu supported the taking of interest on loans and wished it to be made legal (Bk. XXII, Ch. 19; *Pensées* 767).

It is in *De l'esprit des lois* that Montesquieu has most to say about luxury. He gives an important definition: "Luxury is always in proportion to the inequality of incomes. If wealth is equally spread out in a state there will be no luxury; because it is only based on the commodities which one awards oneself from the work of others" (Bk. VII, Ch. 1). Montesquieu had great faith that the hard work that is associated with commerce would prevent luxury from corrupting behaviour. Though he saw the character of republics as depending on equality of wealth and frugality, he made an exception for republics such as ancient Athens, which were based on commerce: "It is true that, when the democratic state is based on trade, it may very well happen that some individuals in it have great wealth, and that behaviour there is not corrupted. This is because the spirit of commerce brings with it that of frugality, of economy, of moderation, work, wisdom, tranquillity, order and law. Thus, so long as this spirit endures, the wealth it produces has no bad effect" (Bk V, Ch. 6). He stated that banks did not have a place in monarchies because any considerable accumulation of their wealth is liable to become the Prince's treasure. His opinions on mercantile companies are interesting as, after arguing that they do not normally suit a monarchy, he continued: "I say further: they are not always appropriate in States where people carry out trade in essentials; and, if enterprises are not so large that they are beyond the scope of individuals, one would do even better not to hinder freedom of trade in any way through exclusive privileges" (Bk. XX, Ch. 10). Montesquieu saw a place for sumptuary laws, especially in republics, which might need to preserve the spirit of frugality. However, he cautioned against their use in monarchies (Bk. VII, Ch. 5). A limit on the ability of governments to regulate their citizens was noticed by Montesquieu (Bk. XIX, Ch. 27) and by Melon (112), who each referred to tax exiles.

While Melon, Voltaire, and Montesquieu were in their different ways sympathetic to the growth of luxury and were comfortable that France should follow Great Britain in its principal manifestations, a powerful adversary, Jean-Jacques Rousseau, entered the debate in the 1750s. The talent he displayed in his *Discours sur les sciences et les arts* brought him patronage from wealthy aristocrats and the protection of Chrétien-Guillaume de Lamoignon de Malesherbes, who was running the censorship. Rousseau argued from a supposed state of nature, in which humans were blessedly ignorant and happy, to the evils of present society: "There you see how luxury, dissoluteness, and enslavement have been in every age the punishment for the presumptuous efforts we have made to leave the happy ignorance in which eternal wisdom had placed us" (40). Rousseau saw luxury as making a nation less able to fight (47). He attacked paintings that did not glorify martial heroes but put forward "with great care all ancient mythology's aberrations of heart and mind" (49–50). This is close to Fénelon. Soon he moved on to attack the evils that printing had brought and to approve the burning of books! (Rousseau 52n). Louis XV's father-in-law, the former King of Poland, replied to this first treatise, and Rousseau in his response said, "Luxury corrupts everything; both the rich man who enjoys it, and the wretch who covets it" (88). In his *Dernière réponse,* Rousseau stated, "Luxury sustains a hundred poor in our towns, and causes the death of a hundred thousand in our countryside: the money which circulates through the hands of the rich and artists to supply their excesses is lost from the farmworker's subsistence; and it is precisely because the others must have braid that he has no cloak. [. . .] We must have powder for our wigs; there you have the reason why so many poor folk have no bread" (107n). Jean le Rond d'Alembert had come to the defence of the arts and sciences in the *Discours préliminaire de l'Encyclopédie* of 1751, arguing that they made society more agreeable even if they did not improve it. Rousseau riposted in the preface to his play *Narcisse* in 1752 that "the appetite for literature, philosophy and the fine arts destroys love for our prime duties and for true glory." He returned to the subject in *The Discours sur l'origine et les fondements de l'inegalité parmi les hommes* of 1755. Not surprisingly, Sparta was his classical model (111). "At the same time as industry and the arts spread out and flourish, the cultivator, disregarded, weighed down by taxes needed to support luxury and condemned to spend his life between work and hunger, abandons his fields to seek in the towns the bread he should be carrying there (*L'origine* 187). In his *Discours sur l'économie politique*, Rousseau proposed that heavy taxes should be placed on luxury goods such as carriages, mirrors, furniture, materials, gilding, the courts and gardens of private residences, on every kind of entertainment. In contrast to Melon, he believed that, once entrapped by luxury, people would not give it up, and they would rather starve than die of shame.

In *Du contrat social*, Rousseau made several references of a laudatory nature to the Marquis d'Argenson, whose *Considérations sur le Gouvernement ancien et présent de la France* he knew in manuscript. They shared an admiration for the republics of the ancient world (Larrère 61–65), and Argenson was eager to increase the popular element in France's government under its monarchy. Both men also advanced views that fit what Galliani has called "l'idéologie nobiliaire" (145). Differences on religion and politics between such nobles as Fénelon, Montesquieu, Argenson, and Mirabeau show the limits to the concept's usefulness.

Argenson's professed aim was to show in his *Considérations sur le Gouvernement* that popular government under the sovereign would increase the state's power and promote the happiness of the people. He wanted to replace royal officers with municipal ones chosen by the people. He also criticized the government for interfering in commerce, echoing Melon's words when he said, "Commerce only needs protection and freedom and perhaps the one should be abandoned in order to enjoy the other more fully." He was not hostile to the arts, but he argued that, whereas a country like Russia needed laws to encourage the arts (the word then included what we would call crafts), France needed to return to agriculture, which it had neglected (15).

Argenson said that it was just that those who consumed most for their own luxury should pay the most to the State whose capital they diminished (*Considérations* 228). He considered that Spain had been ruined by luxury and inequality (78). He blamed financiers and finance ministers since Colbert for policies such as alterations of the coinage, the trickery of false letters of credit, and double assignations of revenue (185). He attacked the sale of offices as impeding democracy (156) as well as for the tax exemptions they entailed, resulting in the tax burden falling on the weakest shoulders. He wanted wealthy men to be ennobled (190) but not through the purchase of offices (311).

Argenson expressed the wish that nobles and wealthy men should reside on their country properties. He wanted lands to be free of feudal dues, and he scorned these personally: "I prefer a good walnut tree which bears fruit to a fief which is just idiocy" (qtd. in Larrère 192). He scorned rank that relied only on birth as leading to laziness, and he wished people to be equal among themselves so that they could work according to their talents (308–09).

In many of his journal entries from 1747 to his final entry in January 1757, Argenson refers to spectacular examples of luxury expenditure on the royal favourite, Madame de Pompadour. In November 1748, he wrote, "Yesterday eight country houses and private residences were counted where work was in progress for the Marquise de Pompadour." In July 1750, he wrote of the King having ordered more than 800,000 livres worth of Vincennes china for his country houses and especially for her Château de Bellevue. In May 1751, he noted that she appeared at Marly in a gown embellished with English lace costing more than 22,500 livres, and he added that the public noticed these expenditures. This was doubly objectionable since in 1752 he reported the fear that the King would have to declare bankruptcy. On 6 February 1753, he noted that the English were building forty new ships and that they had paid off 200 million livres worth of public debt since the war. He prophesied that with these numerous fleets the English would wipe France out in the three areas of the world where it had colonies. Indeed, this largely occurred in 1763 at the end of the Seven Years War, when France lost Canada and various West Indian islands and was marginalized in India.

In December 1754, after describing the taking of royal troops by smugglers, Argenson stated that the people favoured the smugglers because they were at war with the tax farmers, who were considered too rich, and the people wanted goods more cheaply.

In his journal entry for 5 October 1749, Argenson reported his neighbours as saying that the rural population had declined by more than a third in ten years. He blamed the *corvée* for driving labourers to the towns. The towns had their problems too: on 12 July 1750, he noted that Lyon was full of the poor, not because bread was dear but because a fall in the supply of silk from Piedmont had led to layoffs. The farmers-general, he reported in June 1754, had complained to the controller-general of Finances, Machault, that trade and manufactures were decaying and that foreigners were working up French raw materials. Machault's response was, "So much the better! That is all the more workers to return to the land."

This was not everyone's solution, but by the 1750s the luxury debate was increasingly becoming one between agriculture and industry. In 1755, an anonymous work was published entitled, significantly, *L'Abeille, [the bee] ou recueuil de philosophie de littérature et d'histoire*. It had every sign from its contents of seeking to appeal to the circle of Madame de Pompadour and the duc de Choiseul. The author devoted pages to famous women in history and defended tax farmers—her family was involved in tax farming—while he was eager to build up the navy, Choiseul's particular concern.

Chapter 11 of *L'Abeille* begins, "Happy is the State which possesses the Merchant and Manufactures!" After enumerating stages in the preparation of hemp, flax, wool, etc., he continued, "Let us assume that all these activities are suppressed; and cast our eyes on the consequences of so many people being out of work. It is easy to see that we shall soon cease being happy and peaceful: we shall fall bit by bit into the condition of Savages: and the State will suffer from it in many ways. Thus China in her wisdom does not allow anybody to avoid work in the length and breadth of that vast Empire, much more populous than France or Holland" (106). The author of *L'Abeille* suggested that only a third of the population was needed for agriculture. He argued that manufactures brought demand for more animals, fields were brought under cultivation, the soil was improved, income rose and trade expanded (112).

François Véron de Forbonnais argued similarly that luxury assisted the whole economy in *Éléments de commerce*: "It is luxury alone, or the abundance whose fruit it is which gives the spirit this activity which is so prodigious in its effects. If abundance is widespread an equal and lifegiving warmth will spread through all the parts of the body politic" (Ch. 13, "Du luxe"). He added, "The greatest of all abuses would be that the rich spent nothing; all would be poverty-stricken around them, the state would be almost without warmth and lifeless."

There is an interesting contrast between the pro-industrial analyses of Melon and Forbonnais and the pro-agricultural analysis of Argenson, and of Richard Cantillon, which was reinforced a few years later by François Quesnay, physician to Madame de Pompadour, to Louis XV, and indeed to Adam Smith, when his pupil, the Duke of Buccleuch, fell ill in Paris. Cantillon was a brilliant millionaire banker who had understood and exploited the inconsistencies in Law's scheme (Murphy 172–75) and whose *Essai sur la nature du commerce en générale* attempted the first complete account of the financial circulation of an economy. This was widely read in manuscript in the 1740s and published in 1755 through the personal sponsorship of Vincent de Gournay. Cantillon included a devastating account of the economically destructive consequences of imports of luxury manufactures. His argument was founded on the assumption that the land supported the population, and that each one-and-a-half acres had the potential to support an agricultural labourer and his family at the standard of living which had become customary in France. A third of the output of the land was paid to landlords who did not farm, and how they spent their revenues was of immense importance.

If they spent these on imports, the surplus of agricultural output would be diverted to create foreign wealth and employment, "often serving to support the Enemies of the State" (Cantillon 77). To the extent that manufactures were imported, a country in effect sustained the subsistence of potential enemies. In contrast, if the recipients of France's agricultural surplus spent this on domestically manufactured goods and services, it would sustain French employment that would be additional to that provided by agriculture itself. Better still, if French industry achieved an export surplus, French employment and population would benefit further. Cantillon offered a clear answer to a question George

Berkeley had proposed in *The Querist* in 1735 (query 150): "Whether an Irish Lady, set out with French Silks, and Flanders Lace, may not be said to consume more Beef and Butter than fifty of our labouring peasants?"

> If the Ladies of Paris are pleased to wear Brussels Lace, and if France pays for this Lace with Champagne wine, the product of a single Acre of Flax must be paid for with the product of 16,000 acres of land under vines. [. . .] Suffice to say here that in this transaction a great amount of the produce of the Land is withdrawn from the subsistence of the French, and that all the produce sent abroad, unless an equally considerable amount of produce be brought back in exchange, tends to diminish the number of People in the State. (77)

If French goods were superior to those manufactured overseas and produced net inflows of gold and silver, prices would rise, the terms of trade would move in France's favour, and the state would become increasingly powerful. But these favourable conditions would eventually prove unsustainable. Beneficiaries of the favourable export trade and therefore of higher French prices and incomes would adopt habits of luxury that undermined the balance of trade because the goods they bought would mainly be imported.

> Abundance will not arise without many wealthy individuals springing up who will plunge into luxury. They will buy Pictures and Gems from the Foreigner, will procure their Silks and rare objects, and set such an example of luxury in the State that in spite of the advantage of its ordinary trade its money will flow abroad annually to pay for this luxury. This will gradually impoverish the State and cause it to pass from great power into great weakness. (185)

Cantillon's notable successor as an analyst of the economy's complete financial flows, Quesnay, saw still greater risks to the French economy from a taste for manufactures. According to Cantillon, the consumption of manufactures would only damage the economy insofar as they were imported, but Quesnay's analysis actually suggested that an increased demand for manufactures would undermine the economy even if the additional goods were produced by France itself.

QUESNAY'S ANALYSIS OF THE INFLUENCE OF LUXURY CONSUMPTION

By the 1760s, the new excitement about the economy that was inducing so many to publish had begun to centre on Quesnay's powerful and original contributions and those of his physiocrat disciples. They presented an entirely technical approach to the luxury question, which removed it from debate about incentives and social inequality. For Quesnay, all non-agricultural economic activity was "sterile" because it generated no economic surplus or *produit net*, and it was the luxury element in a nation's sterile expenditure that was most liable to undermine the long-term viability of the economy. At the margin, increased sterile expenditure was always attributed to excessive *"luxe de décoration*," which was the element in the expenditure on the products of industry and commerce that might be so high as to destabilize the economy.

In the *Tableau économique*, which Quesnay created in 1758–59 in the Palace of Versailles, where King Louis XV is said to have played a part in the correction of the proofs, the economy was in stationary-state equilibrium when the proportion of expenditure on the products of industry and commerce including luxe was 50 percent, while there would be disastrous consequences if luxe rose above this:

> It can be seen from the distribution delineated in the tableau that if the nation's expenditure went more to the sterile expenditure side than the productive expenditure side, the revenue would fall proportionately, and this fall would increase in the same progression from year to year successively. It follows that a high level of expenditure on luxe de décoration and on conspicuous consumption is ruinous. If on the other hand the nation's expenditure goes on the productive expenditure side the revenue will rise, and this rise will in the same way increase successively from year to year. Thus it is not true that the type of expenditure is a matter of indifference. (12)

In 1760, Quesnay created a detailed series of tableaux that set out precisely how this would occur in "Tableau économique avec ses explications," which he appended to the marquis de Mirabeau's *L'Ami des hommes*. In 1763, further collaboration between Quesnay and Mirabeau led to the publication of *Philosophie rurale*, a comprehensive account of the economics of the growing physiocratic school, over which Quesnay presided intellectually, and Mirabeau socially. It included sequences of tableaux that sought to provide a complete account of the circumstances in which the French economy would grow or decline. One of these describes how it would decline if the propensity to consume manufactures including those that constitute *"luxe de décoration"* came to exceed the critical 50 percent.

By seeking to analyze the effect of luxe within *the Tableau économique*, Mirabeau and Quesnay and other physiocratic writers such as Nicholas Baudeau, the editor of *Les Éphémérides du citoyen* between 1765–1772 and 1774–1776, replaced the large and important questions that had previously dominated the luxury debate with a formula for the luxe that an economy could afford. In essence, Quesnay, Mirabeau, and Baudeau reiterated that an economy in stationary-state equilibrium could afford to spend 50 percent of all incomes on the sterile side of the *Tableau,* which comprised all industrial and commercial activity, including the provision of luxe.

In the series of tableaux from *Philosophie rurale* that are presented in Figs. 1, 2, and 3, Mirabeau and Quesnay set out the full effect on the whole economy of an increase of one-tenth in the propensity to consume the products of industry and commerce. These marginal changes are always referred to as increases in the propensity to consume luxe.

PRÉCIS DES RÉSULTATS
DE LA DISTRIBUTION REPRÉSENTÉE DANS LE TABLEAU

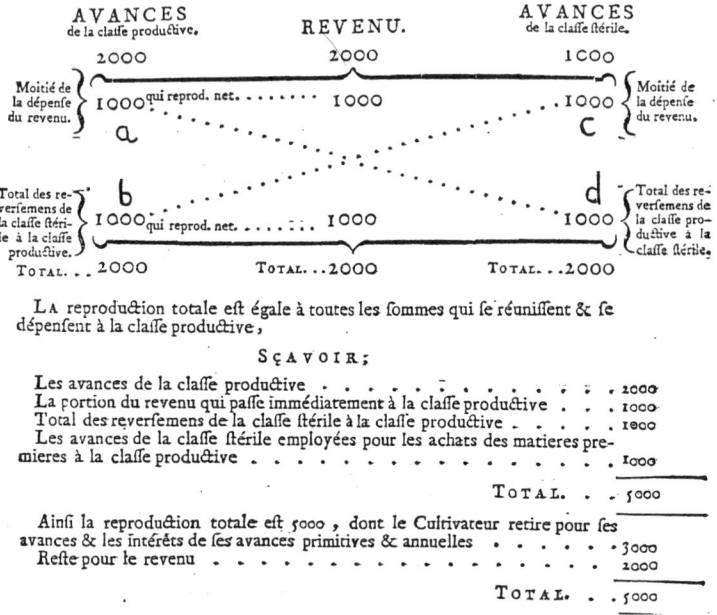

LA reproduction totale eft égale à toutes les fommes qui fe réuniffent & fe dépenfent à la claffe productive,

SÇAVOIR;

Les avances de la claffe productive 2000
La portion du revenu qui paffe immédiatement à la claffe productive . . . 1000
Total des reverfemens de la claffe ftérile à la claffe productive 1000
Les avances de la claffe ftérile employées pour les achats des matieres pre-
mieres à la claffe productive 1000

TOTAL. . . 5000

Ainfi la reproduction totale eft 5000 , dont le Cultivateur retire pour fes
avances & les intérêts de fes avances primitives & annuelles 3000
Refte pour le revenu 2000

TOTAL. . . 5000

Fig. 1 The Tableau in Equilibrium
(*Philosophie rurale* I.123)

Fig. 1 shows the Tableau of *Philosophie rurale* in its equilibrium stationary state. The economy makes advances (i.e., capital investments) of 2,000 in the productive sector (shown at the head of the Tableau on the left), which it invests in agriculture, and advances of 1,000 in the sterile sector (at the head of the Tableau on the right), which it invests in industry and commerce. These investments produce reproducible agricultural wealth of 5,000, which is the total shown at the foot of Fig. 1. This 5,000 is just sufficient to enable farmers to pay rents of 2,000 (the Revenue shown in the centre at the head of the Tableau) and to retain 3,000 for the following year's investments. Rents are 2,000 because annual agricultural advances of 2,000 create a *produit net* of 100 percent, which is the yield that la grande culture generates. Farmers would be able to use the 3,000 of the 5,000, which they retain to invest 2,000 in agricultural advances for the next harvest, while their further 1,000 will cover what Quesnay calls interest to make good the one-tenth rate of depreciation that he assumes on their total farm capital (Avances Primitives et Annuelles) of 10,000 (see Appendix).

Because the initial agricultural investment of 2,000 creates reproducible agricultural wealth of 5,000, this will continue to be just sufficient to pay rents of 2,000, to furnish the following year's farm investments of 2,000 and to provide 1,000 to cover the depreciation of farm capital. The economy can continue to produce these returns and sustain a stationary state in which agricultural investment is always 2,000 and agricultural output is always 5,000.

Fig. 2 shows what would occur if, in a subsequent year, the propensity to consume luxe increased by one-fifth. There would be the same investments at the start of the year as in Fig. 1, of 2,000 in agriculture, and 1,000 in industry and commerce, but, because there is an increased propensity to consume luxe by all classes, less of the economy's effective demand would return to agriculture. As a consequence of the reduced financial flows to agriculture (see Appendix), farmers' reproducible wealth at the foot of Fig. 2 is 4,680 in place of the 5,000 at the foot of Fig. 1. If, out of this reduced reproduction of agricultural wealth, farmers retained the 3,000 they would need to maintain agricultural investment at its previous level, they would have only 1,680 with which to pay rents, 320 less than the 2,000 they were contractually obliged to pay. Quesnay assumed that the shortfall of 320 in the resources available to pay rents would be divided equally between farmer and landlord, who would each lose 160. Hence, in the following year, illustrated in Fig. 3, agricultural investment (Avances) would be 1,840 in place of the former 2,000, and rents (Revenu) would be 1,840 in place of 2,000. Each is therefore reduced by 8 percent.

Hence, at the head of Fig. 3 (p. 78), which shows what would occur in the second year of an increased propensity to consume luxe, because agricultural advances are merely 1,840, and Revenue at the head of the Tableau is also only 1,840, there is an 8 percent reduction in food output (because investment is 8 percent lower) and expenditure on food is also 8 percent lower because purchases of food from the revenue and by farmers themselves are 8 percent less. Total reproducible agricultural wealth (at the foot of Fig. 3) is 4,306 in place of the 4,680 of the previous year (shown at the foot of Fig. 2), which was 8 percent lower than the reproduction of 5,000 in the stationary state, which is illustrated in Fig. 1. Hence, in the second year of increased luxe that is illustrated in Fig. 3, output and the resources available to pay rent and to invest are each reduced by 8 percent from the already reduced levels illustrated in Fig. 2. The economy would continue to decline at a rate of 8 percent per annum for as long as the 60 percent propensity to consume the products of the sterile sector including especially luxe persists.

The rates of decline predicted in Figs. 2 and 3 (and by the equations that explain Quesnay's results in the Appendix) are very large. Quesnay's tableaux demonstrate that an economy's propensity to consume luxe will have a significant impact on its rate of growth and that a propensity that exceeds the equilibrium ratio of 50 percent has the potential to produce a sharp sequence of decline.

PREMIER TABLEAU de la dégradation causée par un cinquieme de surcroît de luxe.

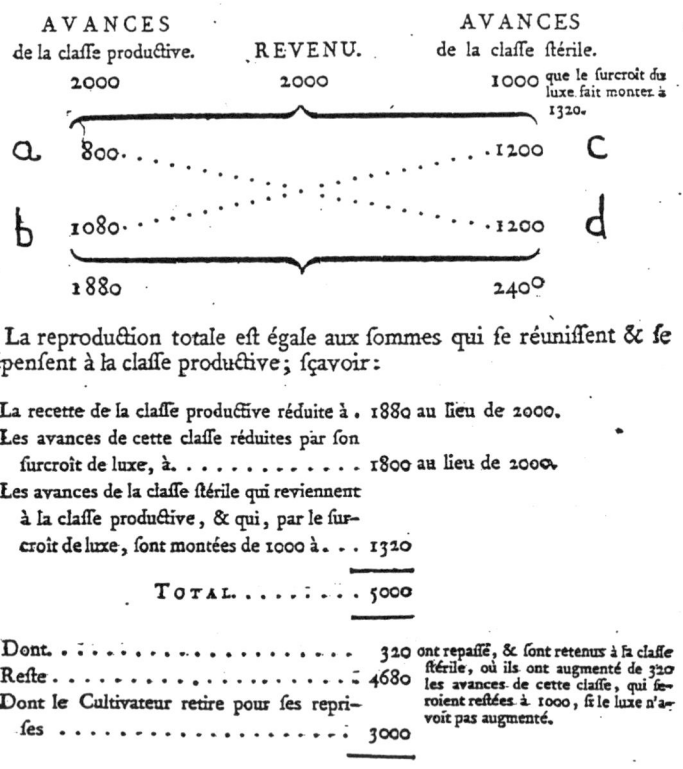

La reproduction totale est égale aux sommes qui se réunissent & se dépensent à la classe productive; sçavoir:

La recette de la classe productive réduite à . 1880 au lieu de 2000.

Les avances de cette classe réduites par son
surcroît de luxe, à. . . . . 1800 au lieu de 2000.

Les avances de la classe stérile qui reviennent
à la classe productive, & qui, par le surcroît de luxe, sont montées de 1000 à . . . 1320

TOTAL. 5000

Dont. 320   ont repassé, & sont retenus à la classe
stérile, où ils ont augmenté de 320

Reste. 4680   les avances de cette classe, qui se-
roient restées à 1000, si le luxe n'a-

Dont le Cultivateur retire pour ses repri-
ses 3000   voit pas augmenté.

Reste pour le revenu. . . . . 1680 au lieu de 2000.

TOTAL. 4680

La perte de 320 livres, que le calcul fait tomber en totalité sur le revenu, étant repartie également sur les avances de la classe productive & sur le revenu, est pour chacun 160 livres; ce qui réduit la reproduction des avances de la classe productive à 1840, & celle du revenu également à 1840.

Fig. 2 Initial Impact of a Twenty-Percent Increase in Luxury Consuption
(*Philosophie rural* III.36–37)

It has been widely argued that Quesnay's assumption that the direction of internal consumption influences the rate of growth is flawed. The essence of Quesnay's argument is that, because only agriculture generates a *produit net*, a diversion of demand away from agriculture and toward luxury manufactures will reduce the economy's investable surplus and therefore its rate of growth. But Negishi in particular has suggested that, if demand within an agricultural kingdom shifts in favour of manufactures, as shown in Figs. 2 and 3, the economy could continue to produce the same quantity of food as before and therefore create an unchanged *produit net*, by selling in world markets the food that is no longer marketable within France. The additional manufactures that the French population desired in place of food could be imported in exchange for these higher exports of food. The use of international markets to export any food that had become surplus to French requirements in order to import the extra manufactures that French consumers now desired would allow the economy to adopt the pattern of production that realizes the highest economic surplus it could achieve. Negishi's solution required an unlimited potential to exchange food for manufactures in world markets at unchanging terms of trade. His assumption is, in effect, that France is a "small country" that faces world prices for food and manufactures that are independent of the quantities it exports and imports.

But eighteenth-century France was not a "small country" that faced export prices for food and import prices of manufactures that were independent of the quantities it sought to export and import. *In Philosophie rurale*, Mirabeau and Quesnay considered the possibility that a shift in consumer preferences from food to manufactures could be met by exporting the food that was no longer in demand in France and importing additional manufactures:

> Could it not be said that an excessive taste for manufactures [luxe de décoration] would be damaging only to nations which lacked the opportunity of freedom of external trade in their own agricultural produce; because these would be unable to compensate by the sale of their foodstuffs abroad for a loss on domestic sales caused by an excessive demand for manufactures? But would the opportunity for foreign trade and all round freedom to conduct it be enough to put right this derangement? Such external trade might perhaps greatly slow the progress of the destructive impact of an excessive demand for manufactures. But even this trade does not extend to the export of every kind of agricultural product; for most of these can only be consumed in the region which produces them. Besides, this external trade itself can only be sustained in so far as it is reciprocal. The merchant himself wishes to transport and bring back goods to cover his costs and gain a profit. Now, through what purchases will a nation, intent on manufactures, carry on with foreigners trade in the sale of its natural products? (III.32–33)

Here Mirabeau and Quesnay demonstrate that they have the same awareness as Negishi that an unlimited potential to trade would allow an economy with a large agricultural *produit net* to remain predominantly agricultural. But they also summarize the difficulties in financing greatly increased imports of manufactures through additional agricultural exports.

When they wrote in the eighteenth century, there was no free trade in agricultural produce in France, or anywhere else in Europe. Much agricultural produce was untradable: it had to be consumed close to where it was harvested, and this was especially the case with the eighteenth century's primitive transport facilities. There were also deep-rooted reasons that many countries would not allow unlimited food imports to undermine their own agriculture. That was as true in the eighteenth century as it still is in the twenty-first. Mirabeau and Quesnay's argument that the propensity to consume agricultural products influences the rate of growth is therefore not flawed in the manner that Negishi supposes.

Mirabeau and Quesnay were convinced that the invention of the tableaux provided a basis for the calculation of the effect of particular policies. They told their critics, "Will you again say that you do not understand what there is to gain in having more income or more revenue, and paying more for what one buys? [. . .] If you are able to calculate, you will easily penetrate this mystery" (I.233). They believed that the tableaux provided a basis for the calculation of the growth that France could achieve through the adoption of appropriate policies. At the same time, inappropriate policies could all too easily cause the continuation of the economic decline from which they believed France was suffering.

Mirabeau and Quesnay's brilliant and sophisticated tableaux show how luxe can be even more damaging to the long-term viability of economies than their many predecessors had supposed. But their argument also suggests, as Baudeau subsequently insisted, that there is a level of luxe that can be afforded in a stationary state, while other opponents of luxe regarded all expenditures of this kind as economically and socially harmful.

It will be evident that the physiocrats abstracted virtually all that was socially and politically significant from the debate about luxury and grafted an economic model of immense originality and sophistication onto their supposition that the manufacture of luxuries generates no kind of economic surplus. This assumption was rapidly shown to be false, not least by Adam Smith in Great Britain in 1776 in *The Nature and Causes of the Wealth of Nations* and in France in the same year by the Abbé de Condillac, who developed "a general theory of the generation of surpluses, of general economic equilibrium, and of maximal efficiency" in *Le Commerce et le Gouvernement: considérés relativement l'un à l'autre* which, in the opinion of French Nobel Prizewinner in Economics Maurice Allais, was superior to Adam Smith (37, 192). Both showed that manufactures can be hugely surplus-generating. Their development of economics beyond the physiocratic model suggests that the contribution of the earlier writers, whom Quesnay and his disciples briefly superseded, should not be overlooked.

APPENDIX

*The Explanation of the Impact of a One-Fifth Increase
in Expenditure on Luxe de Décoration in Quesnay's
Tableaux in* Philosophie Rurale

In what is said below, for expositional simplicity, what Mirabeau and Quesnay describe as the productive sector will be referred to as "agriculture," which produces "food," while the sterile sector will be referred to as "industry," which produces "manufactures."

In Fig. 1, a and b represent the expenditure on food from the non-agricultural classes, while c and d represent the expenditure on manufactures from outside the industrial sector. Half of landowners' total revenue or rents of 2,000 are spent on food and half on manufactures, so a and c are each 1,000. The farmers spend half their advances of 2,000 on manufactures, so d is 1,000. The principal complication in the explanation of Fig. 1 concerns b, manufacturers' expenditures on food. Quesnay states that "the total of the payments of the manufacturing class to the agricultural class equals one-half of the receipts of the manufacturing class" (I.328). As these receipts are represented by c and d, which are each 1,000, b which is ½(c + d) also equals 1,000. Quesnay adds that "the manufacturing class receives 2000 of which 1000 remain to replace its advances, and 1000 are employed for the subsistence of those who work in it" (I.328–29). It is simplest to suppose that b represents the purchases of food by manufacturers for their subsistence, which absorbs 1,000 of the 2,000 that they have received (via c and d), while the remaining 1,000 they receive is used after the completion of the transactions set out in Fig. 1, to purchase the advances that they will require for the following year.

When the tableau becomes more complex in Figs. 2 and 3, the key to whether output will expand or decline is whether the total agricultural wealth that is reproduced rises or falls. It is therefore necessary to understand how this total is arrived at. At the foot of Fig. 1, Quesnay writes, "The total reproduction is equal to all the sums which in combination are spent within agriculture." Viz:

1. Farmers' advances	2,000
2. That part of the revenues of the landlords that is immediately spent on food	1,000
3. Purchases of food by the manufacturers (b)	1,000
4. Advances of the manufacturers that are used to buy raw materials from the farmers	1,000
TOTAL	5,000

TABLEAU de la seconde année de la continuation d'un cinquieme de surcroit du luxe.

| AVANCES de la claffe productive. 1840 | REVENU. 1840 | AVANCES de la claffe ftérile. 1320 qui fe trouvent réduits à 1214 2 cinquiemes. |

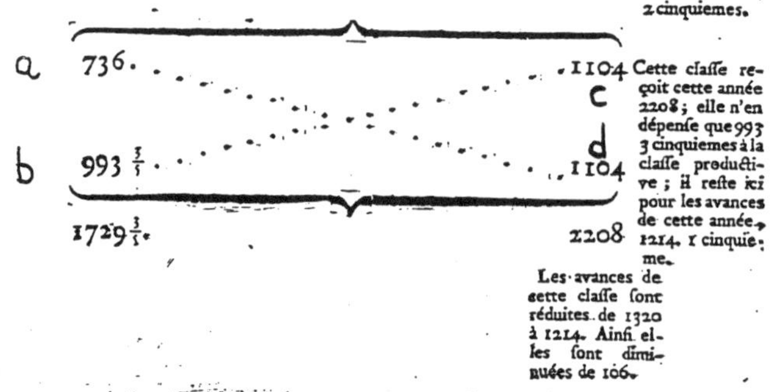

q   736 . .   . . 1104 Cette claffe re-
c çoit cette année
2208; elle n'en
dépenfe que 993
3 cinquiemes à la
b   993 ⅗ . . . . 1104 claffe producti-
d ve ; il refte ici
pour les avances
de cette année.

    1729⅗.   2208 1214. 1 cinquie-
me.

Les avances de
cette claffe font
réduites de 1320
à 1214. Ainfi el-
les font dimi-
nuées de 106.

La reproduction totale eft égale aux fommes qui fe réuniffent & fe dépenfent à la claffe productive; fçavoir :

La recette de la claffe productive. . . . . 1729⅗.
Les avances de cette claffe, réduites par
l'excès de fon luxe, de 1840 à 1656
Les avances de la claffe ftérile de 1320,
defquelles il n'eft dépenfé cetteannée que
1214, dont 106 font pris fur les 1320
de ces mêmes avances, & conformé-
ment à cette reprife, elles fe trouvent
réduites à . . . . 1214⅖.

                    TOTAL 4600

Dont 294   ont repaffé, & font retenus à la claffe
Refte 4306   ftérile, & y foutiennent les avan-
                                                      ces de cette claffe à 1214, lef-
                                                      quelles, fans l'excès de luxe, n'au-
Le Cultivateur retire pour { Avances. . . . . . 1840 l.   roient été que de 920 , c'eft-à-
fes reprifes   { Intérêts 920   dire, égales au quart des fommes
                                                      des avances productives , & du
                                                      revenu, prifes enfemble.
                    TOTAL 2760

Refte pour le produit net . . . . 1546 au lieu de 1840.

            . . . . TOTAL 4306

Ce déchet de 294 étant reparti entre les avances de la claffe productive & le revenu, les réduifent de part & d'autre, à 1703.

Fig. 3 Impact in Second Year of a
Twenty-Percent Increase in Luxury Consumption
(*Philosophie rural* III.39.40)

Thus, the reproduction totals 5,000, of which farmers
   retain for their advances and the "interest" they
   require to maintain their total capital   3,000

There remains for revenue to pay to the landlords   2,000

As the total revenue shown in Fig. 1 in the initial year is 2,000, farmers retain enough to pay a similar rent in the following year. The 3,000 they retain for themselves is sufficient to sustain their annual advances at 2,000 and to provide the 1,000 that Quesnay assumes they will require to cover the depreciation of one-tenth of their total capital of 10,000, which is made up of the annual advances of 2,000 shown in the Tableau, and primary advances (of long-term fixed capital) of 8,000, which are four times as great. Hence, the conditions required to sustain a stationary state will be continually reproduced.

Fig. 2 shows the effect on this basic tableau of an increase of one-fifth in the propensity of all classes to purchase manufactures where these additional manufactures represent luxe. In Quesnay's words, the tableau shows "the deterioration caused by an excess of luxury of one-fifth" (III.36). In Fig. 1, landowners, farmers, and manufacturers each spent half their incomes on food and half on manufactures. Now these each spend four-tenths on food and six-tenths on manufactures, that is, an additional two-tenths, or one-fifth, is now spent by each class on manufactures. The expenditure of landowners on food (a) and manufactures (c) is readily calculable as 800 and 1,200 (that is, 40 and 60 percent of their total rents of 2,000). Farmers' expenditures on manufactures at 1,200 (d) are also a straightforward 60 percent of their advances of 2,000 in place of the previous 50 percent. The figure that is less straightforward to interpret is b, manufacturers' expenditure on food, which Quesnay writes down as 1,080. In the stationary state shown in Fig. 1, they spent one-half of their total receipts of (c + d) on food. If they are now to spend one-fifth less on food because, like the rest of the population, they now have a greater propensity to consume manufactures, they would spend four-tenths of their enhanced receipts of 2,400 on food, that is, 960 in place of the former five-tenths, which would produce 1,200. But Quesnay says that they spend 1,080. The explanation of this discrepancy is that only half of manufacturers' total receipts of 2,400 are allocated to the financing of subsistence, and it is merely to this half that the one-fifth reduction in the propensity to buy food applies. The overall reduction in manufacturers' propensity to buy food will therefore be one-tenth, and not one-fifth, and a one-tenth reduction in the 1,200 that half of (c + d) produces is the 1,080 that Quesnay shows for b in Fig. 2. The economy's total reproduction, which was 5,000 in the stationary state presented in Fig. 2, is now describable as follows:

1. Farmers' expenditures on food from their own advances in place of the former 2,000. Their "interest" [depreciation of capital] of 1,000 is spent entirely in agriculture, and four-tenths of their advances of 2,000 are spent in agriculture, so they spend 1,800 in all on agricultural produce   1,800

2. Farmers' receipts from landowners (a) which are four-tenths of their rents of 2,000   800

3. Purchases of food by manufacturers (b)   1,080

4. Purchases of raw materials by manufacturers [manufacturers' advances of 1,000 at the head of the tableau]   1,000

                    ————

                    4,680

The economy's total reproduction is therefore 4,680 in place of the 5,000 of the previous year when the tableau was in stationary-state equilibrium. Quesnay assumes that the 320 by which farmers' receipts fall short of the 5,000 they would require in a stationary state is divided equally between a 160 reduction in revenues paid to landowners and a reduction of 160 in farmers' annual agricultural advances in the following year.

Manufacturers are in the apparently happy situation that they have received 2,400 and spent 1,080 of this on food, and 1,000 on materials, and they therefore have a financial surplus of 320, which they retain for the future. In Quesnay's words under Fig. 2, "320 have passed to and are retained by the manufacturers."

The key to the economy's rate of growth is that because farmers' total reproduction has fallen from 5,000 to 4,680, they are in financial deficit by 320, and half of this is taken from their annual advances, which therefore fall from 2,000 to 1840, that is, by 8 percent, while rents are also reduced by 8 percent from 2,000 to 1,840. That is precisely what Fig. 3 shows: all the totals in Fig. 2 are reduced in precisely this proportion, for all the totals in a Quesnaysian economy are multiples of annual agricultural advances, and in Quesnay's calculations these have fallen 8 percent.

Thus, the totals in Fig. 3, the Tableau of the second year, of an increase in the propensity to consume luxe from 50 to 60 percent, correspond precisely to the Tableau of the previous year, with a, b, c, and d each 8 percent lower than that shown in Fig. 2. A general formula for the economy's rate of decline in the conditions Quesnay assumes, which confirms his calculations in Figs. 2 and 3, can readily be derived.

Farmers' annual advances in the initial year when the Tableau is in stationary-state equilibrium can be written as A: it is 2,000 in Fig. 1. Total rents or revenues are thus also A with Quesnay's assumption of a rate of return of 100 percent on annual agricultural advances. The propensity to consume food of all classes can be written as q: this is 0.5, as shown in Fig. 1. Then the reproduction of the economy is as follows:

1. Farmers' expenditures on food from their own advances will be ½A from the expenditure of interest plus qA from their expenditures on their own subsistence, i.e.: $(\frac{1}{2} + q)A$

2. A fraction q of total rents of A will be spent in agriculture, i.e.: qA

3. Farmers and landlords each spend (1-q)A on manufactures, so industry receives 2(1-q)A. Half of this is retained to finance advances. Of the remaining (1-q)A, half is sensitive to variation in q, and therefore becomes q(1-q)A, while the remaining half is independent of q and continues as ½(1-q)A. Hence, manufacturers expenditures on food total: $(\frac{1}{2}+q)(1-q)A$

4. Manufacturers' advances are one quarter of the sum of agricultural advances and rents, i.e. ¼ of 2A or: ½A

The economy's total reproduction, for which X can be written, is the sum of 1., 2., 3., and 4. or $(1\frac{1}{2} + 2\frac{1}{2}q - q^2)A$. Hence:

$$X = (1\frac{1}{2} + 2\frac{1}{2}q - q^2)A \tag{1}$$

When the economy is in stationary-state equilibrium, q is 0.5 and X is 2½A, as shown in Fig. 1, where A is 2,000.

When q is 0.4 instead of 0.5, X, the total reproduction, is 2.34A or 4,680 as shown in Fig. 2, where A is initially 2,000. If the extent to which the total reproduction falls is divided equally between reduced agricultural advances and lower rents, as Quesnay assumes, these will each be reduced by half the fall in X, that is, by half of 0.16A or by 0.08A. In Fig. 2, A is 2,000, and agricultural advances fall by 0.08A to 1,840, as shown in Fig. 3.

The formula for the rate of decline (or, conversely, growth) of annual agricultural advances, and therefore of every total in the Tableau, is the change in annual agricultural advances as a fraction of agricultural advances at the start of the year. The change in advances is half the change in the economy's total reproduction.

The reproduction changes from 2½A to $(1\frac{1}{2} + 2\frac{1}{2}q - q^2)A$; i.e. it changes by $(2\frac{1}{2}q - q^2 - 1)A$

The change in annual agricultural advances is half the change in reproduction or $(1\frac{1}{4}q - \frac{1}{2}q^2 - \frac{1}{2})A$ and the economy's rate of growth of annual agricultural advances, g_A, is this as a fraction of A. Hence:

$$g_A = 1\tfrac{1}{4}q - \tfrac{1}{2}q^2 - \tfrac{1}{2} \tag{2}$$

When q = 0.5 as in Fig. 1, g_A is zero, while it is -0.08
When q = 0.4 as in Figs. 2 and 3.

WORKS CITED

Alembert, Jean le Rond d'. *Discours préliminaire de l'Encyclopédie.* 1751. Ed. F. Picavet. Armand Colin: Paris, 1929.

Allais, Maurice. "The general theory of surpluses as a formalization of the underlying theoretical thought of Adam Smith, his predecessors and his contemporaries." *Adam Smith's Legacy.* Ed. Michael Fry. London: Routledge, 1992. 29–62.

L'Abeille, ou recueil de philosophie de littérature et d'histoire. Hague: 1755.

Argenson, René, Louis de Voyer de Paulmy Marquis d'. *Considérations sur le Gouvernement ancien et présent de la France,* Amsterdam: 1764.

_____ . *Journal et Mémoirés.* 9 vols. Ed. E.J.B. Rathery. Paris: 1859–1867.

Baudeau, Nicholas. "Principes de la science morale et politique sur le luxe et les lois somptuaires." *Les Éphémérides du citoyen.* 1767.

Berkeley, George. *The Querist.* 3 vols. Dublin: 1735–1737.

Boisguilbert, Pierre de. *Oeuvres manuscrites et imprimées de Boisguilbert,* vol. II of *Pierre de Boisguilbert ou la naissance de l'Économie Politique.* Paris: L'Institut National d'Études Démographiques, 1966.

Cantillon, Richard. *Essai sur la nature du commerce en général.* Paris: 1755. Rprt. and trans. by Henry Higgs for the Royal Economic Society. London: Macmillan, 1931.

Condillac, E. Bonnot, abbé de. 1776. *Le Commerce et le Gouvernement: considérés relativement l'un à l'autre.* Paris: 1776. Trans. and ed. Shelagh M. Eltis and Walter Eltis. Aldershot: Edward Elgar, 1997.

Eltis, Walter. "Does Luxury Consumption Promote Growth?" *From Classical Economics to the Theory of the Firm: Essays in Honour of D.P. O'Brien.* Ed. Roger E. Backhouse and John Creedy. Cheltenham: Edward Elgar, 1999. 87–103.

Fénelon, François de Salignac de La Mothe. *Les aventures de Télémaque.* Paris: 1699. Paris: Gallimard, 1995.

Forbonnais, François Véron de. *Éléments de commerce.* Amsterdam: 1755.

Galliani, Renato. *Rousseau, le luxe et l'idéologie nobiliaire.* Oxford: Voltaire Foundation at the Taylor Institute, 1989.

Larrère, Catherine. *L'invention de l'économie au XVIIIe siècle.* Paris: PUF Léviathan, 1992.

McManners, John. *Church and Society in Eighteenth-Century France.* 2 vols. Oxford: Clarendon Press, 1998.

Mandeville, Bernard de. *The Fable of the Bees: or Private Vices, Public Benefits.* London: 1714. [After 1729, editions also included the Second Part.]

Melon, Jean-François. *Essai politique sur le commerce.* 1734. Paris: Édition augmentée, 1736.

Mirabeau, Victor Riqueti, Marquis de, and François Quesnay. *L'Ami des hommes.* 8 parts. Avignon: 1756–1760. [Including "Le Tableau économique avec ses explications."]

——— . 1763) *Philosophie rurale.* 1763. 2nd ed. 1764. 3 vols. Paris: Scientia Verlag Aalen, 1972.

Montesquieu, Charles-Louis de Secondat, baron de la Brède. *Lettres persanes.* 1721. Ed. Émile Faguet. Paris: Nelson, 1951.

——— . *Considérations sur les causes de la grandeur des Romains et de leur décadence.* 1734. Rpt. in *Lettres persanes.* Paris: Nelson, 1951. 331–523.

——— . *De l'esprit des lois.* 1748. 2 vols. Paris: Garnier frères, 1961.

——— . *Pensées et Spicilège.* Ed. Louis Desgraves. Paris: Robert Laffont, 1991.

Morize, André. *L'Apologie du luxe au XVIIIe siècle et Le Mondain de Voltaire.* Paris: H. Didier, 1909.

Murphy, Antoin. *Richard Cantillon: Entrepreneur and Economist.* Oxford: Clarendon Press, 1986.

Negishi, T. "Expenditure Patterns and International Trade in Quesnay's *Tableau économique.*" *Developments in Japanese Economics.* Tokyo: Academic Press/Harcourt Brace Jovanovich, 1989. 85–97.

Perrotta, Cosimo. "The Pre-Classical Theory of Development: Increased Consumption Raises Productivity." *History of Political Economy* 29.2 (summer 1997): 295–326.

Quesnay, François. *Tableau économique.* 1758–1759. Republished as *Quesnay's Tableau économique.* Ed. Marguerite Kuczynski and Ronald L. Meek. London: Macmillan, 1972.

Rousseau, Jean-Jacques. *Discours sur les sciences et les arts.* 1750. Ed. Jacques Roger. Paris: Flammarion, 1992. 23–55.

——— . *Dernière réponse de J.J. Rousseau.* 1752. Paris: Flammarion, 1992. 97–126.

——— . *Discours sur l'économiie politique.* 1755. *Oeuvres complètes.* 5 vols. Ed. B. Gagnebin and M. Raymond. Paris: Gallimard, 1959–1995. Vol. III, 241–78.

——— . *Discours sur l'origine et les fondements de l'inégalité, parmi les hommes.* 1755. Paris: Flammarion, 1992. 145–257.

——— . *Du contrat social.* 1762. *Oeuvres complètes.* 5 vols. Ed. B. Gagnebin and M. Raymond. Paris: Gallimard, 1959–1995. Vol. III, 279–470.

——— . Préface to *Narcisse. Oeuvres complètes.* 5 vols. Ed. B. Gagnebin and M. Raymond. Paris: Gallimard, 1959–1995. Vol. II, 959–74.

Smith, Adam. *The Nature and Causes of the Wealth of Nations.* London: 1776.

Steincr, Philippe. *La 'Science Nouvelle' de l'économie politique.* Paris: PUF, 1998.

Théré, Christine. "Economic Publishing and Authors, 1566–1789." *Studies in the History of French Political Economy: From Bodin to Walras*. Ed. Gilbert Faccarello. London: Routledge, 1988. 1–56.

Voltaire, François Marie Arouet de. *Le Mondain*. 1734. Rpt. in *L'Apologie du luxe au XVIIIe siècle et Le Mondain de Voltaire*. By André Morize. Paris: H. Didier, 1909. 133–39.

_____ . *La Défense du Mondain*. 1739. Rpt. in *L'Apologie du luxe au XVIIIe siècle et Le Mondain de Voltaire*. By André Morize. Paris: H. Didier, 1909.

The Idea of a Secular Society Revisited

Ross Emmett

Christian economists should [. . .] read Munby [. . .] for guidance and inspiration in the difficult intellectual and spiritual enterprise of relating economics to the faith.—A.M.C. Waterman, "Denys Munby (1919–1976) on Economics and Christianity"

In March 1962, Denys L. Munby gave the Riddell Memorial Lectures at King's College, University of Durham. The lectures were published a year later, under the title *The Idea of a Secular Society: And its Significance for Christians*. Munby was an applied economist, a fellow of Nuffield College at Oxford, and a Christian (Waterman, "Denys"). The latter was of particular importance for Munby's lectures because they were designed as a response to T.S. Eliot's famous lectures entitled *The Idea of a Christian Society*. Schooled in the Christendom movement, which claimed Eliot as its own, Munby's eventual training in economics brought him to a different understanding of the relation between social science, religion, and social policy. Where Eliot argued for a state that functioned according to Christian principles, Munby said that the church had little to say about the functioning of the state and made the case for specialized roles for religion and economics. Where Eliot believed that the church should comprehend the entire nation and that religious symbols and images were necessary for social unity, Munby argued that a secular society must accept religious diversity and reject unifying symbols that bore the stamp of particular religions. Where Eliot affirmed the permanence of traditional Christian values and worried that the secular trend of social change would lead to a society that worshiped "gods that are not gods," Munby believed that economic progress would lead to the enhanced satisfaction of many social values and could be pursued without necessarily threatening traditions and religious

Faith, Reason, and Economics: Essays in Honour of Anthony Waterman. Ed. Derek Hum. Winnipeg: St. John's College Press, 2003.

practices. In short, the differences between these two Christians' understandings of society could not be more stark.

While the language of both Munby and Eliot sounds naïve and optimistic to us today and was clearly shaped by the contingencies of their historical settings—Britain in the 1930s and the early 1960s—their discussion of the relationship between religion and economics remains relevant to us today. We have seen in recent years that religion has not diminished in the face of secularization and that, far from losing its public authority, it once again shapes global politics. We are now told that the modern political world is a "clash of civilizations" (Huntington), shaped by the religious divide between the Judeo-Christian civilizations of the West and the Islamic and Sinec civilizations of the East. Rather than ending history (Fukuyama, *End*), the conclusion of the battle between the *ideological* West and East—capitalism versus socialism—has transformed global conflict into a clash between the *religious* West and East. In this post–September eleventh world, is there any place for a secular society? Can a society that is neutral to religious beliefs survive in a world shaped by religious difference?

At the same time, we are also told that Munby's chosen profession—economics—is itself a religion, or at least the theology that undergirds the religion of economic progress and the market. In his book *Economics as Religion: From Samuelson to Chicago and Beyond*, economist Robert Nelson argues that "the most vital religion of the modern age has been economic progress. If economists have had a modest impact in actually generating this progress, or even understanding the actual mechanisms by which it has occurred, they have had a large role in giving it social legitimacy. They have been the modern priesthood of the religion of progress" (329).

Can Munby's argument for the specialized roles of religion and the social sciences be upheld in light of the critique offered by Nelson? Does a secular society simply substitute material progress for religious tradition, the market or money for God? Does Munby's vision mean that Eliot's greatest fear—that society will serve Mammon, not God—will be realized?

WHAT IS A SECULAR SOCIETY?

An appropriate starting point for our consideration of Munby's view of the secular society is to contrast his understanding of such a society with that of his contemporaries, whose views are more familiar and have shaped our common understanding of secularization. It was Dietrich Bonhoeffer who spoke of "man's coming of age"—of the human race's maturation to the point that we no longer needed God as a comfort in pain or sorrow, a source of inspiration to act for good, or as someone to blame for the world's misfortunes. We could turn our attention from another world and focus it on the joys and trials of this world, from emancipation *from* this world to emancipation *in* this world (Cox, *Secular*). From the perspective of a secular society, religion "gives not help but hindrance as it keeps man in a state of puerile dependence and holds him back from his maturity" (Ramsey 17). These observations led to the secularization thesis: belief in traditional religion would decline as modern society developed a variety of means to enable its members to live without it. Social scientists and liberal theologians alike adopted the secularization thesis; the former assumed it meant that they could ignore religion as a factor in social and economic development; the latter began to construct theologies more relevant to a secular world than the orthodox formulations.

It was the increasing loss of common beliefs and rationalization of life that Eliot protested in *The Idea of a Christian Society*. Munby puts Eliot's case well when he says that, according to Eliot, a secular society "undermines the cultural values without which men cannot remain permanently satisfied. It uproots men from their traditional stabilities, demands of them a rationality they cannot bear, and continuously disassociates them from their fellow men, as the changing social and economic forces break up any grouping, whether regional or professional, at work, or in the places where people live, almost as soon as they are able to form them. [. . .] Far from being enriched by the new powers, men become the slaves of new and more compelling social and economic processes" (46–47).

However, the notion of a secular society that Munby defended is somewhat different from the one that Eliot attacked. Munby's notion differs from the common understanding of secularization in three ways. The first difference emerges from his use of the term *neutral* as a synonym for secular. A neutral society is one in which the state does not privilege one religion over another (Munby 11–12). Munby extended neutrality to imply that a secular society's decisions about the production and distribution of resources and the administration of human, natural, and financial capital were made via mechanisms that do not depend upon the organization or beliefs of any particular religion. The analogy of the American notion of the separation of church and state comes to mind, but, for Munby, the separation is between church and any form of social macro-organization. At the micro-level, individuals retain the right of free association. One of the implications of Munby's identification of secularization with religious neutrality at the macro-level is that his notion of the secular society does not necessitate the same decline of traditional religious belief that the secularization theorists posited. In fact, he suggests that secularization brings the enlargement of human choices over their beliefs and values rather than the loss of traditional beliefs (77). The difference between a focus on the decline of belief and the enlargement of choice plays a central role in Munby's argument for the secular society.

If we combine Munby's focus on religious neutrality at the macro-level with his assumption that totalitarian states privilege "Communist dogma," we can identify a second difference between Munby's understanding of a secular society and the secularization thesis: the close relationship between liberalism and secularism. While it is never explicitly stated, this close relationship is another underlying theme in Munby's argument. When secularization was seen simply as the decline of religious belief, it could be interpreted to include the totalitarian societies of the post–World War II era. Munby's focus on neutrality provides a different perspective on the communist régimes. These régimes were not neutral, choosing to restrict religious choice and privilege their own dogma. According to Munby, the secular society will not flourish in collectivist environments but only in the liberal societies of the West. Munby does suggest that communist societies could become secularized if "Communist dogma becomes as irrelevant to the concerns of the common man as have the theological pretensions of the Christian Church in the West" (12). In hindsight, one wonders if the secularization of communism, in Munby's sense, helped to bring about its downfall.

Finally, Munby sees secularization as offering new opportunities for orthodox faith. Eliot saw secular society as aiding the onslaught of paganism against the stronghold of orthodoxy (perhaps an appropriate metaphor during the dark days of 1939). Despite the spread of communism, Munby thought:

> It is less easy to be pessimistic about the inherent possibilities of our society, however much we may detest the complacency and vulgarity of the Macmillan era in decline. In spite of the theological prophecies that a people without God will perish, in spite of the condemnations of moralists who point to the allegedly growing laxity of sexual mores and the supposed increase in neuroses, our society has shown signs of vigour that would hardly have been believed in the thirties. The Neutral Society has become more neutral, without as yet showing signs of becoming more aggressively "pagan," at least in the Communist or Fascist/Nazi sense, in which Mr. Eliot may be supposed to have intended his phrase to be interpreted. (10–11)

Like Bonhoeffer, Munby perceived that true Christianity could flourish in a world come of age. God's presence in the world meant that the secular society was not to be feared and resisted, but welcomed.

It may be worth noting that Munby's positive view of the prospects for religion in the secular society has been reinforced by recent studies in the sociology and economics of religion that challenge the secularization thesis. These studies have shown that religious activity increased over the past several decades, although lower growth occurred in countries or regions with an established or dominant church (see Iannacone for a summary). However, where the scholars who undertook these studies usually interpret their results as an attack on the notion of the secular society, Munby would probably see them as an affirmation of his argument for a secular society.

ECONOMICS, PROGRESS, AND THE SECULAR SOCIETY

The reader familiar with *The Idea of a Secular Society* may raise a sceptical eyebrow at this point and ask whether Munby's idea of a secular society is not based simply on the notion that economic progress in a market economy allows all members of society a greater array of choices; a case of prosperity breeding tolerance. Isn't the core of his argument to be found in the second lecture, entitled "Change, Specialization and Human Values"? Perhaps Munby's response to Eliot is more about accepting a form of social organization conducive to economic progress than it is about the society's neutrality to religion? Certainly, progress plays a significant role in Munby's argument; he uses it to counter Eliot's claim that secular change will always be destructive of human values. In his usual understated style, Munby says that, despite all the changes since the 1930s, "it is not at all clear that we are in any unambiguous or generally agreed sense 'worse off'" (48). But he does not make progress the core of his argument for a secular society. In order to understand why, we need to return to the relation of liberal society and secularization and begin to incorporate Munby's economic perspective.

Liberalism is often understood as a political philosophy that seeks to enable the members of a pluralistic society to function together while pursuing their various personal ends (Hall). Munby's training in economics added an additional element to his understanding of liberal society, highlighted by his frequent reference to "specialization." The economics tradition in which Munby was trained made the radical claim that liberal society is held together by the mutual benefits that individuals find from exchange with one another. The *locus classicus* for this claim is the opening chapters of Adam Smith's *Wealth of Nations*, with their eloquent appeal to the division of labour. Specialization, via the division of labour, in an economy regulated by market processes enables the creation of wealth exceeding that available to a closed economy committed to self-sufficiency. While it is tempting to leap immediately to the prospects for the growth of wealth and incomes in a market economy, Smith makes a more subtle point. The market creates interdependencies among the members of such a society (and across societies that trade with each other) that bind people with disparate values, beliefs and commitments to each other. In a market economy, my prosperity depends upon my ability and willingness to serve you. (While Smith was right that we depend on the self-interest of the baker, butcher, and brewer for our supper, it is also the case that they depend on our self-interest for their income.) Interdependency builds upon specialization, and specialization requires trust in our interdependency. No underlying commonality is required to produce social order. It springs, as if by an "invisible hand," from the self-regulating process implicit in market exchange.

Many people, including some economists, have resisted this economic version of the argument for liberalism. Apart from those who reject the argument on efficiency grounds, the most telling criticisms are two sides of the same coin. On one side is Eliot's argument that the market either destroys human values or supports the satisfaction of the "wrong" values. In either case, the market is said to leave us without an underlying philosophy that can animate a rich life for our society as a whole. This argument has a long tradition in British discourse, from Charles Dickens's novels and Thomas Carlyle's debates with J.S. Mill (see Levy) to more recent postmodern accounts (Giddens). It also appears in the North American literature, most forcibly in the work of Frank Knight ("Competition") and Charles Taylor. A new variant of the argument appears in the contemporary literature of environmentalism, which shares Eliot's distress at the fact that the market is unable to distinguish between "right" and "wrong" values and, hence, may allow individuals to make "bad" choices.

Munby's response to Eliot provides us with two counter-arguments to the claim that the market has a destructive effect on human values. I have treated the first of these arguments—his claim that market exchange widens the scope for the realization of human values. Those who wish to be "self-acclaimed spokespersons for humanity" (or the environment) often find it difficult to accept people's willingness to trade the benefits of living in a community with strong social or religious bonds for the benefits of living in a secular society that allows one to select among a larger range of values. But, if we agree with Knight that "the chief thing which the common-sense individual actually wants is not satisfaction for the wants which he has, but more, and better wants" ("Economic" 42), then we may wish to argue that widening the array of choices will allow individuals to adopt better values.

The possibility that people's values may change is the source of Munby's second counter-argument to Eliot. The possibility of new values being adopted provides a specialized mission for the church in a secular society. If the church truly believes that God is in the world, and not just that part of the world that lies outside the market, then the church's task in a secular society is to help its members construct lives within the secular society that are true to the Gospel (Munby 67–77, 85–89). This is not an Anabaptist call for a Christian counterculture (although Christians may adopt some values that others will not) but rather a recognition of the fact that it is in the ordinary business of life that the Gospel is lived out. This argument is also an appropriate response to the environmental movement's attack on the market's neutrality toward "bad" values.

The other side of the moral critique of the market is that a market society works best when its participants do share strong common bonds, like religion. For example, Francis Fukuyama has argued (see *Trust*) that market exchange requires a non-market basis for trust among individuals who are not family members. Fukuyama provides a new version of the Weber thesis with his claim that certain forms of religion (among them Protestantism) build a basis for such trust, and therefore, enhance their societies' prosperity. Nelson extends

Fukuyama's claim as far as to suggest that "investments in religion may be a more effective means than achieving higher levels of physical and human capital in advancing economic growth and development" (301). Much earlier, Josiah Stamp made a similar argument about the role of the Christian ethic in promoting national wealth.

Munby never considers this second side of the moral critique of markets, but there is a fundamental flaw in it. Essentially, the problem is this: if we limit our trade to a group with whom we share common bonds, we may increase the prosperity of that group relative to other groups (notice Fukuyama's and Stamp's focus on *national* prosperity), but we will also curtail the total prosperity of all groups. This is a result that Smith would have appreciated, but that is best known today from game theory. The economist's argument, once again, is that people will trade where they judge there to be an advantage to do so and that such trades will contribute to all participants' prosperity, regardless of national, regional, or even religious affiliation. Group-based differences, such as religion, ethnicity, or nationality, may alter one's estimation of the benefits or costs of trade, but where a net benefit is seen, trade will occur (and grow) if allowed. This argument is not heard enough today in the clamour over the benefits and costs of globalization.

Munby's discussion of progress and the positive aspects of change, therefore, emerge from the core of his argument about the secular society rather than the other way around. Neutrality does not only mean the absence of state privilege for any religion and toleration of diverse values. It also extends to the notion that trade will benefit not only one group but also all participants. Economic progress strengthens the argument for a secular society but is not its foundation.

The core of Munby's argument for a secular society, then, can be restated this way: a market economy, combined with a liberal democratic political system, provides the social processes for the coordination of the available resources across existing human needs and wants. In such a society, the processes of social coordination are independent of, and remain neutral toward, the religious or other value systems that may inform the needs and wants of individuals in the society. Rather than seeking to avoid responsibility for our own choices, we as individuals can welcome a secular society because it provides a setting in which we not only can satisfy our needs most efficiently but also can explore values that we have not adopted before. The church need not fear the widening array of choices provided in a secular society, for God's presence in the world has not changed.

Does Munby's argument retain its currency today? Does the re-appearance of religion as a major social and political force contradict Munby's idea of a secular society as it does the secularization thesis? The short answers are yes to the first question and no to the second. Munby's argument is built around religious neutrality rather than religious decline, and hence his notion of a secular society can accommodate the emergence of religious movements with broad social appeal. What his defence of a secular society stands against is a *religious society*, in which the state gives social privilege to a particular religion. But that, of course, is what Eliot called for. In the midst of the re-appearance of religious societies in various parts of the world, and the strident claims of some within liberal democratic market economies to give religious movements greater political control, the secular society remains an ideal worth pursuing, even by those with religious commitments.

SPECIALIZATION AND THE RELATION BETWEEN ECONOMICS AND THEOLOGY

We have dealt at length with Munby's case for a secular society and have found good reasons to support it. But the argument is not finished. Eliot, in his time, and Nelson, today, argue that economics and religion are not separate realms, as Munby assumed, but overlap in several ways. For Eliot, theology was the queen of the sciences, providing the glue that held all knowledge together. True economic knowledge could be built only upon an orthodox theological base. Nelson goes even further, claiming that economics provides an alternative theology, competing with traditional religious beliefs (and probably winning). Nelson's view is similar to that of theologian Harvey Cox. Cox recently wrote of reading the modern "signs of the time":

> The lexicon of *The Wall Street Journal* and the business sections of *Time* and *Newsweek* turned out to bear a striking resemblance to Genesis, the Epistle to the Romans, and Saint Augustine's City of God. Behind descriptions of market reforms, monetary policy, and the convolutions of the Dow, I gradually made out the pieces of a grand narrative about the inner meaning of human history, why things had gone wrong, and how to put them right. Theologians call these myths of origin, legends of the fall, and doctrines of sin and redemption. But here they were again, and in only thin disguise: chronicles about the creation of wealth, the seductive temptations of statism, captivity to faceless economic cycles, and, ultimately, salvation through the advent of free markets, with a small dose of ascetic belt tightening along the way, especially for the East Asian economies. ("Market" 18)

Can Munby's argument for a distinction between economics and theology be sustained in the face of these claims?

To his credit, Munby does not build his case for the separation of economics and theology on the common notion that they deal with different fields of human knowledge. Scientific inquiry invariably seeks an explanation for every aspect of our world, natural or human, and attempts to barricade some aspect of human activity against the encroachment of science always fail. "There is no field left where we can exclude science and intrude God as an alternative explanation" (Munby 71). Insistence on interpreting religious knowledge as the same type of knowledge as scientific knowledge inevitably runs into difficulty. Munby argues that we can render "to Caesar the things that are Caesar's and to God the things that are God's" (Matthew 22.21) if we acknowledge that science and religion make different types of claims. He states:

> The conclusion is clear. God does not provide explanations of events as does science, whether physical, social, or psychological sciences are in question. We are not to look for the hand of God in any particular fields of experience. He is in all or in none. Providence is universal or nowhere. It does not provide an explanation that we can fall back upon when other explanations fail. [. . .] The tools that [the natural and social sciences have] provided for us, as well as those provided by philosophers in the analysis of language, are necessary and fundamental parts of our everyday life. There can be no conflict in principle between their use and the glory of God. The world they reveal to us has always been there, and it is God's world. (71–72)

Munby's argument that science and religion provide different *types* of knowledge is reminiscent of Richard Whately's *Introductory Lectures on Political Economy*. In his lectures, Whately distinguished between scientific and religious knowledge on epistemological grounds in order to defend the Christian use of the knowledge of political economy from those who would argue that its association with utilitarianism rendered it antithetical to a Christian world view (Waterman, "Whately"). Munby's purpose, and conclusion, is similar. His early experiences with the Christendom movement convinced him that their attempts to establish a Christian sociology were either trivial or misguided. Where a Christian economics (to put it in our terms) agrees with the economic discipline's approach, there is no particular reason to identify it as uniquely Christian. It is simply good economics. And where a so-called Christian economics makes scientific claims that disagree with the findings of the discipline, its conclusions usually prove to be inadequate because its claims are not subjected to the same scientific process.

Whately's lectures provided the first recognition within economics of what is known today as the positive/normative distinction. Munby accepted that distinction and suggested that it provided a basis for the division of labour between economics and religion. Like Whately before him, he argued that Christians could accept the knowledge of the economics profession as a positive tool to be used in advancing their normative ends. But he has little appreciation for organized church bodies that seek to issue statements about current economic policy. He does not say that such bodies are irrelevant, but he does point out that, in a secular world, the pronouncements of such bodies sound altogether too much like the dictates of an Anglican schoolmaster. A world come of age does not wish to be treated as a child again. Rather than putting its energy into public policy pronouncements, the church should turn to the task of assisting the laity in considering the responsibilities of their ordinary lives in light of the normative claims of the Gospel (Munby 85–88). Unfortunately, the tendency of church bodies to continue making pronouncements about public policy on the assumption that the secular world has a responsibility to listen to them has not diminished since Munby's time.

It is interesting to observe that Munby's discussion of the relation between economic and religious knowledge touches only lightly on the theological task. In fact, there is a strong antipathy toward contemporary theology in his lectures. "It is clear that we can expect little help from the theologians," he says (83), just after his discussion of our need to bring the positive knowledge of economics and the norms of Christian religion together. Specialization in theology, while necessary, has also led, he claims, to a discipline removed from the ordinary concerns of Christians. One wonders if he would have had the same concern about specialization in economics had he been writing forty years later.

How, then, would Munby respond to Nelson and Cox today? I suspect his response would be twofold. First, he might argue that Nelson has mistaken commitment for religion. All humans have commitments, which range across the varieties of human knowledge, beliefs, and values. Scientists may be firmly committed to certain scientific propositions, such as those that undergird the theory of evolution or the theory of the market. They may seek to explain every aspect of natural or human activity in the terms of that theory. They may employ their scientific knowledge in support of particular social or economic policies. Yet the knowledge that their science generates is not the same as religious knowledge. Economics is not religion; religion is not economics. Cox's rhetoric creates a powerful analogy, but his conflation of economics and religion re-opens the door to the notion of a religious society that he rejected almost forty years ago in *The Secular City*. We would do better to hold out the ideal of a secular society than to provide fodder for those who want us to return to a religious one.

But Nelson and Cox may persist in their argument, claiming that, whether or not the knowledge of economics constitutes religious belief, many economists not only accept, but also advocate, values that run counter to the basic human values articulated by many religions. Surely, the market's destructive power over basic human values should be restricted. Munby's twofold response to Eliot's claim that the secular society allows the market to destroy human values is clearly as relevant today as it was in his time. The greatest enemy of the secular society is not religion per se, but rather it is those who, with the best of intentions, seek to restrict the operation of the market and liberal democracy in the interest of promoting values that they believe all humans should adopt.

CONCLUSION

"The Church will be seen, if seen at all, in the thick of ordinary life" (Munby 89). Throughout *The Idea of a Secular Society*, Munby refers frequently to the activity of ordinary people going about their ordinary business. The connection to economics is obvious to those familiar with Alfred Marshall's famous definition of economics as "a study of mankind in the ordinary business of life." But Munby's focus on the ordinary things of life was also an explicit criticism of Eliot, who spoke disparagingly of modern culture as a "lower middle class culture" (76) and called for a "Church within the Church" (78)—comprised of "consciously and thoughtfully practising Christians, especially those of intellectual and spiritual superiority" (35)—to provide leadership for the church and the Christian society. Up against Eliot's select group of superior Christians, Munby set the knowledge of economics and the religious beliefs of ordinary people. He then asked the church to assume the role of assisting these people to live the Gospel in the ordinary business of life. In our secular society, what higher calling could there be?

WORKS CITED

Bonhoeffer, D. *Letters and Papers from Prison.* London: SCM Press, 1953.

Cox, H. 1965. *The Secular City: Secularization and Urbanization in Theological Perspective.* New York: Macmillan, 1965.

_____ . "The Market as God." *Atlantic Monthly* 283 (March 1999):18–23.

Eliot, T.S. *The Idea of a Christian Society.* London: Faber and Faber, 1939.

Fukuyama, F. *The End of History and the Last Man.* New York: Free Press, 1991.

_____ . *Trust: The Social Virtues and the Creation of Prosperity.* New York: Free Press, 1995.

Giddens, A. *Modernity and Self-Identity.* Palo Alto: Stanford University Press, 1991.

Hall, J.A. *Liberalism: Politics, Ideology and the Market.* London: Paladin, 1987.

Huntington, S.P. *The Clash of Civilizations and the Remaking of World Order.* New York: Simon and Schuster, 1996.

Iannacone, L.R. "Introduction to the Economics of Religion." *Journal of Economic Literature* 36 (September 1998): 1,465–95.

Knight, F.H. "Ethics and the Economic Interpretation. 1922. *Selected Essays by Frank H. Knight.* Vol. 1: *"What is Truth" in Economics?* Ed. Ross B. Emmett. Chicago: University of Chicago Press, 1999. 40–60.

_____ . "The Ethics of Competition." 1923. *Selected Essays by Frank H. Knight.* Vol. 1: *"What is Truth" in Economics?* Ed. Ross B. Emmett. Chicago: University of Chicago Press, 1999. 61–93.

Levy, D. *How the Dismal Science Got its Name: Classical Economics and the Ur-Text of Racial Politics*. Ann Arbor: University of Michigan Press, 2001.

Marshall, A. *Principles of Economics*. London: Macmillan, 1890.

Munby, D.L. *The Idea of a Secular Society: And its Significance for Christians*. London: Oxford University Press, 1963.

Nelson, R.H. *Economics as Religion: From Samuelson to Chicago and Beyond*. University Park, PA: Pennsylvania State University Press, 2001.

Ramsey, A.M. *God, Christ and the World: A Study in Contemporary Theology*. London: SCM Press, 1969.

Stamp. J. *The Christian Ethic as an Economic Factor*. London: Epworth Press, 1926.

Taylor, C. *Sources of the Self*. Cambridge: Harvard University Press, 1989.

Waterman, A.M.C. "Denys Munby (1919–1976) on Economics and Christianity." *Bulletin of the Association of Christian Economists* 12 (Fall 1988): 5–10.

_____ . "Whately, Senior, and the Methodology of Classical Economics." *Economics and Religion: Are They Distinct?* Ed. H.G. Brennan and A.M.C. Waterman. Boston: Kluwer, 1994. 41–60.

Whately, R. *Introductory Lectures on Political Economy*. London: Fellowes, 1832.

Hearts in the Balance:
Virtue, Gender, and the Enlightenment

Nancy Folbre

I am a dabbler in the history of economic thought, and, unlike the masters of this field, including Anthony Waterman, I have always adopted a shamelessly "presentist" agenda. I use intellectual history to illustrate my own contemporary concerns. For this, I have been scolded by said Waterman, in a most instructive way, and often forced to clarify and (I must hope) improve my arguments. Thus emboldened, I iterate here between the past and the present, arguing that Bishop Butler and Adam Smith, as well as contemporary representatives of the British Enlightenment, were overconfident of human virtue in general and male virtue in particular.

The proposition that we all benefit from the individual pursuit of self-interest within a competitive market economy is central to the discourse of mainstream economics. This proposition can be stated in a variety of forms, and the caveats appended to it largely determine its political implications. Still, those who agree with this proposition can be sorted into two basic groups. Some believe that the individual pursuit of self-interest delivers good results whether or not individuals are virtuous or, in more modern "neoclassical" parlance, regardless of the underlying preference orderings of rational actors. The positive consequences flow purely from institutional design: the magic of competition. This perspective dates from Mandeville, finds eloquent expression in Malthus, and is best represented in the twentieth century by the writings of Hayek and Buchanan. All these famous economists insist that the intentions of economic actors are less important than the outcomes they generate. Indeed, they suggest that markets are the best form of economic organization precisely because men are knaves.

Other economists, often claiming allegiance to Enlightenment ideals, invoke concepts of human nature and suggest that the individual pursuit of self-interest

Faith, Reason, and Economics: Essays in Honour of Anthony Waterman. Ed. Derek Hum. Winnipeg: St. John's College Press, 2003.

will not normally take a purely selfish form. The essentially benevolent character of civilized men ensures that the interests of the self encompass the interests of others. Preferences and motives matter, and altruism and benevolence exert a moderating influence. Shaftesbury offered a secular version of this argument; Butler, a religious one. Smith is the best-known exponent, though his discussion was sufficiently nuanced to generate substantial controversy over what he actually meant.

I am entirely unpersuaded by the first justification of self-interest. Whether or not it applies in idealized competitive markets, it does not obviously apply within the family or the polity, which are indispensable parts of the economic system as a whole. Furthermore, it is difficult to draw strict boundaries among the market, the family, and the polity. By encouraging uninhibited pursuit of individual self-interest in one sphere, we almost certainly encourage it in others. I recently had the opportunity to broach this issue in person with James Buchanan, pointing out that his general condemnation of "dependency" and distrust of altruism has rather different consequences in the typically male arena of the market than in the typically female arena of the home. He declined to engage the point, simply stating that he "had not thought very much about the family."[1] One can see why he would prefer not to.

I am fascinated by the second justification of self-interest, which accounts for my intellectual affinity with Anthony Waterman and others who dare to explore the relationship between the normative and positive, often by addressing the relationship between religion and economics.[2] To apply Adam Smith's felicitous phrase, I believe that the "moral sentiments" influence economic decisions. Individuals are often quite concerned about the welfare of others, especially within the family and the polity. My own view of moral sentiments, however, does not derive from religious convictions or assumptions regarding human nature. Unlike Smith, and those writing in his tradition, I believe that moral sentiments are the outcome of a process of cultural evolution in which many factors, including intellectual discourse, socialization, and economic incentives play an important role.[3]

Sentiments is a slightly anachronistic term, appealing to me but confusing to many modern economists because it implies emotion. For the sake of clarity, I restate the argument in terms of the more familiar neoclassical vocabulary of *preferences*. Sentiments, preferences, values, and norms are not the same, and little is to be gained by suggesting that they are. Nonetheless, I believe it makes sense to speak of "moral preferences" (concern for right and wrong) even though these may be distinct from and perhaps even the product of moral values or moral norms. Furthermore, we can speak of "caring preferences" (reflecting concern for the well-being of others) that are related to values and norms of care. The crucial point, from my perspective, is that moral and caring preferences are culturally constructed. In neoclassical vocabulary, they are at least partially endogenous.

This point leads me to make two related claims. First, the preferences that temper individual pursuit of self-interest are more variable and malleable than most Enlightenment thinkers generally concede. Second, in circumstances in which a powerful social group dominates intellectual discourse, controls most institutions of socialization, and wields disproportionate economic power, these moral and caring preferences are often defined in ways that are distinctly disadvantageous to a less powerful social group. I focus on circumstances in which men are, by the above criteria, more powerful than women. I illustrate these two claims through brief discussion of a contemporary debate that reiterates many Enlightenment themes, followed by a critique of several major Enlightenment thinkers, including Adam Smith.

INVISIBLE HEARTS

As Anthony Waterman points out in his charming description of his experience as a student of Joan Robinson, one of the qualities that fosters communication across different political perspectives is "moral seriousness."[4] This quality characterizes three recent books that are otherwise quite divergent in their treatment of self-interest. Jennifer Roback Morse, an economist once affiliated with James Buchanan at George Mason University, challenges libertarian thinkers to reconsider the importance of love and commitment in *Love and Economics: Why the Laissez-Faire Family Doesn't Work.*[5] Russell Roberts offers a novelistic treatment of the virtuous Smithian hero who is willing to pay a high price for his principles in *The Invisible Heart: An Economic Romance.*[6] My own book, *The Invisible Heart: Economics and Family Values* (published at the same time, with a coincidentally similar title) emerges from the social feminist tradition, arguing that market competition can have the effect of undermining altruism and commitment to others.[7]

Morse challenges the notion that economic theory can be securely based on individual pursuit of self-interest that excludes concern for the welfare of others. Children's interests—indeed their very sense of identity—are shaped by parental love and affection, and children who fail to receive a modicum of such love and affection never develop the kinds of preferences necessary for a market society to function. Framed in terms of the vocabulary described above, her argument is that individuals who lack caring preferences cannot be trusted to engage in reciprocal exchange or to honour their contractual obligations. Furthermore, the cost of explicit monitoring and enforcement of exchange contracts among individuals who are completely opportunistic is prohibitively high.

Morse embraces Adam Smith's emphasis on moral sentiments but criticizes him for arguing that justice is more fundamental than love and for taking caring preferences as a given: "The conditions of his particular time and place induced him to inquire into the nature and causes of the wealth of nations even while those same circumstances allowed him to take sympathy or empathy for granted. Nothing in the social environment of his time led him to inquire into the nature and causes of the disposition to cooperate."[8] Conservatives and individualists, she argues, tend to take love for granted, or to treat it as an irrational emotion (she devotes an entire chapter of her book to the explanation of why the decision to love is reasonable). The principle of laissez-faire, which features in her title, cannot be applied to family life because it requires commitment, obligation, and (at least to some extent) regulation by the state.

This critique of unmitigated self-interest is especially gratifying, coming from an economist who is, in other respects, an acolyte of James Buchanan. But, perhaps because her book is largely addressed to other libertarians, Morse endorses a traditional, conservative, and, I would argue, gender-biased vision of the family. She assumes that the traditional male breadwinner / female caregiver family is the only institutional arrangement adequate to the task of socializing children. She offers explicit criticisms of institutional child care and over-utilization of paid substitutes for family care. But she never considers the possibility that mothers and fathers might share care more equally. Indeed, she avoids any mention of the extensive feminist scholarship suggesting that the traditional division of labour in the family both reflects and reinforces gender inequality.

There is a certain irony to this avoidance, because the feminist critique of the patriarchal state can be interpreted as an instance of the type of collective rent-seeking behaviour that Buchanan and others assail.[9] Just as Smith took norms and preferences of civilized society as a given, Morse takes the ideal typical family as a given, never asking how the rules, norms, and preferences upon which it is based came to be constructed. In this sense, she remains squarely within the Smithian tradition, ignoring the forms of collective identity and action based on gender (or class, or citizenship, or race/ethnicity) that comprise the structures of constraint on individual choice.[10] The result is an a-historical view of the family, which ignores the tremendous significance of collective renegotiation of its rules and responsibilities since Smith's times. Examples of such renegotiation include not only changes in women's rights over property, income, divorce, and child custody but also the cultural transformation of norms regarding appropriate behaviour for women.

I argue, by contrast, that the gradual, ongoing transformation of gender roles, partly driven by the empowerment of women in the market economy, is a major force behind current efforts to reconsider the definition of self-interest. The increasing tendency to encourage women, as well as men, to behave in self-interested ways threatens the viability of traditional family and community life. It pushes some conservative thinkers to re-moralize self-interest by moving away from the libertarian toward the more gentle Smithian tradition. Russell Roberts's *Invisible Heart: An Economic Romance,* though lighter and less ambitious than *Love and Economics*, is also a morality tale.

Roberts conforms to masculine stereotype, choosing a male protagonist and focussing on the nexus between morality and the market, leaving the family out of the picture. He is less interested in caring than in moral preferences. Yet the two categories are related, since the exhortation to "love thy neighbour" invokes both. Furthermore, a romance, by definition, introduces elements of personal affection and emotion. In this romance, a virtuous conservative is relentlessly punished for his faith in the free market but, in the end, wins the heart of a good woman. He also persuades her that she should perhaps renounce her plans to become a lawyer and remain faithful to the more virtuous and caring profession of teaching.

Sam Gordon is a high school economics teacher who is fired from his job and publicly ridiculed for his laissez-faire views. He is attracted to Laura Silver, a liberal English teacher, who finds him intriguing but politically unacceptable. She begins her class with a classic line from Wordsworth: "Getting and spending, we lay waste our powers." He teaches his students to value the discipline and impartiality of the market. Yet he is also attracted to poetry.

Sam Gordon's most distinctive feature, however, is his virtue. The book introduces him as someone who graciously gives money to a street beggar. Sam's favourite movie is *It's a Wonderful Life*, the Frank Capra tale in which Jimmy Stewart plays a banker redeemed by kindness. Sam doesn't mind his low wages because he gets so much intrinsic satisfaction from his work. He never whines about being fired for lack of political correctness. Indeed, he passes up an easy opportunity to avenge himself, because he does not want to hurt one of his students. One could even say that Sam has gender virtue as well as general virtue: he is attracted to Laura as a person, not as a status symbol or sexual object. He would probably even agree to share the child care.

In short, Sam is chock full of the moral sentiments. Reading this novel makes one wonder at the oft-made accusation that left-wing thinkers are utopian. If all the rational actors in a free market were as virtuous as Sam, the pursuit of self-interest would indisputably guarantee the common good. He would never pursue aggressive accounting procedures that would overstate his company's profits. He would never make campaign finance contributions intended to bribe a politician. He would never sell products that were unsafe for consumers or harmful to the environment. The question is, would Sam survive as the CEO of a major corporation fulfilling the Smithian destiny of *Wealth of Nations*?

Let's give Sam the benefit of the doubt and assume that he could. We are still left with the question of how he came to be so virtuous, so impervious to temptation. Where did his moral and caring preferences come from? This is the same question that Adam Smith tried to avoid. If the success of the economic system depends on virtue, one must explain how virtue itself is produced. But even the first step in such an explanation—a definition of virtue—proves remarkably contentious. Its cultural meaning is the product of power and negotiation.

THE BRITISH ENLIGHTENMENT

Unlike most of their successors, the great thinkers of the British Enlightenment never hid behind the feeble claim that facts could be separated from values, the positive from the normative. They felt a strong affinity for religious values. But they also wanted to get on with their worldly affairs. In their efforts to reconcile spiritual with economic well-being, they struggled to encourage just enough self-interest, but not too much. In general, they embraced the notion that either God or some other external force would ensure that moral and caring preferences would temper otherwise selfish pursuits.

At the same time, however, the moral and caring preferences they expressed reflected a highly gendered double standard. Men could pursue their self-interest because women would stay home to provide love and care. Though said to represent the natural order of things, this apparently required the exclusion of women from political participation, the restriction of their opportunities for economic independence, and the strict regulation of family life.

Love Thyself

Butler defended Christianity against the Deist claim that one could believe in the Great Watchmaker, without adherence to the dubious details of inherited scripture. His arguments persuasively emphasized that Nature was even harder to interpret than the scriptures and insisted on the importance of faith and humility. Yet part of Butler's appeal lay in his willingness to interpret scripture in modern terms. In the Rolls Sermons, preached between 1732 and 1735, in the immediate aftermath of *Fable of the Bees*, Butler co-opted Mandeville's argument by declaring self-love a virtue rather than a vice.[11]

Butler explained that a man may be impulsively tempted to indulge an immoral desire, but if he reflects in a calm and considered way upon the likely outcome, he will make the virtuous decision, which is also in his interest. To love oneself is to want to be virtuous. Like the Earl of Shaftesbury, Butler believed duty and self-interest entirely coincident. Unlike Shaftesbury, he invoked both the prospect of salvation and the commandments of Christ. One must love oneself even as one loves one's neighbours. There is no consideration, in his writings, of any trade-off between the two. Descartes feared cognitive deception by a demon; Butler apparently did not fear moral deception by the Devil.

Butler's reasoning sometimes veered close to the Deist emphasis on the divine design of nature: "Conscience and self-love, if we understand our true happiness, always lead us the same way, [. . .] this being implied in the notion of a good and perfect administration of things."[12] Providence itself ensures that self-regarding actions lead to unintended social goods.[13] Reverend Joseph Tucker advanced this argument in terms that strongly anticipate Adam Smith: "The Self-Love and Self-Interest of each Individual will prompt him to seek such Ways of Gain, Trades and Occupations of Life, as by serving himself, will promote the public Welfare at the same Time."[14]

The use of the masculine pronoun in such context was not accidental. Neither Butler nor Tucker urged women to ways of gain or trades or occupations. Most religious instruction for women urged them to love their families, not themselves. One of the most influential mid-eighteenth-century tracts, by the Reverend John Brown, described women's primary virtue as "domestic love and Care, as the first Duty of her life, the very purpose of her being."[15] Only among evangelical groups such as the Methodists were women allowed to preach on the same terms as men. Among those groups, the rhetoric of compassion, charity, and social redemption was more prominent.

Religious acceptance of Enlightenment ideals should not be overstated, especially in the Scottish case.[16] Frances Hutcheson, who held the chair of moral philosophy at Glasgow University, was arraigned before the Presbyterian Church for promoting the dangerous doctrine that the standard of moral goodness was the "promotion of the happiness of others," which could be ascertained without God's explicit assistance.[17] Hutcheson succeeded professionally in part because he was willing to place his work within a Christian context. David Hume was not so lucky. Though a great fan of Butler, his efforts to develop what he called "the moral sciences," along with his religious scepticism, probably contributed to his failure to secure the Chair of Moral Philosophy at Edinburgh in 1744.[18]

Hume developed Butler's arguments in more secular terms, reassuring his readers that self-interested men were not necessarily selfish and describing friendship and generosity as human passions. Criticizing Hobbes and Locke as advocates of the "selfish system of morals," he wrote, "I esteem the man whose self-love, by whatever means, is so directed as to give him a concern for others and render him serviceable to society, as I hate or despise him who has no regard to anything beyond his own gratifications and enjoyments."[19] In another famous quote, he referred to the "particle of the dove" that softened the elements of wolf and serpent in human nature.[20] Another influential figure of the Scottish Enlightenment, Adam Ferguson, reiterated Shaftesbury's argument that benevolence gave pleasure to the giver as well as the receiver.[21] The image suggests a pleasurable intercourse, an exchange in which the boundaries of the self become, at least temporarily, redefined.

The Moral Sentiments

Adam Smith's first book, *The Theory of Moral Sentiments*, lay squarely within this optimistic tradition. Its title was based on a phrase Hume had made famous and the book itself reiterated many popular arguments concerning human nature.[22] At the very outset of the book, Smith postulated that self-interest was subject to natural limits: "How selfish soever man may be supposed, there arc evidently some principles in his nature, which interest him in the fortune of others, and render their happiness necessary to him, though he derives nothing from it, except the pleasure of seeing it."[23] Smith's analysis of the moral sentiments was distinctly gendered. He praised sympathy but argued that feelings alone mattered little; rather, they should be "refracted" through the eyes of an impartial spectator.[24] He explicitly contrasted the female and emotional trait of humanity with the masculine and moral trait of generosity, echoing the traditional distinction between the natural and the social.

> Humanity is the virtue of a woman, generosity of a man. The fair sex, who have commonly much more tenderness than ours, have seldom so much generosity. [. . .] Humanity consists merely in the exquisite fellow-feeling which the spectator entertains with the sentiments of the persons principally concerned, so as to grieve for their sufferings, to resent their injuries, and to rejoice at their good fortune. The most human actions require no self-denial, no self-command, no great exertion of the sense of propriety. They consist only in doing what this exquisite sympathy would of its own accord prompt us to do. But it is otherwise with generosity. We never are generous except when in some respect we prefer some other person to ourselves, and sacrifice some great and important interest of our own to an equal interest of a friend or of a superior.[25]

Smith was more conservative than his Scottish predecessors on all matters pertaining to women's rights. In his lectures on moral philosophy, later amplified and published in 1755, Hutcheson had rebutted Locke's argument that men had a natural right to command within the family; as well, he criticized civil laws that deprived women of property and attacked the sexual double standard. Even Hume had spoken out briefly but decisively against "male tyranny."[26] Smith never expressed opinions on such matters and, in one of his few references to sexual intercourse, described any breach of female chastity as an irreversible disaster: "Even a rape dishonours, and the innocence of the mind, cannot, in our imagination, wash out the pollution of the body."[27]

Either because he was a bachelor, or because he wanted to avoid mention of the bodily passions, Smith seldom alluded to the love of a husband for his wife, or vice versa. But he waxed eloquent, in the *Moral Sentiments*, on the love of parents for children, brothers and sisters for one another, and the family in general for all its members. In an image that evokes Pope's metaphor of the circles of affection, he argued that men's sympathy for others diminished in proportion to his degree of relatedness and extent of social contact with them, and seldom extended beyond his country.[28] Of the possibility of universal benevolence, he promised that "the wise and virtuous man is at all times willing that his own private interest should be sacrificed to the public interest or his own particular order or society."[29] He did not provide a precise estimate of the proportion of men who were actually wise and virtuous.

The Butcher, the Baker, and the Wife

In his more famous book, *The Wealth of Nations*, published in 1776, Smith directly prescribed the individual pursuit of self-interest. He has sometimes been accused of inconsistency on this score, but his earlier book had, after all, made the case that self-interest would generally take a benevolent form. *The Wealth of Nations* emphasized the important role that competitive markets could play in ensuring good social outcomes and is in this respect entirely consistent with the Deist interpretation of providential design.[30] Smith reiterated the Hobbesian notion that self-interest was a mainspring of a "well-contrived machine."[31] It was the gears of human nature that translated that energy into the orderly and civilized movement of the watch's hands.

Within his economic analysis, Smith also found a spatial solution to the tension between virtue and self-interest, assigning one to the family (and to a lesser extent, the state) and the other to the economy. In one of the most famous sentences in the history of economic thought, he wrote, "It is not from the benevolence of the butcher, the brewer, or the baker that we expect our dinner but from regard to their self interest."[32] Smith neglected to mention that none of these tradesmen actually gets dinner on the table. Nor did he ever suggest that wives might prepare dinner for their husbands out of regard for their self-interest. Implicitly rejecting the broader mercantilist approach of Petty and others, Smith confined his attention to market exchanges: those exchanges primarily motivated by individual self-interest. He did not need to consider the process by which dinner was prepared because it was motivated by a combination of moral sentiments and animal-like dependence.[33]

Smith marvelled at the efficiency of specialization in the factory but never in the household. Despite his great attention to the variety of occupations that men pursued in agriculture as well as in manufacturing, he seldom mentioned women's work either in the market or in the home.[34] The institution of domestic service was widespread in his day, and accounted for a significant share of all wage employment for women. In aristocratic families (such as the one in which he briefly served as a tutor), the division of labour was elaborate. But Smith was entirely uninterested in cooks or upstairs maids.

The theoretical counterpart to the lack of descriptive attention was a theory of productive and unproductive labour that ignored domestic work, whether paid or unpaid. Smith argued that only labour devoted to material production could create that all-important key to economic growth: a surplus. He insisted that labour devoted to what we now term "services" was essentially sterile.[35] If cooks and nannies and housekeepers were explicitly deemed unproductive despite their wages, the wives and mothers who often provided similar services to their own families were obviously also unproductive. As Deborah Valenze points out, "domestic chores were tainted by their association with perhaps the most unacknowledged form of women's work, that of simply attending to the needs of others."[36]

Smith judiciously noted that many occupations that failed to meet his standard of productivity—increasing the market value of a tangible commodity—were nonetheless "necessary." Churchmen, lawyers, physicians, men of letters, the army, and the navy all graced the list of those who performed necessary services and therefore deserved the support of productive workers. Neither domestic servants nor wives nor mothers were included. This does not imply that Smith thought these women undeserving of support. Rather, it suggests that, unlike Petty, he was unwilling to consider them workers who made a contribution to economic growth.

Smith called attention to the importance of education and training of children once they had left the natural world of affection and entered the social world of exchange.[37] Furthermore, he realized that some assumptions regarding population growth were necessary to a theory of wages. In the short run, subsistence could be defined as the wages necessary to enable the worker to return to work the next day; in the long run, subsistence required funds sufficient to compensate for the attrition of the adult work force by sickness, old age, and death. A predecessor, Richard Cantillon, had suggested that a man's wage must be sufficient to support two children as well as the wage earner himself (assuming that a mother's productive activities were sufficient to provide for herself but not for her children).[38]

Pursuing this reasoning, Smith added the wise qualification that more than two children must be borne in order for two to survive to maturity. He went on to suggest that economic factors sometimes affected decisions about family size. Where land was plentiful, as in England's colonies in the United States, families were large. Observing that children there were a "source of opulence and prosperity," Smith calculated their economic rate of return, noting that the "labour of each child, before it can leave their [parents'] home, is computed to be worth a hundred pounds clear gain to them."[39] Men, therefore, pursued their own self-interest when they married early and began to propagate.

But, despite his summary claim that the "demand for men, like that for any other commodity, necessarily regulates the production of men," Smith offered an asymmetric treatment of fertility decisions.[40] Rational responses to changing prices failed to come into play when children became an economic burden. Infanticide or high infant mortality were the only factors Smith named as means of curtailing the size of families among the labouring poor. His reluctance to explore the possibility that men and women might choose to limit their fertility within marriage—a choice that conventional morality still deemed immoral—set the stage for later Malthusian assumptions.[41]

Smith is most famous for his criticisms of state intervention in the economy. In the *Wealth of Nations*, he roundly criticized policies that interfered with free trade or the free mobility of labour. As he made clear in his discussion of the poor laws, he regarded the state as a moral institution that could, like an overprotective mother, stifle male initiative. Yet he had few quarrels with the state's

106

hold on women, including the denial of independent property rights to married women and children, or restrictions on access to education and apprenticeships.

In this respect, he was typical of his day and age. The journalist and dictionary author Samuel Johnson, with whom Smith dined at least once, was famous for his social repartee, much of which was recorded by the randy but articulate James Boswell. At one party at a Mr. Dilly's home in the late 1770s, the conversation turned to cookbooks, and Mr. Johnson opined that men (including himself) could doubtless do a much better job on this subject than women. He provoked a Quaker woman named Mrs. Knowles, who was one of the dinner guests.

> Mrs. Knowles affected to complain that men had much more liberty allowed them than women.
>
> Johnson: "Why Madam, women have all the liberty they should wish to have . . ."
>
> Mrs. Knowles: "Still, Doctor, I cannot help thinking it a hardship that more indulgence is allowed to men than to women. It gives a superiority to men, to which I do not see how they are entitled."
>
> Johnson: "It is plain, Madam, one or the other must have the superiority. As Shakespear[e] says, 'If two men ride on a horse, one must ride behind.'"
>
> Dilly: "I suppose, Sir, Mrs. Knowles would have them to ride in panniers, one on each side."
>
> Johnson: "Then, Sir, the horse would throw them both."
>
> Mrs. Knowles: "Well, I hope that in another world the sexes will be equal."
>
> Boswell: "That is being too ambitious, Madam. We might as well desire to be equal with the angels."[42]

I read this exchange as an example of the ease with which feminist concerns could be rebuked.

Anthony Waterman suggests that my reading may be too harsh, since Johnson's affection for Mrs. Knowles was well-known. But, if the tone of the exchange is ambiguous, its content is not. Women are inferior to men in the political and economic sphere precisely because they are sweet angels of superior morality.

In his lively discussion of eighteenth-century confidence in the civilizing effects of commerce, Albert Hirschman repeats one of Samuel Johnson's most famous quotes: "There are few ways in which a man can be more innocently employed than in getting money."[43] Neither Johnson nor Smith would have agreed that this was true for women as well as men, and this inconsistency calls their larger world view into question. It also helps explain why their modern-day fans face a political dilemma. Women today have virtually the same rights as men to be self-interested; more importantly, women live in a cultural milieu that increasingly encourages them to exercise those rights. This makes it increasingly unlikely that we will continue to accept the sexual and moral double standard that has been central to the traditional organization of family life. Yet a reorganization of family life requires a renegotiation of the meaning of virtue.

THE BALANCE

Truly libertarian thinkers remain confident of individual self-interest in its most naked form. The Enlightenment tradition, on the other hand, reassures us that self-interest is safely clothed by moral and caring preferences. Both views are simplistic in their optimism. Many of the changes we have witnessed in the cultural construction of morality and obligation are linked to changes in the economic position of women. This makes it easy for us to look upon the past with our "presentist" agenda and criticize the moral and sexual double standard. But my point here is not to finger-wag.

The more important reason to study the transformation of moral and caring preferences is to ask how they might be reconstructed in more equitable and durable forms. We should define a balance between self-interest, morality, and care for others that is consistent with our ideals of gender-neutral justice. This is, of course, an idealistic demand based on the possibility of secular redemption, for if we lack virtue now, how can we teach ourselves to acquire it in the future? Perhaps we cannot. But the Enlightenment tradition tells us that we should at least try, with all the moral seriousness we can command.

NOTES

1. These exchanges took place in February 2002 at the Research School of Social Sciences at Australian National University, in two separate events organized by Geoffrey Brennan.

2. See, for instance: Geoffrey Brennan and A.M.C. Waterman, eds., *Economics and Religion: Are They Distinct?* (Boston: Kluwer, 1994); Daniel M. Hausman and Michael S. McPherson, *Economic Analysis and Moral Philosophy* (New York: Cambridge University Press, 1996).

3. For an example of how evolutionary game theory can help explain principles such as justice and mutual aid, see Brian Skryms, *Evolution of the Social Contract* (New York: Cambridge University Press, 1996).

4. A.M.C. Waterman, "Joan Robinson as a Teacher," ms., Boston College and St. John's College, Winnipeg.

5. Jennifer Roback Morse, *Love and Economics: Why the Laissez-Faire Family Doesn't Work* (Dallas: Spence Publishing, 2001).

6. Russell Roberts, *The Invisible Heart: An Economic Romance* (Cambridge: MIT Press, 2001).

7. Nancy Folbre, *The Invisible Heart: Economics and Family Values* (New York: The New Press, 2001).

8. Morse, p. 222.

9. Further discussion of rent-seeking as a way of conceptualizing patriarchal power can be found in: Nancy Folbre, "Engendering Economics: New Perspectives on Women, Work, and Demographic Change," in *Proceedings of the Annual World Bank Conference on*

Development Economics (Washington, DC: The International Bank for Reconstruction and Development, 1996); and "Gender Coalitions: Extrafamily Influences on Intrafamily Inequality," in *Intrahousehold Resource Allocation in Developing Countries: Methods, Models and Policy,* ed. Lawrence Haddad, John Hoddinott, and Harold Alderman (Baltimore: Johns Hopkins University Press, 1998).

10. For more discussion of structures of constraint, see Nancy Folbre, *Who Pays for the Kids? Gender and the Structures of Constraint* (New York: Routledge, 1994).

11. A.M.C. Waterman, "The Beginning of 'Boundaries': The Sudden Separation of Economics from Christian Theology," pp. 41–63 in *Economics and Interdisciplinary Research,* ed. G. Erreygers (New York: Routledge, 2001); and "Recycling Old Ideas: Economics among the Humanities," *Research in the History of Economic Thought and Methodology* 15 (1997): 237–49.

12. Joseph Butler, Sermon 3.9, *The Works of Bishop Butler,* ed. S. Halifax, vol. 1 (Oxford: 1874), p. 57.

13. Waterman, "Beginning," p. 3.

14. Josiah Tucker, *Instructions for Travelers,* in *The Collected Works of Josiah Tucker,* with a new introduction by Jeffery Stern, 6 vols. (London: Routlege, 1993 [first published in 1757]), p. 48.

15. John Brown, D.D., *On the Female Character and Education* (London: 1765), pp. 13–14.

16. Waterman states, "The Enlightenment in Britain was regarded as an opportunity rather than as a threat to established religion" ("Beginning," p. 1). Likewise, Gertrude Himmelfarb idealizes the British Enlightenment even more, stating, "Secular and religious institutions, civil society and the state, public relief and private charity complemented and cooperated with one another" ("The Idea of Compassion: The British vs. the French Enlightenment," *The Public Interest* [Fall 2001]: 9).

17. Jane Rendall, *The Origins of the Scottish Enlightenment* (New York: St. Martin's Press, 1978), p. 74. See also A.W. Coats, "Adam Smith, the Modern Reappraisal," in *On the History of American Thought: British and American Economic Essays,* vol. 1, ed. Coats (New York: Routledge, 1992), p. 124.

18. Peter Gay, *The Enlightenment, An Interpretation: The Science of Freedom* (New York: W.W. Norton, 1969), p. 8. See also Rendall, *Origins,* p. 32.

19. David Hume, *An Inquiry Concerning the Principles of Morals,* ed. Charles W. Hendel (Indianapolis: Bobbs-Merrill Educational Publishing, 1957), p. 115.

20. Ibid., p. 109.

21. Gay, p. 341.

22. On Smith's contributions relative to his predecessors, see Coats.

23. Adam Smith, *The Theory of Moral Sentiments,* with a biographical and critical memoir of the author by Dugald Stewart (London: G. Bell and Sons, 1911), p. 3. See also p. 27: "And hence it is, that to feel much for others, and little for ourselves, that to restrain our selfish, and to indulge our benevolent affections, constitutes the perfection of human nature"; and p. 214: "The man of the most perfect virtue, the man whom we love and revere the most, is he who joins, to the most perfect command of his own original and selfish feelings, the most exquisite sensibility both to the original and sympathetic feelings of others."

24. Samuel Fleischacker, "Adam Smith," *A Companion to Early Modern Philosophy*, ed. Steven M. Nadler (New York: Blackwell, 2002), p. 4.

25. See Jane Rendall, "Virtue and Commerce: Women in the Making of Adam Smith's Political Economy," in *Women in Western Political Philosophy*, ed. Ellen Kennedy and Susan Mendus (New York: St. Martin's Press, 1987), p. 59.

26. Gay, p. 34.

27. Rendall, "Virtue," p. 60.

28. Smith, , pp. 321–44.

29. Ibid., p. 346.

30. Anthony Waterman, *Revolution, Economics, and Religion: Christian Political Economy, 1798–1833* (Cambridge: Cambridge University Press, 1991).

31. T.D. Campbell, *Adam Smith's Science of Morals* (London: George Allen and Unwin, 1971), p. 220.

32. Adam Smith, *An Inquiry into the Nature and Causes of the Wealth of Nations*, 3rd. ed. (Edinburgh: Mundell, Pig, and Sevenson, 1809), p. 19.

33. "A puppy fawns upon its dam, and a spaniel endeavours by a thousand attractions to engage the attention of its master who is at dinner, when it wants to be fed by him" (ibid., p. 18).

34. For a discussion of the few instances in which Smith does discuss women's work, see: Michèle Pujol, *Feminism and Anti-Feminism in Early Economic Thought* (Aldershot: Edward Elgar, 1992); and Rendall, "Virtue." For a more detailed critique of his masculinist assumptions, see: Ulla Grapard, "Robinson Crusoe: The Quintessential Economic Man?" *Feminist Economics* 1.1 (Spring 1995): 33–52; and "The Benevolence of the Butcher's Wife," ms., Department of Economics, Colgate University.

35. Smith, *Wealth*, II, p. 84.

36. Deborah Valenze, *The First Industrial Woman* (New York: Oxford University Press, 1995). Note, however, that Valenze offers a more generous interpretation of Smith than I do here.

37. Pujol, , p. 19.

38. Smith, *Wealth*, I, p. 91.

39. Ibid., p. 95.

40. Ibid., p. 108.

41. For a more detailed discussion of attitudes toward contraception, see Nancy Folbre, "'The Improper Arts': Sex in Classical Political Economy," *Population and Development Review* 18.1 (1992), pp. 105–21.

42. James Boswell, *Boswell's Life of Johnson*, ed. George Birkbeck Hill, 6 vols. (Oxford: The Clarendon Press, 1934), pp. 286–87.

43. Albert Hirschman, *The Passions and the Interests: Political Arguments for Capitalism before its Triumph* (Princeton: Princeton University Press, 1977), p. 57.

Sophie Condorcet: Four Portraits

Evelyn L. Forget

This story is for Anthony. It is a story about the eighteenth century, the source from which our world emerged. Anthony and I both believe the economics of the past two centuries to be very largely the result of trying to come to terms with challenges raised during the French Revolution. One of us thinks the Revolution was probably a good idea. It is a story about the peculiar experience of reflecting on a life and trying to discover and to create the multiple narratives that give meaning to lived experience. And it is a story about Sophie de Grouchy, marquise de Condorcet, who lived from 1764 to 1822, and whose self-portrait as a young woman still has an extraordinary effect on men of a certain age 200 years after its creation.

Historians of economic thought have always made use of life writing. We draw upon memoirs, correspondence, interviews, diaries, minutes of committee meetings, notebooks, and autobiographies as source material in our histories. But not since the multi-volume biographical tomes of the Victorian age, skewered so definitively by Lytton Strachey, has there been such an outpouring of biography and autobiography in all fields of inquiry as in recent decades. We have seen, over the past twenty years, full-length biographies of some of the major figures of our past supplemented by collections of biographies of less well-known figures and volumes of autobiography, interviews, and oral histories. Neither the status nor influence of life writing, nor the methodological challenges of the genre, has attracted much comment in the history of economic thought.

The most astonishing aspect of the recent revival of biography is that it exists at all. Since the end of the eighteenth century, the role of the merely

Faith, Reason, and Economics: Essays in Honour of Anthony Waterman. Ed. Derek Hum. Winnipeg: St. John's College Press, 2003.

personal in historical study has been an uneasy one. During the twentieth century, biographical writing in the history of economic thought has weathered at least three significant challenges. The personality of the individual theorist was attenuated in histories that made use of rational reconstruction. The sociology-of-knowledge literature undermined the role of the individual writer, who became a pawn in thrall to forces much greater than any individual. And the most devastating attack, from a philosophical perspective, emerged from postmodern literary criticism in the form of the "contested self." If the subject itself is neither stable nor recoverable, the biographer's task becomes impossible. And yet, biographies, autobiographies, and memoirs proliferate.

I am writing the life of Sophie de Grouchy for many reasons. She (with her husband, Nicolas Condorcet) was an important figure in the development of late-eighteenth- and nineteenth-century French feminism. She was an intimate friend of the political revolutionary Thomas Paine and, as his translator and confidante, played a significant role in political events surrounding the French Revolution. Her *salon* was an important meeting place for republicans and revolutionary theorists. She was persecuted, and her husband died in custody, for political activities during the Terror.

Her intellectual work involved the idea of sympathy. She translated into French Adam Smith's *Theory of Moral Sentiments*, a key social text on the topic, and annotated the work with a series of essays that made the links between social theory, physiology, and literature much clearer than Smith had left them. These essays actually involve a rather complex cultural translation, in that Sophie Condorcet locates in Adam Smith's work not only a critical evaluation of the institution of monarchy but also the roots of the "rights-of-man" rhetoric that cost her husband his life. Most students of Smith have not found these ideas in the *Theory of Moral Sentiments*. Her commentary is less an error of interpretation than it is an attempt to adapt a philosophical innovation developed in one society and written in one language, to another quite distinct society through a careful and sensitive translation into a different language (Forget, "Cultivating").

In physiology, sympathy referred to the somatic communication of non-contiguous bodily organs: the sympathy of the nerves. Physiologists investigated the mechanisms by which a human body coordinates the operation of a number of separate systems and organs, which they labelled *sympathy* and, in the process, learned a great deal about the operation of the nervous system. Sympathy may be of antiquarian interest to historians of medicine, but it still intrigues philosophers and historians of the social sciences. In social theory, sympathy was introduced as the counterpart of the economic idea of self-interest. Sympathy was used to denote fellow feeling, or the (often but not always) non-conscious communication between different parts of the social body, that is, different people in the same society. Social philosophers investigated the ways in which society can behave as a coordinated organism, notwithstanding the distinct interests and activities of its separate parts. These are not simple analogies; physicians writing medical textbooks referred to social theorists, who in turn cited physiologists and their experiments (Forget, "Evocations").

Sympathy enters French intellectual discourse largely on the basis of Sophie's work. Her essays influenced a generation of social scientists and especially her brother-in-law, French physiologist P.-J.-G. Cabanis, who began to investigate the biological correlates of sympathy. Nineteenth-century socialist writers such as Charles Fourier, as well as some liberal writers, including economist Jean-Baptiste Say and sociologist Auguste Comte, picked up her insights (Forget: *Social*; "Cultivating; "Saint-Simonian"; "Jean-Baptist"). Nevertheless, she is virtually absent from the historical record as other than a *salonnière*.

There is no English-language biography of Sophie Condorcet. There are three book-length biographies in French. The first, by Antoine Guillois, is written in a nineteenth-century style for the explicit purpose of supporting a particular political agenda. It focusses on her salon and her social network. Henri Valentino's focusses on her lovers, friends, and acquaintances. And the most recent, by Thierry Boissel, is an imaginative, but ahistorical, reconstruction that contains many undocumented and unverifiable events.

The best recent account of Sophie Condorcet's life is found in an introductory essay written by Jean-Paul de LaGrave in *Lettres sur la sympathie, suivies des letters d'amour*. Shorter biographical accounts can be found in Isambert, Chaussinand-Nogaret and Winifred Stephens. Her daughter, Éliza Condorcet-O'Connor, wrote biographical notes on Sophie's life, which are reproduced in F. Robinet. This account is not factually correct, but is, for that very reason, an interesting piece. Robinet's biography of Nicolas Condorcet discusses the reception of their joint work as well as some of the very many rumours related to their personal lives. There is also a five-volume memoir written by Sophie Condorcet's brother, Emmanuel de Grouchy, that documents several generations of family history. It is based on documentation that would have been required as proof of nobility, both when Emmanuel was admitted to military training and when Sophie was admitted to the convent in which she spent almost eighteen months before her marriage. Because it was written after Bonaparte's defeat at Waterloo, it is also an interesting exercise in narrative reconstruction. Grouchy served as a senior officer in Bonaparte's army and was scapegoated by the latter for the defeat. Emmanuel left France for America shortly after the incident and shortly before his scheduled court martial.

Sophie Condorcet's intellectual contribution has received less attention than is its due. Lynn McDonald (*Women Founders*; "Classical"; *Women Theorists*) has attempted to restore her to a position of some influence in Western intellectual history. Condorcet's *Letters on Sympathy* were discussed by LaGrave and have occasioned a few essays in the literature (Ando; Dawson; Marshall). I have discussed these pieces, and Condorcet's work on sympathy, in "Cultivating Sympathy: Sophie Condorcet's *Letters on Sympathy*." I argued that her relative neglect can be attributed to the then-common practice of not citing sources, attributing citations to intellectual colleagues (in her case to Cabanis), and, most tellingly, to "citing" Condorcet in footnotes to scholarly articles without mentioning her name. For example, physiologist Pierre Roussel, according to an *éloge* published by J.L. Alibert, was induced to insert "in the *Actes de la Société médicale*, a curious note on Sympathies" (Alibert xiv): "He had been especially determined to address this matter, by the publication of eight letters on the same subject, at the end of an excellent translation of Smith, by a woman of his intimate society, who, at that time, seemed to hold aloft at once the scepter of beauty and the torch of philosophy" (xiv, trans. mine). Alibert adds a footnote in which he claims that "Smith himself," were he still alive, would translate these letters from French into English, because they were "full of novel insights." Alibert does not name her, and Roussel does not cite her. The political situation in nineteenth-century France was volatile, and there were periods when the name Condorcet (or Grouchy) would have been more a liability than an asset to a writer.

My special interest in writing the life of Sophie, however, is not the result of her translations or her essays. One of the most profound insights of the social sciences over the past forty years has been the recognition that we live our lives immersed in narrative (e.g.: Geertz; MacIntyre; Fish; Clifford and Marcus). Living a life involves the creation and re-creation of stories that give our lived experiences meaning.

Dorinda Outram has documented a very large outpouring of autobiographical writing, particularly among the middle-aged, immediately after the French Revolution. Political expedience is only part of the explanation. Antonia Fraser, in her recent biography of Marie Antoinette, notes that "the women who survived felt an urgent need to relive the trauma and record the truth, a compulsion often modestly disguised as a little gift to their descendents: "'c'est pour vous, mes enfants'" (xx). The massive disruption of society created a breach in the ways in which individuals understood themselves and their social roles. When our experiences exceed our capacity to process them, and become unintelligible within the narratives we understand, we become physically and mentally ill (Donald). The need for psychic stability in the midst of social chaos drove many to life writing after the Revolution. This personal reconstruction is inadequately portrayed in terms of simple "truth" and "fabrication." There are undoubted fabrications, some (but not all) of which were politically motivated, but there are a variety of true narratives.

Personal reconstruction in the shape of life writing is a form of historical reconstruction. Hayden White, among others, has often argued that all historical reconstruction, including biography, requires events and figures to be conceptualized in terms of narrative genres with which we are familiar: tragedies, comedies, epic poetry, fairy tales (White). Personal narratives, however, are not unique and stable. Personal reconstruction is ongoing. At any point in time there will be multiple, more or less consistent, narrative strains. Over time, and especially in response to particularly traumatic events, these constructions are reconsidered and revised.

Many literary theorists and philosophers have emphasized the multiplicity of the narratives we create at any point in time, and their changes over time, and focussed on the incoherence of our various selves (Clifford; Barthes; Rorty). Clifford, for example, challenges the entire genre of biography, denouncing biographies based on "the myth of personal coherence" (44–45). The postmodern challenge claims that human subjects are "merely an effect of language" (Barthes 56): "incarnated vocabularies" (Rorty 88).

David Nye, for example, in his fascinating attempt to create an "autobiography" of Thomas Edison, claims that "the fundamental error of biography lies in the attempt to construct a definitive figure at all" (17–18): "If [the subject] can be expressed as sixteen different figures, [the biographer] will do so rather than perform a reduction" (19). This calls to mind the old anatomy textbooks where a series of transparencies showing bone structure, musculature, and so on, build up a "visible man." But, in contrast to the multi-layered but ultimately coherent textbook character, Nye proposes a multi-layered and incoherent subject in which the creator of the portrait does not trouble herself to search for any consistency.

This perspective creates a particular problem for biographers. In the context of narrative-based medicine, however, we can find a partial solution. While human beings create multiple stories and multiple selves, many gerontologists have argued that healthy human beings struggle over their life course to create a coherent, if not unified, narrative that gives their lived experiences meaning (e,g., Kenyon and Randall). This insight allows us to recreate the richness of lived experience while finding enough solid ground that writing life stories becomes possible.

Narrative-based medicine, recognized and legitimized by a series of articles in the *British Medical Journal*, is founded on the premise that patients' narratives "provide us with far more than factual information of the kind that might be more efficiently obtained when they [. . .] carry electronic smart cards encoded with their entire 'medical history'" (Greenhalgh and Hurwitz 6). Perhaps, ironically, the movement rests on the notions that "illness" and "wellness" are, like individuals, rhetorical constructs, and that the narrative interplay between patient and physician is important. That recognition, however, is used to argue for, rather than against, some narrative unity. "Diagnosis" involves the joint construction of a coherent narrative by patient and physician to replace the "broken narratives" the patient arrives with (Elwyn and Gwyn). "Healing" involves substituting a coherent narrative of wellness, or at least a story of coping, for one of ill health and suffering (Bolton; Bayliss). And narrative, of course, is central to some forms of psychotherapy where the reconstruction of stories is essential to the process (Launer; Holmes). Ian Hacking has delineated the consequences of trying to live a life without a reasonably coherent narrative structure within which an individual might find meaning.

This treatment paradigm is offered as a response to too great a reliance in contemporary practice on "evidence-based medicine," typified by population-cohort studies or randomized clinical trials. This "scientific" approach, ironically, finds its roots in the late eighteenth century—Sophie's lifetime—when physicians, emboldened by new developments in physiology, stopped listening to the unique histories of their patients and instead searched for that which is common between patients (Hogarth and Marks 142). Narrative-based medicine seeks to restore the individual patient and her story, created interactively with the physician, to the centre of treatment. The relationship between the physician and the patient parallels that between the biographer and the subject. The "story" need not disintegrate simply because we recognize the importance of language or notice that neither the physician/biographer nor the patient/subject tells an unchanging and objective story independently of the efforts of the other.

Sophie was aware of the power of narrative. She was a *salonnière*. Her entire existence was devoted to the art of storytelling. And, like her contemporaries, she faced a personally devastating political disruption. The world that existed before the Revolution was not the same as the world that emerged from Terror. The people who inhabited that earlier world could not continue to exist unchanged in the new. Not everyone survived. Some were guillotined or otherwise murdered. Some, like Nicolas Condorcet, committed suicide. Some went mad. One of the largest categories of "lunatics" listed by Philippe Pinel, the man who as superintendent of the Parisian asylums for men and women revolutionized the treatment of the mentally ill, consisted of people "driven mad by the Revolution" (Forget, *Social* 56-60). Some were, no doubt, political prisoners. Not all were.

And some individuals, such as Sophie Condorcet, survived physically and psychologically by seizing and transforming the narratives out of which their lives were constructed.

Narratives take many forms, and only the most literal will insist on words. Sophie was a gifted amateur portraitist. During the Terror, with her husband imprisoned and his property seized and frozen by the state, she found herself the sole supporter of an infant daughter and a younger sister. She fed them by creating two jobs for herself. She opened a shop and sold lingerie. And she was commissioned by individuals imprisoned and queued up for the guillotine to paint their portraits so they could leave a likeness for those they left behind.

As an adolescent, Sophie had studied with Elisabeth-Louise Vigée-Lebrun, who painted portraits of the European rich and famous. Granted patronage by Marie Antoinette, of whom she painted more than thirty portraits, she fled from Paris on the eve of the Revolution and returned to great honour in 1805. Frances Borzello characterizes the teacher's multiple self-portraits: "Underrated today for their high sugar content, they are examples of a sophisticated woman manipulating the imagery of fine art to illustrate her ambition and artistic intelligence without upsetting the rules of artistic and social acceptability" (74). Are Sophie's portraits merely an imperfect forerunner of snapshots, or is there more to see?

I want you to imagine four different portraits, three painted by Sophie Condorcet. All are reproduced in Leger. The first is the self-portrait to which I referred above. It shows a pretty woman with long, loose, undressed and unpowdered hair. This is a powerful political statement. Her skin is clear. I mention this only because Sophie survived smallpox at the age of twelve. Sophie's illness was the occasion for a very affecting letter from her mother to her aunt, published in Guillois (15–16). Her mother considers without equivocation and with little handwringing whether it would be better for her eldest and much loved daughter to die than to live scarred in a society in which her only currency would be her beauty. Sophie was a beautiful woman.

The portrait, which is currently in the private collection of a descendent, is interesting for another reason. It has been dated in the secondary literature to 1794. This was the height of Terror. Nicolas Condorcet died that year, in the custody of the secret police, after several months spent in hiding. Sophie would have been thirty—not a young woman—in 1794. The subject of the portrait has both the appearance and demeanour of a much younger, more innocent, and more carefree woman. In 1794, Sophie was hard at work on the subject of "sympathy." Her translation of Smith and the accompanying interpretive essays that later appeared as *Letters on Sympathy* were ultimately published in 1798. If the dating of the self-portrait is correct, it is a fascinating exercise in narrative reconstruction, or at least in psychological self-preservation.

The second pair of portraits should be considered together. The first is the official portrait of Nicolas Condorcet created for the *Académie*. It shows a severe face beneath a very formal powdered wig. He looks much older than the fifty-one he was at his death. The marriage of this dry and unworldly academic to a beautiful woman twenty-one years his junior occasioned a good deal of gossip and speculation. Her family was aristocratic but not of the stature of his, and she had no dowry. The marriage produced one child, a daughter called Éliza, and a well-known anglophile *salon* that became a meeting place for moderate republicans. During this marriage, Sophie claimed her intellectual gifts.

Its partner is a portrait by Sophie of Claude Fauriel, called *Le Fauve* (the wild one? the untamed?) by his contemporaries. He was her three-decade younger lover and protegé at the time of her death in 1822. This was not a great love match. The perpetual adolescent broods in this portrait, his dark eyes challenging beneath a mass of Byronesque curls. The relationship was stormy, but the worries he created for Sophie were maternal ones. Would he ever find work worthy of his efforts? Could he ever be relied upon?

Together, the portraits of Nicolas Condorcet and Claude Fauriel frame an era and frame Sophie's life. The formality of the *Académie* portrait of Nicolas Condorcet recalls the world as it was before 1789: ordered and comprehensible. The portrait of *Le Fauve* shows the world after 1795: dangerous, challenging and never to be taken as fixed again.

The final portrait—another self-portrait by Sophie, this time as a thirty-six-year-old widow—is more disturbing. Painted as a gift for journalist Maillia Garat, her second serious relationship, this woman has survived Revolution, Terror, and financial turmoil. She has challenged conventional ideas about marriage and family life. She has acted as translator and confidante for revolutionary Thomas Paine. She has published a translation and commentary on Adam Smith. She has published (anonymously) political commentary. This is the woman whose tart tongue, not too many years later, challenged Bonaparte directly on his political exclusion of women by telling him that, if women were to lose their heads over politics, they might want a say in the matter.

In this portrait, Sophie is posed in the manner of Titian's *Olympia* series. This is a standard pose for female nudes in European art history, although unusual for a self-portrait by a self-consciously intellectual woman. She is reclining upon a sofa, looking out at the viewer. Only one thing differentiates the subject of this self-portrait from Titian's model, but its effect is immediate and striking. In place of the wide, moist, modestly averted eyes and inviting pout of the model in the master's work, Sophie's subject has a direct gaze and an unmistakable smirk.

WORKS CITED

Alibert, J.L. "Éloge historique de Pierre Roussel." *Système physique et moral de la femme, suivi d'un fragment du système physique et moral de l'homme, et d'un essai sur la sensibilité, et . . . d'une note sur les sympathies . . .* 1806. By Pierre Roussel. 11th ed. Paris: Caille et Ravier, 1820.

Ando, Takaho. "Mme de Condorcet et la philosophie de la 'sympathie.'" *Studies on Voltaire and the Eighteenth Century* 216 (1983): 335–36.

Barthes, R. *Roland Barthes by Roland Barthes.* New York: Farrar, 1977.

Bayliss, R. "Pain Narratives." *Narrative Based Medicine.* Ed. T. Greenhalgh and B. Hurwitz. London: BMJ Books, 1998. 75–82.

Boissel, Thierry. *Sophie de Condorcet, femme des lumières.* Paris: Presses de la Renaissance, 1988.

Bolton, G. "Stories of Dying: Therapeutic Writing in Hospice Care." *Narrative Based Medicine.* Ed. T. Greenhalgh and B. Hurwitz: London: BMJ Books, 1998. 45–54.

Borzello, F. *Seeing Ourselves: Women's Self-Portraits.* New York: Harry N. Abrams, 1998.

Chaussinand-Nogaret, G. "La Marquise de Condorcet, la révolution et la république." *Histoire* 71 (1984): 30–38.

Clifford, J. "'Hanging up Looking Glasses at Odd Corners': Ethnobiographical Prospects." *Studies in Biography*. Ed. D. Aaron. Cambridge, MA: Harvard University Press, 1978.

Clifford, J., and G.E. Marcus, eds. *Writing Culture: The Poetics and Politics of Ethnography*. Berkeley: University of California Press, 1986.

Condorcet, S. de Grouchy, marquise de. "Lettres à C[abanis], sur la théorie des sentimens moraux." *Théorie des sentimens moraux*. By Adam Smith. Trans. from the 7th ed. [1792] by Sophie Condorcet. Paris: F. Buisson, 1798.

Condorcet-O'Connor, E. "Notes biographiques sur Mme de Condorcet et sur Mme Vernet." (1841) 1893. *Condorcet: Sa Vie, Son Œuvre*. By F. Robinet. Geneva: Slatkine Reprints, 1968.

Dawson, D. "Is Sympathy So Surprising? Adam Smith and French Fictions of Sympathy." *Eighteenth-Century Life* 15.1–2 (1991): 147–62.

Donald, A. "The Words We Live In." *Narrative Based Medicine*. Ed. T. Greenhalgh and B. Hurwitz. London: BMJ Books, 1998. 17–26.

Elwyn, G., and R. Gwyn. "Stories We Hear and Stories We tell: Analysing Talk in Clinical Practice." *Narrative Based Medicine*. Ed. T. Greenhalgh and B. Hurwitz: London: BMJ Books, 1998. 165–75.

Fish, S. *Doing What Comes Naturally: Change, Rhetoric, and the Practice of Theory in Literary and Legal Studies*. Durham: Duke University Press, 1995.

Forget, E.L. *The Social Economics of Jean-Baptiste Say: Markets and Virtue*. London: Routledge, 1999.

_____ . "Cultivating Sympathy: Sophie Condorcet's *Letters on Sympathy*." *Journal of the History of Economic Thought* 28.3 (2001): 319–37.

_____ . "Saint-Simonian Feminism." *Feminist Economics* 7.1 (2001): 79–96.

_____ . "Jean-Baptiste Say and Spontaneous Order." *History of Political Economy* 33.2 (2001): 193–218.

_____ . "Evocations of Sympathy: Sympathetic Imagery in Eighteenth-Century Social Theory and Physiology." Unpublished manuscript. 2001.

Fraser, A. *Marie Antoinette: The Journey*. Toronto: Doubleday Canada, 2001.

Geertz, C. *The Interpretation of Cultures*. New York: Basic Books, 1973.

Greenhalgh, T., and B. Hurwitz, eds. *Narrative Based Medicine*. London: BMJ Books, 1998.

Grouchy, Emmanuel, marquis de, maréchal de France. *Mémoires*. 5 vols., n.p., 1873.

Guillois, A. *La Marquise de Condorcet: Sa Famille, Son Salon, Ses Amis*. Paris: Paul Ollendorf, 1897.

Hacking, I. *Rewriting the Soul: Multiple Personality and the Sciences of Memory*. Princeton: Princeton University Press, 1995.

Hogarth, S., and L. Marks. "The Golden Narrative in British Medicine." *Narrative Based Medicine*. Ed. T. Greenhalgh and B. Hurwitz. London: BMJ Books, 1998.140–48.

Holmes, J. "Narrative in Psychotherapy." *Narrative Based Medicine.* Ed. T. Greenhalgh and B. Hurwitz. London: BMJ Books, 1998. 176–84.

Isambert, F.A. "Condorcet (Marie-Louise-Sophie de Grouchy de)." *Nouvelle Biographie Générale depuis les temps les plus reculés jusqu'a nos jours.* 46 vols. Ed. M. Le Dr. Hoefer. Paris: Firmin Didot Frères, 1855.

Kenyon, G.M., and W.L. Randall. *Restorying Our Lives: Personal Growth through Autobiographical Reflection.* Westport, CT: Praeger Publishers, 1997.

LaGrave, Jean-Paul de. *Lettres sur la sympathie, suivies des lettres d'amour.* Montreal: L'Étincelle, 1994.

_____ . "Sophie de Condorcet, marquise des Lumières et adepte de la sympathie." *Lettres sur la sympathie, suivies des lettres d'amour.* Montreal: L'Étincelle, 1994. 15–44.

Launer, J. "Narrative and Mental Health in Primary Care." *Narrative Based Medicine.* Ed. T. Greenhalgh and B. Hurwitz. London: BMJ Books, 1998. 93–102.

Leger, C. *Captives de L'Amour d'aprés des documents inédits. Lettres intimes de Sophie de Condorcet, d'Aimée de Coigny et de quelques autres coeurs sensibles.* Paris: C. Gaillandre, 1933.

MacIntyre, A. "The Virtues, the Unity of a Human Life and the Concept of a Tradition." *Liberalism and Its Critics.* Ed. M. Sandel. Oxford: Blackwell, 1984.

Marshall, D. *The Surprising Effects of Sympathy: Marivaux, Diderot, Rousseau and Mary Shelley.* Chicago: University of Chicago Press, 1988.

McDonald, L. *The Women Founders of the Social Sciences.* Ottawa: Carleton University Press, 1994.

_____ . "Classical Social Theory with the Women Founders Included." *Reclaiming the Sociological Classics.* Ed. Charles Camic. Oxford: Blackwell, 1998.

_____ . *Women Theorists on Society and Politics.* Waterloo: Wilfrid Laurier University Press, 1998.

Nye, D. *The Invented Self: An Autobiography from Documents of Thomas A. Edison.* Odense: Odense University Press, 1983.

Outram, D. "Life-Paths: Autobiography, Science and the French Revolution." *Telling Lives in Science: Essays on Scientific Biography.* Ed. M. Shortland and R. Yeo. Cambridge, UK: Cambridge University Press, 1996.

Robinet, F. *Condorcet: Sa Vie, son Œuvre.* 1893. Geneva: Slatkine Reprints, 1968.

Rorty, R. *Contingency, Irony, Solidarity.* Cambridge, UK: Cambridge University Press, 1989.

Smith, Adam. *Theory of Moral Sentiments.* 1759. Oxford: Oxford University Press, 1976.

Stephens, W. *Women of the French Revolution.* New York: E.P. Dutton, 1922.

Strachey, L. *Eminent Victorians.* London: Chatto and Windus, 1918.

Valentino, H. *Madame de Condorcet, ses amis et ses amours.* Paris: Perrin, 1950.

White, Hayden. "History as Fulfillment." Keynote address to the Interdisciplinary Scholars Network, Tulane University, 12 November 1999. <http://www.tulane.edu/~isn/hwkeynote.htm>

Adam Smith and "Civil Society"

Knud Haakonssen

It is with Adam Smith and civil society somewhat as it is with Smith and religion; he did not have a declared theory on either, yet both topics have been too interesting for scholars to leave alone. But, while in the case of religion one might argue, and I would so argue, that the silence is the message, in the case of civil society the neglect is, as I suggest, due to the much more pedestrian circumstance that Smith had little use for the concept as understood at the time. Furthermore, in this argument one is assisted by the relatively well-defined meaning of "civil society" that Smith ignored, whereas it is impossible to say with any certainty what were the theological options that Smith might have made part of his public argument but chose not to. This relative definiteness of the concept of civil society enables us to make a negative fact, the absence of the concept, into a useful means of throwing some light on central features of Smith's political theory.

In the seventeenth and eighteenth centuries, "civil society" was undoubtedly often used loosely and vaguely, but in moral and political theory it did have a fairly definite core meaning, also in Smith's immediate intellectual circle in Scotland. In this meaning, the concept had ancient provenance but had been formalized and made common currency, in particular by the various modern schools of natural law. This was civil society as an ordered composite of individual *cives*, that is, the politically organized society. The detail of this was spelled out through contrast with what was not civil society, namely the state of nature and the familial society. The former was the starting point for the various well-known contractarian theories of the basis for political authority; through entering a contract the natural person was transformed into a constituent part of a politically governed unity, the civil society. The family as a contrast

Faith, Reason, and Economics: Essays in Honour of Anthony Waterman. Ed. Derek Hum. Winnipeg: St. John's College Press, 2003.

to civil society was, of course, common to contractarian and non-contractarian theories, and, in both, the family was seen as a smaller society functionally and foundationally different from but, in some sense, constituent of civil society.

It is not necessary to go into the detail and the great variety of these theories in order to make my points about Smith in this context. First, Smith did not and could not have the former concept of civil society as the obverse of the state of nature. Secondly, he entirely transformed the notion of the relationship between family and civil society. In both cases he, so to speak, historicized the issue, subjecting conceptual to temporal relations, a move characteristic of his philosophy as a whole.

Smith firmly rejected the idea of a state of nature. This rejection was rooted in one of the most fundamental features of his philosophy, that is, his concept of personhood. While the philosopher can specify universal features of human nature, no constellation of these makes us into persons. Perhaps the most basic feature of our natural humanity is our predisposition to sympathize with fellow beings, both imagined and real, both human and non-human. But this alone does not make us into persons; it is no more than a presupposition for us becoming persons. As this formulation indicates, personhood is not something we *have* or are endowed with from the hand of God or nature; it is something we acquire; it is the result of a process. That process is social in nature, in the sense that it consists in interaction with other people and the interaction in question is an exercise of our imagination.

Smith took over and elaborated Hume's theory of the imagination as a mental faculty by means of which people create a distinctively human sphere within the natural world. It is the imagination that enables us to make connections between the perceived elements of both the physical and the moral world, ranging from binary relations between particular events and things to complex systems such as the national or international economy, the idea of the cosmos or of humanity as a whole. The activity of the imagination is a spontaneous search for order, coherence and agreement in the world; satisfaction of it carries its own pleasure, while frustration brings "wonder and surprise" and, if prolonged, anxiety and unease.

Sympathy is characterized as an act of the imagination because we do not have access to another person's mind. What we have access to is the other person's observable circumstances, including his or her behaviour. The act of sympathetic understanding is a creation of order in the observer's perceptions by means of an imagined rationale for the observed behaviour. As agents or moral beings, other people are, therefore, the creation of our imagination. But the most remarkable feature of Smith's theory of sympathy is that the same can be said of ourselves; as moral agents we are acts of creative imagination. The central point is that we become aware of ourselves—gain self-consciousness— only through our relationship to others. When we observe others, we notice that they observe us, and one of the most urgently felt needs for sympathetic understanding is to appreciate how they see us. This need is heightened by the inevitability that we and our fellows have different views of our relations to each other, to third persons, and to the environment. Our imagination craves order in these actual or potential conflicts, and that means a workable degree of agreement about personal relations and things, as in questions of who is boss and who owns or has the use of what. Our understanding of how others see us in these circumstances shapes our view of who we are and how we stand in such relationships in life.

Through sympathy we try to anticipate the assessment by others of ourselves, thus enabling us to adjust our behaviour before conflict arises. We internalize the external spectator and respond to this figure of the sympathetic imagination. The internal spectator has the force to prompt such adjustment of behaviour as would otherwise be demanded by external spectators in order to satisfy the inclination to or the need for agreement or conformity. In other words, one learns to see oneself as a person and as a member of a moral universe of agents only through sympathy with others' views of one's identity and situation in the world. Society is, as Smith says, the mirror in which one catches sight of oneself, morally speaking.[1]

This is in its nature an historically changing mirror. What our imagination is able to see as another person or as oneself will depend on what people are doing in relation to their surroundings; and, vice versa, what people do to their surroundings depends on what they can imagine doing. Until someone happens upon the act of claiming a tract of land as his or hers in analogy with the private possession of a tool or a weapon, we cannot imagine ourselves as land-owners. Smith's historical approach, with its central conceptual tool, the four-stages theory, is, therefore, much more than a history of government and its foundation; at least, it was intended to be more. Smith's later, and in the end unfinished, book projects confirm the inference that we may draw from the social theory of personhood put forward in the *Theory of Moral Sentiments* and in the opening parts of the *Lectures on Jurisprudence*. He was apparently aiming at a comprehensive history of culture that should include the fruits of our aesthetic as well as of our moral imagination.[2]

In this scheme of things, there is clearly no room for sharp dividing lines between natural and social states. Human life is inevitably social; otherwise it would not be recognizably human. It is a further thesis of Smith's that the dynamic interchange between agent and spectator constituted through sympathy inevitably leads to relations of authority. There are, according to Smith, two general sources of authority, namely the personal qualities of people—summed up as "authority"—and the benefits hoped for from the exercise of authority: "utility," for short.[3] In some of his most intricate, but also well-known, analyses, Smith shows how the former, "authority," is a feature of all human togetherness, feeding off and being fed by our tendency to vanity and obsequiousness. Since the "personal quality" that is the principal object and tool of vanity is people's relationship to the things of the external world, there is an intimate link between government and property. All government is, as Smith says, a means of protecting property. This applies to the earliest hunter-gatherer society as well as to the later "stages" of the nomadic, farming, and commercial societies. In short, just as there is always "society," so there is always "government." The intellectual challenge is to explain the sorts of government that there are, and this challenge is not met by the traditional contractarian device of looking at the spurious idea of a situation without government.

Although civil society in a sense *is* the human condition, this does not mean that everything "essentially" remains the same through all time. In keeping with his basic analysis of personhood, the question of the human condition is, for Smith, an historical one, and it is one that he answers with intricate tableaux of continuity and change, in the process setting aside traditional ideas of the relationship between family and civil society. Smith initiates an analysis of the family as a scene of power-relations; this analysis was eventually brought to full development by his former student John Millar in *The Origin of the Distinction of Ranks: Or, an Inquiry into the Circumstances Which Give Rise to Influence and Authority, in the Different Members of Society*.[4] It is a theory that undermines all idea of the family as in some sense a "natural" society that, through its (male) head, constitutes the building block of politically organized society. Rather, the family is in itself "political" in the sense that its form and function reflect the socio-economic needs of a given cultural stage.

The family is, therefore, a phenomenon that has to be understood historically in its interaction with other, civil forms of governance. By and large, this has been a story of greater and greater disentanglement of the two forms of government, from the near identification in tribal society, through the dramatic expansion of the family to meet political needs in nomadic and in feudal society, to the dwindling political role of the family in commercial society. Put differently, this is a transformation from direct and personal rule to distant and anonymous rule, often from small to large society. In the process, the relative weight between the two sources of government—authority and utility—is prone to shift toward the latter: the less we know our rulers personally, the more we have to assess them by their performance. Furthermore, without personal relations to regulate behaviour, especially in conflict situations, societies become more dependent upon the replacement of personal and intimate virtues with more abstract ideas of public interest and, especially, with the rules of justice as adopted into a legal system.

This well-known account of the emergence of the modern world may lead—undoubtedly has led—to the idea that there is a civil-society story in Smith after all, one of much greater excitement than the eighteenth-century ideas that we now have seen to be irrelevant to Smith. Is not Smith, in fact, putting forward a vision of commercial society in which the state is identified with the government and the government with the administration of justice that provides a framework within which the social forces of civil society spontaneously operate in the domestic sphere of the family and the economic sphere of the market? If interpreted as the *telos* of the historical process, this vision needed only a touch of Hegelian dusk to set the owl flying; if read as a norm, it seemed to stop us on our road to the serfdom in which private would become public and civil society a state department.

Such a reading of Smith may seem to find deeper philosophical support in his sharp distinction between the positive virtues, such as benevolence, and the negative virtue of justice, an aspect of Smith that I emphasized in earlier work on him.[5] Smith insisted that the latter—justice—provided the basis for all government as the institutionalized regulation of humanity's propensity to violence, and I suggested that this theory of justice was the core of his system of jurisprudence that again provided the connecting link between his ethics and his unfinished theory of government. By leaving open the question of the political role of the positive virtues, as I did, such an interpretation could be— and has been—taken to be lamentably reductionist. It has been read as a re-statement of the old idea of Smith as a proponent of the minimal state, or as someone who merely elaborated Hume's hyperbole of government as little other than the paymaster of the twelve judges.[6]

This was far from my intentions. I did not have a reductionist but only a limited agenda. I wanted to understand Smith's jurisprudence and to interpret it as a central link in his overall system of thought. However, even that case in-volved a more ambitious claim for Smith's political agenda, for I tried to show that his jurisprudence in itself was political in nature. That is to say, Smith did not simply present a theory of law in the abstract; his jurisprudence was centrally a theory of the means of criticizing and reforming the positive law of the land; it was not so much a general theory of the administration of justice as of the *making* of justice in historical context. Viewed in this light, the theory of justice as the basis for government is simply an element of the comprehensive view of politics that Donald Winch already, in 1978, had attributed to Smith in a book that should have made reductionist simplifications impossible once and for all.[7]

While the idea that justice in itself is an object of the political process is crucial to an understanding of Smith's political theory, a fuller picture of that theory requires that we find a role for the positive virtues. Once we have achieved that, however, we will also see that we cannot put Smith on a simple formula in which there is a neat division between government based on justice and civil society based on positive virtue. As a first step, we have to make a brief review of the basis for the distinction between the two kinds of virtue. Smith looked at morality from an historical point of view, suggesting, as we have seen, that the features of personality and lines of action that people approve and disapprove of in others and in themselves vary from one culture and period to another. A major task for philosophy is accordingly to look at humanity historically and compara-tively. This will make it apparent that in one sphere of man's reactions to his fellows there is a great deal in common among all of humankind, namely *moral* approval and disapproval (as opposed to, say, aesthetic reactions to others). The moral philosopher is able, therefore, to identify a number of basic virtues and vices, the tone and composition of which may vary significantly with time and place, but which are nevertheless universally recognizable and comparable.

Smith revised the traditional schema of the cardinal virtues, which in his hands become prudence, benevolence, justice, and self-command. Of these, benevolence is, generally, too individualistic and context-specific in its exercise to be constitutive of any social regularities or social forms; but this does not, of course, mean that it is without social and political importance. Self-command is a sort of meta-virtue that is presupposed in all the other virtues. Prudence and justice are different in that they both are the basis for social structures that can be accounted for in empirical terms. Prudence is concerned with the pursuit of our interests, and this is the subject of political economy. Justice is concerned with the avoidance of injury to our interests, and this is the subject of jurisprudence. In both cases, history plays a crucial role because interest is an historically determined concept; the hunter-gatherer cannot have any interest in the stock market and, consequently, can neither pursue nor be injured in that interest.

This analysis of the four basic virtues is compatible with the division between positive and negative virtues on which Smith, like Hume, laid particular emphasis. That distinction was based upon spectator reactions. When the spectator, whether the actual or the imagined impartial one, sympathetically enters into the situation of an agent, the result is approval or disapproval of the agent's judgement and action. When the agent tries to promote the good of someone, whether self or other, the spectatorial approval or disapproval generally varies from person to person, for, while we tend to agree on what is good in broad outline, we have great difficulty agreeing on what is good for particular persons in specific situations, unless we are connected in some moral community. By contrast, people tend to agree on what is harmful not only in general but also in each case, and the pattern of reaction to harmful behaviour, therefore, has a high degree of uniformity, known as resentment. The negative virtue of avoiding harm or injury is, according to Smith, *justice*, which is the foundation of law and the subject of jurisprudence.

The personal attributes and actions that are protected in each person when others show them justice, that is, abstain from injuring them, are their rights. A right is a sphere of freedom to *be* or *do* or *have* something that the individual can maintain against all others because the spectatorial resentment of infringement of this sphere is so strong that it has been institutionalized in the form of the legal system. This line of argument puts Smith in a tradition of subjective rights-thinking from Hobbes. In this tradition, the—or, at least, a—primary moral characteristic of the individual is self-assertion vis-à-vis the rest of humanity with the implication that common or social morality can arise only through "negotiation" between conflicting claims. A central point in the development of the tradition was the transformation of the idea of "negotiation" from that of contract, as in Hobbes, to that of spontaneous social adaptation in Hume and, more explicitly, in Smith. It is a tradition in which natural *law* is a secondary concept to that of *right*, in contrast to the ideas of much of Protestant natural-law thought.[8] While Hume in some respects was close to this tradition, he never found a way of accommodating the concept of rights within his sentimentalist theory of morality. This was left to Smith's theory of the spectatorial regulation of our moral sentiments.

For Smith, the concepts of *rights, injury*, and *personality* are linked. The imagination depends, as we have seen, on social experience and hence varies from one stage of society to another. All consideration of our moral characteristics must therefore include the social setting; this applies not least to claim rights as a primary characteristic of humanity.

Even so, certain minimal rights appear to be common to all social living. A social group is viable only if it, in general, recognizes rights to physical, moral, and some kind of social personality. These may accordingly be considered "universal" and "natural" rights in the sense that life without them would not be a recognizably *human* one. But it is important to appreciate that basic rights and, hence, justice in no other sense are necessary or have any special metaphysical status.[9] They are as dependent upon the spectatorial recognition in social intercourse as are all other, "positive" parts of morality. In this basic question, Smith is a completely consistent conventionalist. Morality in all its parts is introduced into the world through the modulations of human living; and the distinction between positive and negative virtues is *only* between such modulations, namely between degrees of moral urgency and between degrees of uniformity of expression and recognition.

When Smith suggests that justice is the virtue of respecting rights, that these rights have a natural core, and that justice in this sense is basic to government, he is, therefore, not elevating jurisprudence and politics above the basis in opinion that his friend David Hume had begun to work out. Like Hume, Smith was simply trying to characterize different types of opinion according to their malleability, suggesting that the hard, "natural" core of justice, namely elementary rights, is the least changeable of our moral opinions. Furthermore, the more abstract rights—such as elaborate property rights and contractual rights—which are crucial for commercial society, are highly vulnerable to change as the many historical reversals of the history of liberty demonstrated, according to Smith.

Concluding these remarks on the metaphysical—or, rather, non-metaphysical—status of justice and rights, I might indicate the complicated historical crossroads at which Smith stands. On the one hand, he can be seen as heir to a subjective rights-tradition whose main modern representative was Hobbes, preceded, according to some scholars, by Hugo Grotius.[10] According to this tradition of thought, it is a primary feature of humanity to approach the world, including other people, with demands or claims and to see morality and its political and social institutions as negotiated settlements of the conflicts among such claims. It was a tradition transformed from a contractarian to an evolutionary mode by Hume and Smith himself.

In this tradition, the status of humanity's natural claims, called rights, was always ambiguous. In Grotius, they often seemed to have some absolute moral status within a religious view of human agency. They were, so to speak, the divinely sanctioned exercise of each individual person's moral judgement (or conscience). By contrast, in Hobbes, they were naturalized as the expressions of self-preservation of each individual. Smith dissolves this ambiguity by firmly asserting rights (and, hence, justice) to be the outcome of any social intercourse. Rights themselves are, in that sense, conventional, not just the basis for conventions, as in contract theory.

In making this argumentative move, Smith was probably influenced, at least in a general way, by another important aspect of early-modern Protestant natural-law theory, namely the voluntarism that, as a philosophical theory, was introduced most effectively into the debate by Samuel von Pufendorf. As Pufendorf saw it, humanity was mandated by God to live socially. However, the divinity had not provided any detail as to what that might mean, and moral-political life, accordingly, was a matter of humanity implementing its duty according to its own lights—its own understanding of its situation in the world.

Smith saw humanity's social brief not as a divine but as a human demand. We demand sociability of each other, not because we already have a right to do so, nor because God has ordered us to do so, but because we would not otherwise be able to recognize each other and ourselves as persons, as moral agents. In this regard, rights and justice are parts of morality in general; they are part of the infinitely varied responses we make to each other and to ourselves. But they are nothing *more* than that.

I turn now from the basic question of the metaphysical status of justice and rights among the rest of morality to the question of the political significance of the negative versus the positive virtues. This goes to the heart of the issue of whether, and in what sense, Smith may be said to have had a politics proper and, in that connection, what room he might have for a concept of civil society. Put simply, the issue is whether Smith has a theory of politics that goes beyond the institutionalization of the virtue of justice through the legal protection of rights; and whether such a richer politics may be seen as the stage for some aspect of the positive virtues. Let me begin by drawing attention to an elementary distinction. One thing is the question of whether the policies pursued by government should be limited to strict laws of negative justice or whether a wider agenda should be maintained. That is to say, whether the citizenry, *qua* citizens, should be characterized as or be seen as "owners" of anything more than negative rights. Quite another question is whether those who wield governmental power should exhibit a wider set of virtues than those pertaining to justice.

On the former issue, it is clear that, while Smith thought that a society in principle could *survive* as an association of individuals holding merely negative rights against each other, he found this a dismal prospect. A great deal of his concern was to promote a far richer politics that encompassed fiscal policy, economic infrastructure, defence, education, and social and cultural policies. This has been comprehensively demonstrated by Donald Winch and needs no further discussion for present purposes. But, while Smith might have thought a negative-rights society imaginable though not desirable, nobody could seriously maintain that he would contemplate a governing class based upon and motivated by nothing but the drive for negative justice. In fact, it is hard to see exactly what this could mean, and there is, therefore, a need for a Smithan political theory in the sense of a theory of the foundations of government, as distinct from the exercise of government.

As mentioned, Smith thought that there were two principles of governance that operated on the human mind, namely "authority" and "utility." While the tendency was for the former to predominate in the earlier, and the latter in the later, stages of society, both play some role in all societies, and Smith does in fact have a great deal to say about the principle of authority in commercial society. This becomes clear when we remember that he analyzed this principle in terms of its four "causes": "The first of those causes [. . .] is the superiority of personal qualifications, of strength, beauty, and agility of body; of wisdom, and virtue, of prudence, justice, fortitude and moderation of mind. [. . .] The second [. . .] is the superiority of age. [. . .] The third [. . .] the superiority of fortune. [. . .] The fourth [. . .] the superiority of birth."[11]

Much of what Smith has to say about civic and political leadership in contemporary society, such as his well-known contrast between the true statesman and the mere politician, is held in terms of such qualities. Closely intertwined with them is the principle of utility, for this is not, as we might expect, a matter of calculation of the common benefits of public policy but, rather, the citizenry's estimate of the governors' "public spirit"—and that was always a good deal richer than merely a matter of the will to accord each citizen his or her negative rights.

Neither the four "causes" of authority nor public spiritedness could exist in a moral vacuum. Like all moral qualities, these exist only through the medium of a set of spectators. A great deal of Smith's politics concerns the spectating that is necessary for a governing class to have a chance of possessing the marks of authority and of being public spirited. In other words, even if we ascribed to Smith a minimalist policy of implementing and maintaining a system of natural liberty, he would still need a wider politics, namely one that makes it possible to have and to run a governmental system at all. This creates a kind of dialectic between positive virtue and justice that makes it meaningless to speak of one as more *politically* basic than the other. The point is, in other words, that what Smith calls the system of natural liberty, that is, the institution of a system of negative justice, cannot be implemented unless it is the object of public spirit in a government that has sufficient of the marks of authority to make it effective, whatever the constellation of such marks may happen to be at any given time.

When talking about the relationship between positive and negative virtues, it is important to be clear that we are here dealing with ideals to be striven for, not given social facts. Just as the system of natural liberty is an ideal that, in its purity, is utopian, in Smith's eyes, so public benevolence is something the world sees only in fragments. This is well reflected in the very ambiguity with which Smith speaks of public spirit. The minimal defining characteristic of public spirit is that it is concerned with the public interest and, as such, the obverse of a concern with private interest. However, this can mean very different things. On the one hand, public spirit can be "founded upon the love of humanity, upon a real fellow-feeling with the inconveniences and distresses to which some of our fellow citizens may be exposed."[12] On the other hand, public spirit may arise from a "love of system," from a desire to see things organized in an orderly way, more than from a concern with the purpose served by such organization. "There have been men of the greatest public spirit, who have shown themselves in other respects not very sensitive to the feelings of humanity. And on the contrary, there have been men of the greatest humanity, who seem to have been entirely devoid of public spirit."[13]

Smith sees public spirit understood in this way as something very important. In fact, a major point in writing and teaching about politics is to promote concern with the public interest by appealing to people's attraction to system and organization:

> Nothing tends so much to promote public spirit as the study of politics, of the several systems of civil government, their advantages and disadvantages, of the constitution of our own country, its situation, and interest with regard to foreign nations, its commerce, its defence. [. . .] Upon this account political disquisitions, if just, and reasonable, and practicable, are of all the works of speculation the most useful. Even the weakest and the worst of them are not altogether without their utility. They serve at least to animate the public passions of men, and rouse them to seek out the means of promoting the happiness of the society."[14]

The trouble is that in times of crisis, especially of civil strife, the spirit of system is prone to turn to fanaticism and thus distort the public spirit to its very opposite, namely factionalism.[15] In other words, the concept of public spirit indicates the framework within which the politics of opinion takes place. Making the opinion upon which government rests public spirited is itself a political task and one in which we may fail. At the heart of the matter is the idea that effective moral agency depends upon one's ability to participate in mutual sympathetic spectatorship, which, again, presupposes an appraisal of one's knowledge and a willingness to be impartial. However, in the large, "anonymous" society where governors and governed know little about each other as persons, it is difficult to maintain effective mutual spectatorship between government and citizens. The goods that the former can pursue and the latter can assess must be fairly general or abstract and the ability and willingness to appreciate this on both sides is correspondingly difficult to achieve. Therein lies the challenge of politics in commercial society.

Smith suggests that there are three great "orders" that make up modern society: the land-owners, who live on rent; the labouring classes, who live on wages; and the commercial classes, who live on profit. The sectional interests of the first two tend to coincide with the public interest, while the commercial interests generally are the very opposite of those of the public. However, commonly neither labourers nor land-owners understand their situation, although for different reasons, and to make them understand the harmony between the public interest and their own true interests is an ongoing political task, one that Smith is involved in.

One fundamental problem arises from the circumstance that commerce tends to dissolve traditional communities through the division of labour, the associated fragmentation of knowledge, and the drift of population to the city. This means that "the common people" no longer are either subject to or agents of the social discipline of a local community. The loss of this spectator-function deprives society of one of the main supports for that orderliness and decency, as Smith calls it, that exists side by side with the formal dispensation of justice. Smith saw this as a serious problem that had to be countered by government policy in the form of elementary schooling of society at large, and his hope was exactly that this would lead to some minimally enlightened understanding not only of private interest but also of public policy, that is, to a broad spectatorship of governance.[16] This was closely associated with the maintenance of a militia that would inculcate a set of civic virtues, even if the actual military value of such an institution was dwindling in modern warfare.

However, while Smith saw the problem of public spiritedness in the common people as an important challenge to the government of commercial society, his hopes were evidently limited, and he was certainly no democrat. The problem was how to maintain a politically more relevant spectatorship of government and thus, in a sense, government itself. With the higher social groups, the problem was not so much education and information, though Smith did complain of the intellectual laziness of the landed class due to its socio-economic security and even contemplated the idea of imposing educational tests for the practice of the liberal professions and the holding of public and semi-public office.[17] The more important issue was impartiality and independence. The need was for a social group that was independent enough of factional interests to make the public interest their own.

In general, Smith thought that such independence, to the extent that it was possible at all, could derive only from land-ownership, but the problem was that government in commercial society tended to become dependent upon the emerging moneyed interest associated with merchants and manufacturers. These were, he suggested, "an order of men, whose interest is never exactly the same with that of the publick, who have generally an interest to deceive and even to oppress the publick, and who accordingly have, upon many occasions, both deceived and oppressed it."[18]

The remedy was, of course, the prevention of monopolies through the enforcement of a strict system of justice. In other words, the point of the natural system of liberty was not just to keep government out of the market but also, and not least, to keep the market-operators out of government.

However, no government had the strength to enforce such justice unless it rested upon the secure opinion of public-spirited men. The landed gentlemen, both the traditional gentry and those buying into land with commercial capital, had an interest in the country as a coherent whole—as a country—because only this made landed property—real estate—possible. Defence of land and defence of country was one and the same thing; and prosperity of land depended upon prosperity of country. Land, in contrast to capital, moves nowhere. Furthermore, land-ownership provided a higher degree of independence than any other form of property.

It was these factors that *in principle* could make the landed gentlemen into a natural—as opposed to an hereditary—aristocracy, provided this was not hindered by political action and legislation, such as primogeniture. It was this class that was the recruiting ground for government itself. It was also from this social group that military officers were found and, because of their economic and social independence, they provided a potential bulwark against tyrannical government as well as leadership in case of foreign invasion or domestic revolution. In fact, it was the virtue of these gentlemen that could make a standing army politically innocuous, thus setting aside as irrelevant traditional republican fears. So, despite all their traditional failings, the land-owners had the best potential for making up the politically relevant class of spectators surrounding government. However, a fundamental point in Smith's analysis is that in order to function as proper spectators with a clear eye for the public interest, the land-owners and their public spirit could not be taken for granted in the way in which primogeniture and hereditary nobility made them be taken for granted. The creation and maintenance of a land-owning class of public spirit was a political objective to be pursued by a variety of means, both juridical and political, such as reform of laws of succession in order to subject land to the market and cultivation of the proper esteem and prestige of land-ownership in order to encourage the moneyed classes to become land-owners and in order to secure their role as civic leaders.

It should here be remembered what the concept of a landed gentleman with a role in public life meant for Smith and his contemporaries. The landed gentlemen were local magistrates, justices of the peace, officers in the militia and the like; or they chose or greatly influenced the choice of such officials, as well as of ministers of the church and schoolteachers.

Furthermore, as members of Parliament they, in effect, provided much of what today is local government. In the eighteenth century, the overwhelming proportion of Parliamentary business had nothing to do with executive government but consisted of private members' bills providing for, often minor, local matters of no national significance and often without implications for government revenue— the widening of a street, the building of a bridge, the tearing down of a city structure. Parliament, therefore, was a forum not only for the conduct of national policy but also for the display of civic leadership of local communities.

It is hard not to see this wide range of activities as political, and, yet, it had little or nothing to do with the exercise of sovereign government or with matters of state. Furthermore, these activities were carried out by men who certainly saw themselves, and were seen by others, as occupying public offices and public roles but not offices of government. This sphere was the forum for a wide variety of civic virtues, of which justice was only one, that were essential to the social and political stability without which government would hardly have the strength to dispense justice.

There is no indication whatever that Smith deviated from this traditional concept of the landed gentleman, and with it he of course floated the sort of sharp distinction between government and civil society that came to the fore in subsequent generations. Government was still a much more fluid phenomenon for Smith and his contemporaries than it is for us. What is more, also in his innovatory moves does Smith defy the attempt to read him as a theorist of civil society. It was onto the traditional concept of the landed gentleman that he grafted his new ideals for how to make this class politically relevant, public-spirited. However, as we have seen, this meant that the creation and maintenance of a central constituent of the state was a matter of politicking, a part of the ongoing political process, which seems to be a way of thinking entirely alien to any reduction of state and government to juridical machinery.

Against the background of these considerations, it seems as impossible to see in Smith a progenitor of nineteenth-century ideas of state versus civil society as it is to see in him much use for the idea of civil society that was common in his own time and in the preceding century. Smith's emphasis on negative justice as the backbone of *government* had nothing to do with the idea of the *state* as a juridical person. And the limitations on government that he saw as beneficial cannot be seen as a de-politicization of society but, rather, as a political objective.

NOTES

A slightly different version of this essay is forthcoming in French as "Adam Smith et 'société civile,'" in *Adam Smith, Adam Ferguson: Libéralisme, Etat et société civile*, edited by Michaël Biziou, Presses universitaires de France, 2002.

1. *The Theory of Moral Sentiments* [*TMS*], art. III, ch. 1, para. iii.

2. For this distinction, see my Introduction to Adam Smith, *The Theory of Moral Sentiments*, ed. Knud Haakonssen (Cambridge, UK; Cambridge University Press, 2002). A few paragraphs in the present essay derive from this introduction.

3. R.L. Meek, D.D. Raphael, and P.D. Stein, eds., *Lectures on Jurisprudence* (Oxford: Clarendon Press, 1978); report of 1762–63, v. 118–32; report of 1763–64, v. 12–15.

4. John Millar, *The Origin of the Distinction of Ranks: Or, an Inquiry into the Circumstances Which Give Rise to Influence and Authority, in the Different Members of Society* (1771) 4th edition, Edinburgh 1806, esp. chs. 1-2. Cf. Haakonssen, *Natural Law and Moral Philosophy: From Grotius to the Scottish Enlightenment* (Cambridge: Cambridge University Press 1996), ch. 5.

5. Knud Haakonssen, *The Science of a Legislator: The Natural Jurisprudence of David Hume and Adam Smith* (Cambridge: Cambridge University Press, 1981).

6. David Hume, "Of the Origin of Government," in *Political Essays*, ed. K. Haakonssen (Cambridge: Cambridge University Press, 1994), p. 37.

7. Donald Winch, *Adam Smith's Politics: An Essay in Historiographical Revision* (Cambridge: Cambridge University Press, 1978).

8. See Haakonssen, "The Significance of Protestant Natural Law," in *Reading Autonomy*, ed. Natalie Brender and Larry Krasnoff (Cambridge: Cambridge University Press, forthcoming).

9. In *The Science of a Legislator* and in *Natural Law and Moral Philosophy*, I toyed with the idea of seeing the impartial spectator as the embodiment of elementary rules of practical argument that are necessary in the sense that it would be self-defeating to try to deny them, a standard argument on the part of mitigated scepticism against pyrrhonian scepticism. However, that is entirely different from any metaphysical or transcendental necessity.

10. See especially: Richard Tuck, *Natural Rights Theories* (Cambridge: Cambridge University Press, 1979); *Philosophy and Government, 1572–1651* (Cambridge: Cambridge University Press, 1993); and *The Rights of War and Peace: Political Thought and the International Order from Grotius to Kant.* Oxford: Oxford University Press, 2000). For some doubts about Grotius's position in this tradition, see Knud Haakonssen, "The Moral Conservatism of Natural Rights," in *Natural Law and Civil Sovereignty: Moral Right and State Authority in Early Modern Political Thought*, ed. Ian Hunter and David Saunders (Basingstoke: Palgrave, 2002 [27–42]).

11. R.H. Campbell and A.S. Skinner, eds. *An Inquiry into the Nature and Causes of the Wealth of Nations* [*WN*] (Oxford: Clarendon Press, 1976), bk. V, ch. 1, part ii, sects. 5–8.

12. *TMS*, part IV, ch. 1, para. 11.

13. Ibid.

14. Ibid.

15. Ibid., part VI, sect. ii, ch. 2, para. 15.

16. *WN*, bk. V, chap. 1, art. ii, paras. 51–61.

17. Ibid., bk. I, ch. xi, conclusion para. 8; bk. V, ch.1, art. iii, para. 14.

18. Ibid., bk. I, chap. xi, conclusion para. 10.

Engels-Marx Versus Malthus on Distribution and the Population Issue

Samuel Hollander

In this essay I document the dramatic contrast between the prediction by Marx and Engels of the disappearance of the middle class and a bifurcation of income distribution with continual reductions in real wages and no hope of upward mobility on the part of labour—all the inevitable outcome of capitalist development—and the more qualified prospect envisaged by Malthus of a strengthening of the middle class accompanied by rising wages and a prospect of upward mobility. I compare the respective "scientific" analyses leading to these outcomes and trace out certain "objective" arguments by Engels and Marx against Malthus's recommendations, especially those relating to population control. It emerges that Marx himself attributes a major role to population pressure in accounting for the "necessary" trends, as he perceived them, supplementing the descent of the middle classes into the proletariat. As for prospects regarding population control under communism, the roles are shown to be reversed; while Engels considered excess population growth to be at least a potential problem in such a régime with a solution in moral restraint, Malthus saw it as inevitable with no solution conceivable other than unacceptable legal intervention.

Absolute impoverishment and growing inequality played the central role in the Engels-Marx prediction of an ultimate breakdown of capitalist arrangement. Engels's *Outlines of a Critique of Political Economy* of 1844 provides the earliest formulation of the Marxian falling real-wage trend with its clear implications for growing inequality of income distribution between property and labour:

Faith, Reason, and Economics: Essays in Honour of Anthony Waterman. Ed. Derek Hum. Winnipeg: St. John's College Press, 2003.

Thus, competition sets capital against capital, labour against labour, landed property against landed property; and likewise each of these elements against the other two. In the struggle, the stronger wins; and in order to predict the outcome of the struggle, we need to investigate the strength of the contestants. First of all, labour is weaker than either landed property or capital, for the worker must work to live, whilst the landowner can live on his rent and the capitalist on his interest, or, if the need arises, on his capital or on capitalized property in land. *The result is that only the very barest necessities, the mere means of subsistence, fall to the lot of labour; whilst the largest part of the products is shared between capital and landed property.* (Engels, *Outlines* 440–41; emph. mine)

A key feature of the prognostication is the *disappearance of the middle-class*— and a corresponding expansion of the labour supply—under pressure of "centralization" exacerbated by crises:

In general, large property increases much more rapidly than small property, since a much smaller portion is deducted from this proceeds as property expenses. This law of the centralisation of private property is as immanent in private property as all the others. *The middle classes must increasingly disappear until the world is divided into millionaires and paupers, into large landowners and poor farm labourers.* All the laws, all the dividing of landed property, all the possible splitting-up of capital, are of no avail: this result must and will come, unless it is anticipated by a total transformation of social conditions, a fusion of opposed interests, an abolition of private property. (441)

As long as you continue to produce in the present unconscious, thoughtless manner, at the mercy of chance—for just so long trade crises will remain; and each successive crisis is bound to become more universal and therefore worse than the preceding one; *is bound to impoverish a larger body of small capitalists, and to augment in increasing proportion the numbers of the class who live by labour alone, thus considerably enlarging the mass of labour to be employed* (the major problem of our economists) and finally causing a social revolution such as has never been dreamt of in the philosophy of the economists. (433–34, emph. mine)

The *Holy Family*, formally a joint composition with Engels but in fact composed by Marx, contains brief remarks on the undermining of Britain's international competitiveness; and on *centralization* with its dire consequences for labour (14). In his *The Condition of the Working Class in England*, Engels describes the working man of the new propertyless class as having no hope of rising into the middle class, in contrast with a degree of upward social movement existing under the original organization of hand-workers (321). As before, the demise of the lower, or "petty," middle class—the outcome of "centralization"—left only "rich capitalists" and "poor workers"; there is an added illusion to a prospective overthrow of the new governing class or "the elect of the middle-class" (325).

Subsequently in the same document, Engels elaborates on the worsening outlook for labour. First, he raises the threat of American industrial pre-eminence, rejecting McCulloch's position in this respect. In the event of an undermining of British competitiveness—and provided "the present conditions remain unchanged" (a troublesome proviso indeed)—the "proletariat must become forever superfluous and has no other choice than starve or to rebel." But, even had England retained its industrial supremacy, there remained the prospect of worsening cycles. And here Engels again expatiates eloquently on the inevitable inflow into the work force from the middle classes as a result of rising industrial "concentration," presuming now that the depth of crisis is related to the *absolute magnitude* of the "industrial system" based on a capital-labour relation: "The proletariat would increase in geometrical proportion, in consequence of the progressive ruin of the lower middle-class and the giant strides with which capital is concentrating itself in the hands of the few; and the proletariat would soon embrace the whole nation, with the exception of a few millionaires" (580).

Accordingly, a rather more optimistic vision that also is to be found in the text—that full employment is achieved at cyclical peaks with population growth stimulated by good wages (384)—is qualified. This outcome is no longer so certain, considering that the demise of the middle classes implied an expansion of the proletariat "in geometric proportion," in obvious imitation of Malthus. In any event, that somewhat brighter perspective was already undermined by a degradation of standards induced by massive Irish immigration: "another cause of abasement [. . .] a cause *permanently active in forcing the whole class downwards*" (388, emph. mine). Indeed, "the Irish have [. . .] discovered the minimum of the necessities of life, and are now making the English workers acquainted with it" (390–01).

Other forces contributing to the downward pressure on wages emerge in the course of Engels's rejection of the *re-employment argument* often encountered in standard analyses of labour-displacing and cost-reducing technical change, namely its neglect of (1) the lag between expansion of final demand and capital construction; (2) the supplanting of adult male labour by female and child labour; and (3) the necessity for retraining (431).

The problem of *agricultural* unemployment also originated in large-scale farming, machinery, and the employment of female and child labour: "The constant extension of farming on a large scale, the introduction of threshing and other machines, and the employment of women and children (which is now so general that its effects have recently been investigated by a special official commission), threw a large number of men out of employment." The "system of industrial production ha[d] made its entrance." But there is a contrast with industry—that *land scarcity* exacerbated the problem: "New factories could always be built, if there were consumers for their products, but new land could not be created" (Engels, *Condition* 550).

Question 4 of Engels's *Principles of Communism* describes the origins of the "proletariat" in "the industrial revolution which took place in England in the latter half of the [eighteenth] century and which has repeated itself since then in all the civilized countries of the world" (341). Again the implications for severe and growing inequality are rehearsed: "The capitalists soon had their hands on everything and the workers were left with nothing" (342). The new processes entailed increased *division of labour*, and this in turn encouraged further mechanization (an idea to be found, incidentally, in Smith's *The Wealth of Nations*). The same transition occurred in the handicrafts, in addition to manufacture, which "likewise fell increasingly under the domination of the factory system, for here also the big capitalists more and more supplanted the small craftsmen by the establishment of large workshops, in which many savings on costs can be made and there can be a very high division of labour," the outcome being the ruination of "the smaller master handicraftsman," and a transformation in the position of the workers, essentially leaving in place "two new classes" (342–43).

Interestingly, along with growing absolute poverty, there develops labour's growing *political power*, Question 11 dealing with "the immediate results" of industrialization with an eye not only to the political and economic power of the bourgeoisie, but also the "power" of the proletariat, considering its growth and its concentration, leading to revolution (346).

All these themes are repeated in Engels and Marx's *Manifesto of the Communist Party*, namely: the destruction of the "lower strata" of the middle classes (491) the "concentration" of labour with a consequential growth of its political and social power (492–93); the deterioration of real living standards notwithstanding (495–96); and prospective revolution (496). Marx added nothing to all this some twenty years later in *Capital: A Critique of Political Economy.* (35.748–51).

It is illuminating to compare this prognostication regarding the disappearance of the middle class and bifurcation of income distribution, and falling real wages leading to revolution, with Malthus's perspective on the future. The contrast is striking though not in the manner usually portrayed. Malthus, too, perceived a danger of revolution—or rather of abortive revolution, *if the causes of poverty were not well understood*; but he also envisaged rising living standards for labour, greater distributive equality involving a relative expansion of the middle classes, and upward social mobility on the part of labour *if they are understood*.

As for the former concern, Malthus feared that if workers had unrealistic expectations awakened as to what can be done for them by society, their disappointment would be such as to explode in anarchic violence, only to be crushed by despotic governments supported even by those in principle sympathetic to reform: "The habit of expecting too much, and the irritation occasioned by disappointments, continually give a wrong direction to [. . .] efforts in favour of liberty, and constantly tend to defeat the accomplishments of those gradual reforms in government, and that slow melioration of the condition of the lower classes of society, which are really attainable" (*Essay*, 3rd ed. 2.390–01; see also *Essay*, 5th ed. 3.173).

All this should be seen within a broader context relating to the Constitution. In the *Principles of Political Economy*, Malthus made out a case against abolition of primogeniture and the consequent break-up of great estates on "higher considerations [. . .] than those which relate to mere wealth" (437), for the British constitution was "mainly due to a landed aristocracy"; and "if we think that, whatever may be its theoretical imperfections, it has practically given a better government, and more liberty to a greater mass of people for a longer time than any which history records, it would be most unwise to venture upon any such change as would risk the whole structure, and throw us upon a wide sea of experiment, where the chances are so dreadfully against our attaining the object of our search" (437–38). The revisions designed for a second edition, however, recognize the extension of the franchise to "a great majority of the middle classes" (the 1832 Reform Act), *and allow that, though perhaps premature, it might turn out for the best* provided it was not a prelude to "turbulence" (2nd ed. 380n).

Assuming, then, the absence of "turbulence," what are the prospects for progress from labour's perspective? Throughout, Malthus emphasized private property, the marriage institution, and self-interest generally as providing the key to working-class standards. "That the principal and most permanent cause of poverty, has little or no [3rd ed.: direct] relation to forms of government, or the unequal division of property," followed "from the principle of population" (*Essay* 3rd ed. *Works* 3.574; 3rd ed. 2.498). Yet this was not to be read as a case against the feasibility of improvement within a class-structured society, *including a more equable income distribution*: "The structure of society, in its great features, will probably always remain unchanged. We have every reason to believe, that it will always consist of a class of proprietors and a class of labourers; but the condition of each, and the proportion which they bear to each other, may be so altered, as greatly to improve the harmony and beauty of the whole" (575). Indeed, Malthus attributed desirable consequences from labour's perspective to the abolition of various feudal institutions during the French Revolution—including "the sale of church lands and other national domains"—insofar as these measures went hand in hand with, in fact actually encouraged, profound changes in behavioural attitude on the part of labour extending to demographic patterns (*Essay*, 5th ed. 2.378–79). Consistent with this positive reaction to the French Revolution is Malthus's critical view of "feudal" society, which shows him to be a champion of the middle classes partly with an eye to labour's advantage rather than—as is his reputation to this day—a sycophantic apologist of the landlords (3.21–22).

That the growth of "commerce" carried with it an expanded middle at the expense of the upper class is thus a major theme. So, too, are the *advantages* attributed to greater equality from the perspective of aggregate demand and thus for economic growth. This is easily shown from the *Principles of Political Economy,* where prospects are said to be bright despite the law of primogeniture, it being "generally acknowledged that the country, in its actual state and under its actual laws, presents a picture of greater wealth, especially when compared with its natural resources, than any large territorial state of modern times" (1st ed. 435); for by "the natural extinction of some great families, and the natural imprudence of some others, but, above all, by the extraordinary growth of manufactures and commerce, the immense landed properties that formerly prevailed all over the country have been in a great degree broken down" notwithstanding the law. A "large body of [. . .] the middle classes" had been firmly established, and constituted a "large class of effective demanders, who derive their power of purchasing from the various professions, from commerce, from manufactures, from wholesale and retail trade, from salaries of various kinds, and from the interest of public and private debts" (1st ed. 436–37). It was perhaps not inconceivable "for a nation with a comparatively small body of very rich proprietors, and a large body of very poor workmen, to push both the produce of the land and of the manufactures to the greatest extent, that the resources and ingenuity of the country would admit"; but this supposed "a passion among the rich for the consumption of manufactures, and the results of productive labour, much more excessive than has ever been witnessed in human society" whereas, in practice, "it has always been found that the excessive wealth of the few is in no respect equivalent, with regard to effective [2nd ed.: effectual] demand, to the more moderate wealth of the many" (1st ed. 430–31; 2nd ed. 374–75). Too great a degree of equality, however, would prove an impediment on the supply side, an illustration of Malthus's famous doctrine of "proportions": "But though it be true that the division of landed property, and the diffusion of manufacturing and mercantile capital to a certain extent, are of the utmost importance to the increase of wealth; yet it is equally true that, beyond a certain extent, they would impede the progress of wealth as much as they had before accelerated it" (1st ed. 431; 2nd ed. 375).

Malthus goes further. To abolish formally the law of primogeniture and achieve a more equal distribution of *landed* property and consequential "increase [in] the exchangeable value of the national produce" (*Principles,* 1st ed. 507) might—Malthus cautioned—do more harm than good, for the obligation created by the law for *younger sons* "to be the founders of their own fortune" implied reinforcement of the "middle classes of society" (intending here the commercial sector), which was more likely to "acquire tastes more favourable to the encouragement of wealth than the owners of small properties on the land" (436–37). That sort of evaluation also rendered it undesirable to attempt to pay off the national debt since, at least in the going circumstances, this would contribute to a weakening of the middle classes, with adverse effects on the level of effective demand. On a balance of considerations relating to British circumstances, a policy entailing in effect a transfer from the spending class of fundholders to landlords would be dangerous (483–84).

There is also a "moral" dimension, for in 1823 Malthus showed marked impatience with the pretensions of the landlords—their proposal to adjust contracts to their own benefit at the expense of fundholders—which is unlike anything he wrote earlier and as sharp as anything written by David Ricardo (Malthus, *Works* 7.220–21). And there are other broad considerations underlying Malthus's satisfaction with the expansion of the middle classes and smallholders at the expense of the great landed families that "naturally" accompanied the development of commercial society, encouraged by appropriate policy. These already emerge in the 1798 essay in the course of a qualification to its "principal argument" pointing to "the necessity of a class of proprietors, and a class of labourers" (1.102n). The qualification denied "that the present great inequality of property, is either necessary or useful to society. On the contrary, it must certainly be considered as an evil, and every institution that promotes it is essentially bad and impolitic." Similarly: "Though in every civilized state, a class of proprietors and a class of labourers must exist; yet one permanent advantage would always result from a nearer equalization of property. The greater the number of proprietors, the smaller must be the number of labourers; a greater part of society would be in the happy state of possessing property; and a smaller part in the unhappy state of possessing no property other than their labour" (121).

Malthus reiterated the desirability of a more equal income distribution in 1803, with something of an aesthetic rationale in terms of the improved "harmony and beauty" of society. But much more than that was intended. That some degree of inequality was essential is not in question from the perspective of *motivation*. At the same time, in current circumstances greater equality was justified on Utilitarian grounds: "Our best-grounded expectations of an increase in the happiness of the mass of human society are founded in the prospect of an increase in the relative proportions of the middle parts." This case relates partly to those "virtuous and industrious habits" attributed to the middle classes. But, furthermore, with a large middle class—and also assuming a diminution by way of population control of those employed "in severe toil"— the prospects for upward mobility by labour would be more conspicuous and inviting: "If the lowest classes of society were thus diminished, and the middle classes increased, each labourer might indulge a more rational hope of rising by diligence and exertion into a better station; the rewards of industry and virtue would be increased in number; human society would appear to consist of fewer blanks and more prizes; and the sum of social happiness would be evidently augmented" (Malthus, *Works* 3.567).

Despite the wording, it is not *appearance* that is at issue. As is explained in

Principles of Political Economy, after emphasizing the quantitative superiority of the labouring class, "under the prevalence of habits of prudence, the whole of this vast mass might be nearly as happy as the individuals of the other two classes, and probably a greater number of them, though not a greater proportion of them, happier" (1st ed. 423). Similarly: "It is most desirable that the labouring classes should be well paid, for a much more important reason than any that can relate to wealth; namely the happiness of the great mass of society" (472). Malthus's essay on rent of 1815 in fact contains the explicit declaration that the labouring classes are "the foundation on which the whole [social] fabric rests; and from their numbers, unquestionably of the greatest weight, in any estimate of national happiness" (*Works* 7.162). This, of course, is an "Enlightenment" perspective illustrated by David Hume who, for example, had argued against the so-called mercantilist pamphleteers that, even were it true that a wage increase is undesirable because it reduced competitiveness abroad, this outcome was "not to be put in competition with the happiness of so many millions" (16). Adam Smith stated the matter firmly in discussing an observed upward trend in real wages (78–79). And so did Ricardo, who rejoiced at any prospect of increasing "the happiness of the most numerous and therefore the most important part of the people" (179).

Malthus's position can best be appreciated if contrasted—as he himself contrasted it first in the 1803 edition of the essay—with Paley's case favouring inequality, "that the condition most favourable to the population of a country, and at the same time to its general happiness, is 'that of a laborious frugal people ministering to the demands of an opulent, luxurious nation'" (*Works* 3.566). Indeed, Malthus's arithmetic and geometric rates implied for Paley the impossibility "[of peopling] a country with inhabitants who shall be all in easy circumstances," leading to a justification of "the distinctions of civil life" (Paley 340–41). This interpretation of his own essay Malthus denied, having in mind both national wealth and national happiness and the high likelihood of instability with a narrowly based luxury-producing sector.

There is a further consideration. Malthus makes much of the desirability of rising real wages as a stimulus toward the generation of those very prudential habits that are the key to *permanent* improvement; conversely, slow growth (and *a fortiori* stationariness) carries with it the danger of a degeneration of standards (*Principles*, 1st ed. 248–50). Allowance was made in the essay on population for a state-financed education program designed to inculcate the principle of prudential control considering the externalities generated by such public investment (*Works* 3.525), though educational programs had the limited potential of assuring the maintenance of standards already achieved rather than their actual increase, since the rising generation must know in practice what it is that by imprudence it would be surrendering (Hollander 895–96).

To summarize: What mattered for Malthus in his application to social policy of the Greatest Good of the Greatest Number was not some fictitious mean but *median income*, with labour's interest rated highest because of its quantitative significance. All in all, his version of the Benthamite rule—as with Bentham himself, Ricardo, and the Mills—is opposed to the upper-class, military, and Church ideology that rejected population control; and in this he stood poles apart from Paley, who had used the utility principle to defend "accredited doctrines," as J.S. Mill put it in 1852 (10.173–74). Nor was the case for private property based on Natural Law or any such absolutist appeal but, rather, on a calculus of the social benefits deriving from the institution with particular weight placed on wage income.

There is a minor element of inevitability in Malthus's prognostications re garding the growth of the middle class when he talks of the "natural extinction of some great families, and the natural imprudence of some others," or of "the increase in the proportion of the middle classes of society, which the growth of manufacturing and mercantile capital cannot fail to create." But intelligently designed social policy encouraged these trends. Thus, though abolition of the law of primogeniture was an obvious means to break up the great landed estates, to retain it had the advantage of reinforcing the middle classes in the manufacturing and commercial sectors to even greater advantage. Again, to pay off the National Debt had "supply-side" advantages, yet to do so in going circumstances would weaken middle-class fundholders in favour of the landed upper class to the national detriment from the perspective of the volume of spending. Moreover, one crucial fact stands out in all of this: there was nothing *inevitable* for Malthus about falling (or minimal) living standards of the masses (which was Marx's famous charge), for Marx, in his *Theories of Surplus Value* of 1861–63, represented Malthus as a *ruthless* and *cynical* spokesman of the propertied class, in delighting to make a case for the impossibility of improvement on the part of the "poor wretches" (31.349–50). The "natural" trend toward the growth of a middle class at the expense of the very rich was, Malthus recommended, to be encouraged by policy primarily because it was to *labour's* advantage—by encouraging growth and thus demand for labour on the one hand, and opening up the prospect for upward mobility out of the labouring class on the other—*provided that such advantage was not dissipated by irresponsible population growth.* And the entire purpose of his so-called population-mongering was to assure that the natural trends supplemented by appropriate policy were indeed permanently advantageous to labour by way of prudential practice. This is how Malthus was read by the mature J.S. Mill (of the *Principles of Political Economy*) at least regarding versions of the essay other than the first (3.753). In 1859, Mill protested against Edwin Chadwick's "slur" on Malthus (15.590). But already in Malthus's *own lifetime,* Nassau Senior had publicly apologized for having lectured on population under a false impression of his position (a "caricature") and hoped that the misconceptions "unsupported as they are by your authority [. . .] will gradually wear away" (55–57, 81–82, 88–89). Senior was too optimistic. In our day, Salim Rashid, for example, continues to insist on Malthus as "the original economic determinist" in the sense of the inevitability of irremediable population pressure (319); and Craufurd D. Goodwin seeks to solve the "puzzle why nineteenth century political economists were quite so gloomy" referring *inter alia* to "the negative effects of diminishing returns," a "gloom [. . .] [that] seems to have begun with Malthus and Ricardo" (406).

The Marxian charges directed against Malthus relating to an *inevitable* fall in wages can in fact be returned to the sender, to whom they apply with a vengeance, for the striking feature of the Engels-Marx position is precisely the *inevitability* attributed to the predicted outcome of capitalist development, namely falling real wages and extreme bifurcation of income distribution—"imminent laws" Engels called them (but recall the problematic proviso that "the present conditions remain unchanged")—pointing to ultimate collapse of the capitalist system against which human intervention is unavailing.

It is the undermining by the developmental forces of prospects for upward mobility out of the working class, coupled with the degradation of living standards, that provides the key to revolution, for otherwise why would labourers wish to escape from their going situation? To ask this question is to suggest the possibility that *relative impoverishment*, green-eye, would suffice to engender the appropriate reaction. But this is academic, for Engels and Marx insisted on *absolute* impoverishment as one of the objective outcomes of capitalist development—downward pressure on the real wage, engendered in part by the entry into the work force of erstwhile members of the *bourgeoisie*. And one can appreciate why relative impoverishment would *not* suffice, for it would still allow upward mobility by labour into the middle class by dint of the steady accumulation of property out of the "surplus" element in the wage—precisely *Malthus's* hope for the future. This prospect was closed off by the Engels-Marx perception of things.

Marx's charges against Malthus's motivation extend further. His case for prudential population control was wholly hypocritical. Setting aside the slur, there is merit to the objective point in question that involves the free-riding problem. An early instance of this sort of reaction is provided in "Wages": "The [. . .] theory [. . .] which is also expressed as a law of nature, that population grows faster than the means of subsistence, is the more welcome to the bourgeois as it silences his conscience, makes hard-heartedness into a moral duty and the consequences of society into the consequences of nature, and finally gives him the opportunity to watch the destruction of the proletariat by starvation as calmly as other natural events without bestirring himself, and, on the other hand, to regard the misery of the proletariat as its own fault and to punish it" (6.433–34). And just here Marx adds that to assert that "the proletarian can restrain his natural instinct by reason, and so, by moral supervision, halt the law of nature in its injurious course of development" (434), was sheer hypocracy: "The entire working class cannot possibly take the decision not to make any children. [. . .] The bourgeoisie [. . .] does not and cannot mean these phrases and counsels [relating to population control] seriously"; indeed, "overpopulation is [. . .] in the interest of the bourgeoisie, and it gives the workers good advice which it knows it to be impossible to carry out" (433).

Now it was indeed Malthus's position that population growth would be adequately controlled in a system of private property under the rule of self-interest, where each individual was "responsible for the maintenance of his own children" and "subjected to the natural inconveniences and difficulties arising from the indulgence of his inclinations [in too early marriage] and to no other whatever" (*Essay,* 5th ed. 2.284). This holds good, apparently, presuming an adequate educational program—Malthus supported a state-financed system—one designed to inculcate the principle of moral restraint, that the wage depends on checks to the marriage and birth rates. But he seems not to have appreciated that even assuming the success of such a program, each self-interested individual has a motive to marry young—accepting the basic assumption of a desire for marriage and procreation—if he believes others will behave responsibly and delay marriage, thereby raising or maintaining the wage. It is surely not the case that the responsible individual will "reap the full fruits" of his good behaviour "whatever may be the number of others who fail" (*Works* 3.483), since his expectations of future earnings may be ruined by the irresponsible behaviour of others.

Marx was certainly not the first to raise the problem. One formulation in Malthus's lifetime is by William Forster Lloyd who, in a lecture of 1832 entitled "On the Checks to Population," questioned the dependency on moral restraint as a means of raising real wages—or protecting high real wages—on the grounds that "there is no adequate individual benefit to be derived from abstinence," for "what is there to hinder individuals, who do not enter into the common feeling"—supposing such to reign—"from taking advantage of the general forbearance" (34–35). Carlyle made the same point, and may have been Marx's source, since in brief observations on *Chartism* in his "Wages," Marx notes that "the entire theory of Malthus and the economists amounts to saying that it lies with the workers to reduce the demand [sic!] by not making children" (416).

The neglect of free-riding illustrates a point made by James Bonar: "It has been said that Malthus was Utilitarian, but not Utilitarian enough; he should have kept more constantly before him the Greatest Happiness of the Greatest Number. But Malthus was a Utilitarian of the old school; the greatest happiness of the great body of the people seemed to him to be best secured by the devotion of the individual members of it, each of his own permanent and real happiness" (213). We should modify this position, since support of appropriate state-supported education implies *some* social intervention. But any remaining explanation for Malthus's stance should probably best be sought along Bonar's line and certainly not in the alleged "hypocracy" of a spokesman of the "ruling classes."

We turn now to a second aspect of Marx's objective case against Malthus in 1847, namely that labour's condition "makes the sexual instinct their chief pleasure and develops it one-sidedly" ("Wages" 433), or in *Capital*, that a fall in wages creates "a breeding ground for a really swift propagation of the population since under capitalist production misery produces population" (37.217). The same point was made earlier at least implicitly by Engels in his *The Condition of the Working Class in England*: "The moral training which is not given to the worker in school is not supplied by the other conditions of his life; that moral training, at least which alone has worth in the eyes of the bourgeoisie; his whole position and environment involves the strongest temptation to immorality. [. . .] And, when the poverty of the proletarian is intensified to the point of actual lack of the barest necessaries of life, to want and hunger, the temptation to disregard all social order does but gain power" (412).

Engels and Marx were apparently unaware that Malthus had spelled much of this out, *as early as 1803*, in arriving at the conclusion that even simple "prudence," accompanied by the "vice" of "irregular gratification," in contrast with strict "moral restraint," was socially desirable on a balance of moral costs and benefits considering the vicious consequences flowing from *poverty*: degradation of character, pre-eminently female promiscuity, theft, murder (and, in Benthamite fashion, their punishment), and premature mortality (Hollander 887–90). Moreover—and this is a closely related point—Malthus himself we have seen had recognized the *poverty trap* and was concerned with a possible degeneration of standards, desiring rapid economic growth for that very reason. He was not as naïve as his neglect of free-riding may suggest, a conclusion that is reinforced by the role accorded state-funded education.

Other "objective" criticisms of Malthus are raised in *Capital*, where Marx cites Irish experience as providing a clear empirical refutation of Malthus (35.645-46). The objection turns on the "disturbing cause" of technical or organizational change, though population control was never seen by orthodox economists to be a *sufficient* condition to assure against falling wages. And there is also the matter of wage-induced substitution against labour (35.632; see also *Theories* 32.202).

Now, substitution against labour in the event of an absolute fall in labour supply of the foregoing kind could only limit the resultant wage increase, there being no reason to expect the creation of an excess labour supply with downward pressure on the wage. The simple point is that substitution against labour is already reflected in the negative slope of the demand curve. This principle, applied to the dynamic context, implies that there is no reason that a reduced population growth rate cannot retard the falling wage trend even if some substitution against labour, with an impact on the labour-demand growth rate, is induced.

I turn now to the complexity that the demographic dimension is to be found in Marx himself. Consider in particular a formulation in "Wages" of increasing Organic Composition (as it came to be known) generating a lag in the growth rate of wage-fund capital behind that of total capital but not an absolute decline. When, then, Marx proceeds to a fall in the wage rate *in consequence of growing excess supply of labour*, he implicitly presumes that labour supply grows faster than the presumed positive growth of the wages fund:

> It is, therefore, a general law which necessarily arises from the nature of the relation between capital and labour that in the course of the growth of the productive forces *the part of productive capital which is transformed into machinery and raw material, i.e., capital as such, increases in disproportion to the part which is intended for wages*; i.e., in other words, the workers must share among themselves an ever smaller part of the productive capital in relation to its total mass. Their competition, therefore, becomes more and more violent. In other words; *the more productive capital grows, the more, in proportion, the means of employment and the means of subsistence for the workers are reduced, and the more rapidly, in other words, the working population grows in proportion to its means of employment*. And this increases in the same measure in which the productive capital as a whole grows. (432, emph. mine)

To appreciate *why* labour supply rises faster than wages fund—why "the increase of the proletariat must proceed relatively even faster" than wage-fund capital (Marx, "Wages" 433)—we may refer to the inflow into the work force from "ruined sectors of the bourgeoisie" and also to the use of female and child labour, tendencies endogenous to capital accumulation. *But, in addition, there is an explicit demographic dimension*: "The growth of the productive forces therefore leads to increased power of big capital, to the machine called the worker becoming more and more simple, to an increase in direct competition among the workers through greater division of labour and use of machinery, *through a positive premium being placed on the production of people*, through the competition of the ruined sections of the bourgeois class, etc." (430, emph. mine). And, by the "positive premium," it is clear that Marx intended one of the implications of the use of child labour: "By replacing adults with children, modern industry places a veritable premium on the making of children." As for the "premium" itself, that seems to refer to the mere technical opportunity created by industry for child labour; it is not clear that it is the *level* of wages that is responsible, that is, low wages *necessitating*, as it were, larger families to assure "adequate" family income. (We may note in passing Smith's position that it was the *high* earnings, available in North America, that rendered "the value of children [. . .] the greatest of all encouragements to marriage," labour being so well paid that "a numerous family of children, instead of being a burden is a source of opulence and prosperity to the parents" [71].) The same notion is also found in the course of a critique of proposals for the solution to

147

poverty by way of "industrial education": "We shall not draw attention to the trite contradiction which lies in the fact that modern industry replaces compound labour more and more with simple labour which requires no education; we shall not draw attention to the fact that it throws more and more children from the age of seven upwards behind the machine and turns them into a source of income not only for the bourgeois class but for their own proletarian parents" (427). And to this we may add Marx's two-fold objection to Malthus, already referred to, "that the entire working class cannot possibly take the decision not to make any children," but, to the contrary, "their condition makes the sexual instinct their chief pleasure" (433).

The demographic dimension to his secular real-wage decline must, however (as with Engels), be seen as part of the broader picture of capital accumulation, not as an independent "law of nature" reflecting land scarcity as it is with Malthus (Marx, "Wages" 432–33). It is not clear that Marx was aware of the implications of his own adoption of a *sort* of pessimistic "Malthusianism" during the course of his refutation of the efficacy of prudential population control under capitalism. He might well have responded that population control would not be the solution considering substitution against labour engendered thereby, that the proposed remedy was as bad as the disease. In any event, paradoxical as it may appear, it is fair to say that he accorded greater weight than did Malthus to *actual* population pressure in contemporary capitalism, since Malthus was confident regarding the prospects for population control *provided* a significant rise in real wages could be initially assured making prudential habits sufficiently inviting and thus rendering any initial improvement permanent, to which we should add the prospects of growing upward mobility out of the labouring class that would further encourage a desirable outcome.

Malthus's original objective in writing *An Essay on the Principle of Population* was, of course, to counter various utopian reformers. A system of "perfect equality"—one without private property and the marriage institution whereby couples bear the cost of raising their own children (more generally a system governed by "benevolence" rather than "self-interest")—would inevitably fail in consequence of population pressure on scarce land (*Works* 1.67–68); and failure of the experiment reflected in the collapse of living standards and consequential social chaos would lead to the re-establishment of a private-property system and the reinstitution of marriage (72). In all this Malthus made no serious attempt to consider prospects for population control *under communal arrangements*; unlike Godwin, he simply took for granted that people would not act with an eye to the social consequences of their private behaviour (Levy 279). Nonetheless, rejection of utopian communism was not based upon the *inevitability* under all arrangement of population pressure but, rather, its inevitability in the absence of an institutional framework requiring private calculation; prudential behaviour was a cultural variable, the advantage lying with the private-property system—assuming always that it is allowed to function effectively, for which very reason Malthus castigated the contemporary Poor Laws as an ill-thought-out stimulus to early marriage (*Works* 1.32f).

Later editions of *An Essay on the Principle of Population* introduce the question of legal restraint on population growth. Malthus's objections to "systems of equality and community of goods"—he had in mind Robert Owen, not only Godwin's scheme, which, lacking a state, was essentially anarchical—is (as always) that self-interested calculations regarding age of marriage are precluded, and (he now adds) would have to be replaced by legal restraints involving rigorous enforcement and punishment of an "unnatural, immoral, or cruel" order (*Essay*, 5th ed. 2.285). His "greatest objection to a system of equality and the system of the poor laws (two systems which, however different in their outset, are of a nature calculated to produce the same results)" was "that the society in which they are effectively carried into execution, will ultimately be reduced to the miserable alternative of choosing between universal want and the enactment of *direct* laws against marriage" (368–69). Poverty, in brief, was not *inevitable* under communism any more than under capitalism; but any solution in a communist society would entail in his judgement *unacceptable* constraints on personal freedom. Legal restraints might have seemed less objectionable to him if countenanced by public opinion, as J.S. Mill later maintained, but of this we cannot be sure.

Marx had little to say regarding population under communism. Engels said more, but his position is not always clear. As a preliminary, we note that the contrast between excess population relative to "means of production" and excess relative to "subsistence" is to be found in the *Outlines of a Critique of Political Economy* and was apparently Marx's source. In rejecting Malthusian concerns strictly defined, Engels cites Archibald Alison to the effect that "the productivity of the soil can be increased *ad infinitum* by the application of capital, labour and science" (436). Diminishing (average) returns were at the very least matched by "science": "science increases at least as much as population. The latter increases in proportion to the size of the previous generation, science advances in proportion to the knowledge bequeathed to it by the previous generation, and thus under the most ordinary conditions also in a geometric progression" (440). More generally, Alison had demonstrated "that each adult can provide more than he himself needs—a fact without which mankind could not multiply, indeed could not even exist; if it were not so how could those still growing up live?" (438). Indeed, "if it is a fact that every adult produces more than he himself can consume, that children are like trees which give superabundant returns on the outlays invested in them—and these certainly are facts, are they not?—then it must be assumed that each worker ought to be able to produce far more than he needs and that the community, therefore, ought to be very glad to provide him with everything he needs; one must consider a large family to be a very welcome gift to the community" (438–39).

His objections to Malthus's neglect of the contrast between means of employment and means of subsistence and the foregoing elaboration based on
Alison convey an impression that Engels envisaged no *"Malthusian"* over-
population problem *in the sense of pressure on scarce natural resources* (actual or potential) even in society as it existed. Yet the term "ought to be" in the
passage just encountered might suggest otherwise, namely that the notion of
surplus food necessarily generated by each worker *rendering high population
socially advantageous* applies specifically to rationally organized, not actual,
society. Here is a grey area. And the problem is seriously compounded by the
fact that Engels actually goes on to refer to the necessity for Moral Restraint in
a "transformed" society that *alone could provide the education required to
instill an appropriate sense of responsibility,* implying a "Malthusian" population problem, namely excess population relative to means of "subsistence,"
as an *actual* problem in existing society (with no hope of solution), and a
prospective problem in a reformed system (with a solution at hand):

> The Malthusian theory has certainly been a necessary point of transition which
> has taken us an immense step further. Thanks to this theory, as to economics as
> a whole, our attention has been drawn to the productive power of the earth and
> of mankind; and after overcoming this economic despair we have been made
> forever secure against the fear of over-population. *We derive from it the most
> powerful economic arguments for a social transformation. For even if Malthus
> were completely right, this transformation would have to be undertaken straight
> away; for only this transformation, only the education of the masses which it
> provides, make possible that moral restraint of the propagative instinct which
> Malthus himself presents as the most effective and easiest remedy for over-
> population.* (439–40, emph. mine)

The need for Moral Restraint is said here to apply only *if Malthus is supposed to be right.* But one has the impression that Engels must have presumed
this to be the case. Why else claim that Malthusian theory based on "the fear of
over-population"—and the context seems to relate to "the productive power of
the earth and mankind," that is, to population relative to means of subsistence,
not means of employment—provided "the most powerful economic arguments
for a social transformation"? And why bother to mention the efficacy of education under communal arrangement? Nonetheless, if for Engels there is a potential problem of Malthusian over-population under communism (to be resolved
by Moral Restraint) what is the *source* of the problem? He, after all, had also
indicated that "each worker ought to be able to produce far more than he needs
[. . .] [so that] one must consider a large family to be a very welcome gift for the
community" Engels's position remains unclear.

The affirmation of 1844 that, "even if Malthus were completely right," only
communism could assure moral restraint is referred to by Engels nearly forty
years later (1 February 1881) in a letter to Kautsky, where he allows "the abstract

possibility that the number of people will become so great that limits will have to be set to their increase." But he adds that "if at some stage communist society finds itself obliged to regulate the production of human beings, just as it has already come to regulate the production of things, it will be precisely this society, and this society alone, which can carry this out without difficulty. It does not seem to me that it would be at all difficult in such a society to achieve by planning a result which has already been produced spontaneously, without planning, in France and Lower Austria" (Meek 120). Perhaps here he had in mind moral restraint as in 1844. Unfortunately, the affirmation appears in the context of a deliberate refusal to elaborate: "At any rate, it is for the people in the communist society themselves to decide whether, when, and how this is to be done, and what means they wish to employ for the purpose. I do not feel called upon to make proposals or give them advice about it. These people, in any case, will surely not be any less intelligent than we are." It is remarkable that in taking this position Engels was, in effect, duplicating what Mill had written on the issue in 1851 (Mill 5.449), except in his insistence that *only* communist society could provide a solution to any population problem. Both certainly show the same reluctance to elaborate.

There is one further complexity. Engels and Marx came to recognize the deceleration of population growth in capitalist economies, Marx pointing out in *Capital* that, "although the absolute increase of the English population in the last half century was very great, the relative increase or rate of growth fell constantly" (35.642); and Engels implying as much by affirming that "it does not seem to me that it would be at all difficult in such a [Communist] society to achieve by planning a result which has already been produced *spontaneously without planning*, in France and Lower Austria." To this extent, they undermined part of their case against Malthus's proposals for population control and even against their own reading of capitalist development—that wages were depressed by excess population growth *stimulated* by such development.

WORKS CITED

Bonar, James. *Malthus and his Work*. 2nd ed. London: Frank Cass, 1924.

Engels, Frederick. *Outlines of a Critique of Political Economy*. 1844. Vol. 3 of *Marx-Engels Collected Works*. New York: International Publishers, 1975. 418–43.

_____ . *The Condition of the Working Class in England*. 1845. Vol. 4 of *Marx-Engels Collected Works*. New York: International Publishers, 1975. 295–583.

_____ . *Principles of Communism*. 1847. Vol. 6 of *Marx-Engels Collected Works*. New York: International Publishers, 1976. 341–57.

Engels, Frederick, and Karl Marx. *The Holy Family*. 1845. Vol. 4 of *Marx-Engels Collected Works*. New York: International Publishers, 1975. 5–211.

_____ . *Manifesto of the Communist Party*. 1848. Vol. 6 of *Marx-Engels Collected Works*. New York: International Publishers, 1976. 477–519.

Goodwin, Craufurd D. "Economic Man in the Garden of Eden." *Journal of the History of Economic Thought* 22.4 (2000): 405–32.

Hollander, Samuel. *The Economics of Thomas Robert Malthus*. Toronto: University of Toronto Press, 1997.

Hume, David. "Of Commerce." 1752. *Writings on Economics*. Ed. E. Rotwein. London: Nelson, 1955. 3–18.

Levy, David. "Some Normative Aspects of the Malthusian Controversy." *History of Political Economy* 10.2 (1978): 271–85.

Lloyd, William Forster. "On the Checks to Population." *Two Lectures on the Checks to Population*. Oxford: S. Collingswood, 1832.

Malthus, Thomas Robert. *An Essay on the Principle of Population*. 3rd ed. 2 vols. London: J. Johnson, 1806.

_____ . *An Essay on the Principle of Population*. 5th ed. 3 vols. London: John Murray, 1817.

_____ . *Principles of Political Economy*. 1st ed. London: John Murray, 1820.

_____ . *Principles of Political Economy*. 2nd ed. London: William Pickering, 1836.

_____ . *Works*. 8 vols. Ed. E.A. Wrigley and David Souden. London: William Pickering, 1986.

Marx, Karl. "Wages." 1847. *Marx-Engels Collected Works*. Vol. 6. New York: International Publishers, 1976. 415–37.

_____ . *Capital: A Critique of Political Economy*. *Marx-Engels Collected Works*. Vol. 35 (1867); Vol. 37 (1894). London: Lawrence and Wishart, 1996, 1998.

_____ . *Theories of Surplus Value*. 1861–63. *Marx-Engels Collected Works*. Vols. 30–34 (1988–94). 1968.

Meek, Ronald L., ed. *Marx and Engels on the Population Bomb*. Berkeley: The Ramparts Press, 1971.

Mill, John Stuart. *Collected Works*. 30 vols. Toronto: University of Toronto Press, 1963–91.

Paley, Richard. *Natural Theology or Evidences of the Existence and Attributes of the Deity*. 1st ed. London: 1802.

Rashid, Salim. "Hollander on Malthus." *Journal of the History of Economic Thought* 21.3 (1999): 315–24.

Ricardo, David. *Notes on Malthus's Principles*. 1820. Vol. 2 of *Works and Correspondence*. Ed. P. Sraffa. Cambridge: Cambridge University Press, 1951.

Senior, Nassau. *Two Lectures on Population . . . to which is added, a Correspondence between the Author and the Rev. T.R. Malthus*. London: Saunders and Otley, 1829.

Smith, Adam. *The Wealth of Nations*. 1st ed. 1776. New York: Modern Library, 1937.

Is Biography History?
Mary McGeachy, 1901–1991

Mary Kinnear

Overlooking Professor Anthony Waterman's work in his St. John's College office is a portrait of Dr. Samuel Johnson. Anthony greatly admires Dr. Johnson's sense, his Christianity, his conversation, his friendships, his Tory principles, and his prose. Johnson was more than a moralist and lexicographer. He was also a pioneer of modern biography, with *Lives of the Poets* and his *Life of Savage*. Just as pathbreaking was the biography of which he was subject, Boswell's *Life of Johnson*.

Anthony Waterman, too, is a man of multiple interests. Economics, theology, music, and the humanities are among the disciplines that have competed for his attention along with history. His work on Christian social thought has made him into an intellectual historian, and his criticisms of my own historical work over the years have invariably resulted in a greater clarity of expression. Always he has urged the importance of theory in any academic enterprise. My current work in progress is a biography, and I offer this paper in recognition of Anthony's wide-ranging help as mentor and friend over the years.

In this essay I explore the criteria under which biography can be history, and I examine the life of one woman whose life story fulfills such criteria. First, I survey the fluctuating fashions linking biography with history, and then I consider the particular ways in which the international career of a twentieth-century Canadian reflected the historical currents of her time.

The relation between biography and history revolves around the idea of the importance, or not, of individual agency. History tries to understand and explain the past to the present and is critically engaged with understanding change. Do individual human beings change the world? Or is the proper subject for the historian the analysis of general political, economic, and social concepts such

Faith, Reason, and Economics: Essays in Honour of Anthony Waterman. Ed. Derek Hum. Winnipeg: St. John's College Press, 2003.

as, for example, nationalism, class, ethnicity, or sexuality? Can history include an examination of the achievement and identity of an individual human being?

Historians are influenced by the attitude toward biography of writers from other disciplines. Men of letters have long considered biography as their territory. Respect for biography as a genre in the academy has fluctuated just as much in departments of literature as in departments of history.

When Johnson prepared his biographies, there was no doubt that individual agency mattered. Biography justified itself by reference to moral didacticism. Seventeenth-century biographer Izaak Walton chose for his biographies men of blameless credentials as examples for the "next age." "No part of history is more instructive and delighting than the lives of great and worthy men," wrote Bishop Burnet in 1682. Dryden thought biography in comparison with "history and annals [. . .] equals, or even excels both of them" (qtd. in Shelston 6). These writers were following the centuries-old tradition of Plutarch, whose *Lives of the Noble Greeks and Romans* was intended to provide models of how the good man should live his life. Although eighteenth-century biographers were not as uncritical as the mediaeval hagiographers, who wrote lives of the saints in order for readers to understand God's will for man, Johnson's predecessors saw their purpose as edifying and uplifting their readers (Shelston 9).

Johnson did not disagree that biography should provide moral instruction. However, he differed from many biographers before and after him by disputing that moral instruction could be imparted solely by accounts of great and good deeds. Contemporaries were mistaken, he thought, to believe that biography should necessarily concentrate on exciting adventures or important public events. Moral improvement could be gained from reading about "domestic privacies and [. . .] the minute details of daily life" (Johnson, "Rambler" 358).

Moreover, Johnson believed, the subject chosen for a biography need not be famous. "There has rarely passed a life of which a judicious and faithful narrative would not be useful" (Johnson, "Rambler" 356–57). Johnson condemned the prevailing "piety" of refraining from mentioning a subject's weaknesses (360). He believed that the value of any story lay in its truth. Candour, vivid detail, and psychological insight into motivation were, he thought, the hallmarks of a good biography. A reader could apply lessons learned from the lives of others to his own predicaments. This sort of history could teach ordinary human beings how to live better ("Idler" 369).

Eighty years later, Thomas Carlyle came to write a review of Croker's new edition of Boswell's *Life of Johnson* and echoed Johnson's own fascination with the idea of knowing the lives of others. "How inexpressibly comfortable," he wrote, "to know our fellow-creature, to see into him, understand his goings-forth, decipher the whole heart of his mystery [and] [. . .] to view the world altogether as he views it" (Carlyle, "Biography" IV. 3). Biography was "almost the one thing needful" for life (5). Carlyle went as far as to pronounce that history was "the essence of innumerable biographies" (Carlyle, "History" II.348).

Carlyle himself was influenced by German romanticism and its elevation of the individual. His book on heroes and hero worship argued that "every advance which humanity had made was due to special individuals supremely gifted in mind and character, whom Providence sent among them at favoured epochs" (Carlyle, *Heroes* xxxv). His remarks helped give rise to a Great Man theory of history: that events are shaped and formed by great men and that, in order to understand history, we must know about the great leaders of the time. Biography in such a schema was central to history.

These ideas were simultaneously put at risk by Karl Marx, a German writer who was beginning to formulate a theory of historical change that owed little to individual men and much to impersonal forces. Marx identified the dialectic of class struggle as the force triggering economic and political change throughout history. Individuals acted as the human agents for forces beyond their own individual control. Irresistible currents generated by economic forces resulted in a determinism that it was folly to deny (Rigby).

Victorian biographers followed the ideas of Carlyle rather than Marx and tended to overlook Johnson's insistence on frankness, comprehensiveness, and the significance of mundane details of everyday existence. Just as certain topics (including, most notably, sex) were taboo in the conversations of polite society, so too were they kept off the pages of nineteenth-century biographies, regardless of their significance in helping to explain behaviour and motivation. And Johnson's insistence that people other than great men might provide good biographical subjects was ignored. "Let us now praise great men" was the keynote of most biography before the First World War.

In 1918, Lytton Strachey created a furor with the publication of his book *Eminent Victorians*. In short, sharp pieces, he echoed Johnson's insistence on telling the truth by debunking some of the famous names of Victorian society and exposing them as humbugs or prisoners of what he considered false values. Like previous biographers, he followed in the tradition of moral instruction, but he wished to teach about the vice of hypocrisy and the worship of idols. Strachey was confident in his own ethical judgements, and his book, which caused warriors and statesmen to tumble from their pedestals, fitted the public mood in the aftermath of the First World War (Skidelsky 6). His insistence on truth-telling was poetic: it did not extend to fastidiousness regarding factual accuracy.

During the first half of the twentieth century, Freud's ideas reinforced Strachey's excoriation of hypocrisy by suggesting that achievement was displaced sexuality. Freud believed that the will to achieve was the sublimated expression of sexual drives, diverted from immediate gratification into tasks of culture and world improvement. It was therefore relevant for a biographer to delve into the private lives of their subjects (Skidelsky 10–11). Freud succeeded in encouraging authors to discover and write about sexuality. In the wake of Strachey and psychoanalysis, biography became as much a quest for understanding individual motivation and an analysis of personal identity as the critical observation of public achievement.

In the mid-twentieth century, literary theorists following the lead of Dr. F.R. Leavis in Cambridge were less concerned about the content of a biography and more inclined to question the relevance of biography at all. For a couple of generations, students in university literature departments were trained in the New Criticism, which held that the best way to study any work of literature was to treat it "scientifically" as an ideal, timeless object that must be analyzed without reference to any context. The intentions of the author or details of historical context were distractions from the text. The right way to read a text was to discover its own paradoxes and ironies, and the reader's job was to unify and reconcile internal tensions. An underlying assumption was that a single true meaning lay within the text itself. The texts selected for study were great works of art of the past, whose values were eternal and universal, forming a canon of civilization (Cameron 74–75; Hutcheon 148–49).

During the twentieth century, as people from a wider variety of social backgrounds gained access to higher education, the assumptions underpinning many of the traditional confident certainties were queried and attacked. Why should the culture that belonged to the old ruling classes of Europe be considered as eternal and universal, relevant for all? Why should people in all parts of the world venerate a single concept of civilization? Why should people who grew up in a working-class culture necessarily believe that the values of aristocrats and the upper middle class should be the models for literature and life? Why should women learn that the model for the good life was that of the cultivated man? It was plain that the ways of life of non-Europeans, manual workers, and women of all classes were different from those celebrated in the canon. Why was the one culture considered superior to all others?

In the wake of such questions, which disturbed the guardians of literature and culture, universities became the site for an interrogation of values previously held dear. The battles continue into the twenty-first century, but one lesson was learned: context mattered. It helped a reader to know a writer's assumptions and the circumstances under which a book was written. Just as historians had evaluated their main primary sources of archives to establish the particular circumstances under which documents were created, literary scholars became more curious about the production of a text. Derogatory modernist comments about biography could be set aside now that that it was important to understand the circumstances that resulted in a work of literature.

Historians had never forgotten that context was not only relevant but also essential for understanding events, trends, and people. Changes in the theory and practice of history came more from an expansion of topics that were considered appropriate for historical enquiry. In Canada, for instance, the focus shifted "from political survival, nation-building, and biography, toward a systematic examination of the day-to-day struggles of ordinary men, women, and children. There is a populist, and in some cases an explicit Marxist, thrust to the literature" (Nelles). Historians such as Ferdinand Braudel of the French *Annales* school wrote of the "longue durée," the long continuities and trends that fashioned societies and mentalities, particularly with reference to the peoples surrounding the Mediterranean. Historians began to analyze the behaviours and assumptions of groups previously hidden from history, like peasants, labourers, factory workers, families, and women. Historians were still expected to investigate trends, processes, and groups rather than individual events and people.

One of the most influential theorists of history in the English-speaking world was E.H. Carr. A historian of the Russian Revolution, he gave the 1961 Trevelyan Lectures at Cambridge university on the question What is history? The resulting book is still consulted by students of historiography forty years later (Richard Evans 1–4). Carr tended toward the Marxist view that, in history, the individual was a vessel for impersonal forces. He dismissed the "Bad King John theory of history—the view that what matters in history is the character and behaviour of individuals" (39). However, he subsequently moderated his sympathy for determinism and came to attribute a substantial role to accident and personality (xxx–xxxi). On the topic, for instance, of the early death of Lenin, he wrote: "Even if you maintain that in the long run everything would have turned out much the same, there is a short run which is important, and makes a great deal of difference to a great many people" (Haslam 202).

A more radical attack on history itself came from postmodernists under the influence of the French deconstructionists. Some questioned the existence of historical facts. Was there any difference between fact and fiction? In the early 1970s, American scholar Hayden White gave rise to what became known as the "linguistic turn." "By suggesting alternative emplotments of a given sequence of historical events, historians provide historical events with all of the possible meanings with which the literary art of their culture is capable of endowing them" (White 25). He argued that the vulgar distinction between fiction and history, where fiction was conceived as the representation of the imaginable and history as the representation of the actual, "must give place to the recognition that we can only know the *actual* by contrasting it with or likening it to the *imaginable*" (31).

Postmodernists interrogated what we know and how we know it. Some went as far as to deny the possibility of history. If facts could not be objectively agreed, they pointed out, there could be no history, nor biography, either, in an absolute sense. Writers made up what was true for them. Historians, whether writing about forces or individuals, were doing the same as novelists (Nadel 7–12). An intellectual nihilism, argued some postmodernists, was the only conclusion to draw from living without absolute certainties (see: Ankersmit; Zagorin). Meaning resided not in authors' intentions, nor in the written word, but in the readers' acts of interpretation. Consequently, historical events had no independent validity outside of an observer's impression while reading about them (see: Novick 544–45; Caplan).

But counter-arguments were made. Some postmodernists found themselves denying the existence of events. This proved nonsensical when, for example, they would deny that the Holocaust ever happened (Lipstadt 17–20). Few reputable scholars would ally themselves with Holocaust deniers.

Unease at the shifting and confusing pluralities of modern discourse need not result in an abdication of reason altogether. Intellectual enquiry may result in provisional and partial conclusions, but historians have for years accepted, with more or less humility, that history—and by extension most forms of knowledge—will be constantly reinterpreted in the light of new information and different sorts of questions (Perry).

Victoria Glendinning describes novelists as "licensed liars" (57). They are expected to invent their stories. In contrast, the historian has a different function. The historian has to work within what is known and cannot invent the past. There will always be different interpretations, but, as Richard Evans notes, "the past really happened, we really can, if we are very scrupulous and careful and self-critical, find out how it happened and reach some tenable though always less than final conclusions about what it all meant" (253). Some postmodernists may say that "we cannot tolerate the ambiguity of human existence" (Mary Evans 143), but historians must.

The mandate of historians includes making sense of both the toleration and the ambiguities. At two levels, the scholarly and the popular, history not only survives but also prospers. As the president of the Canadian Historical Association noted in 2000, "whether judged by best-seller lists, television ratings, newspaper articles, Web site expansion, scholarly production, or educational activity, History is hot" (Gaffield 2).

History as a discipline is set to continue. But what of biography?

In a presentation to the 2001 Canadian Historical Association, Brian McKillop observed that biography was in strong public demand: "With the new attention to the cultural and the quotidian, we witness [. . .] a rediscovery of human agency and human drama" (8, 20).

Biography has greatly benefitted from the concerns of feminists who made inroads into scholarship in the late twentieth century. Their agenda was to insist on women's equality with men, while acknowledging that women, like men, differed among themselves. Developing Virginia Woolf's 1929 critique of the traditional canon, feminist scholars have wondered where women were in the European tradition. The twentieth-century expansion of history to include social history permitted historians to see and examine the place of women in society. Biography can clearly aid in bringing the achievements of women to our attention.

There are still lingering doubts among historians regarding the overall usefulness of biography. Historians still examine trends, aggregates, and generalized concepts, but as Derek Beales pointed out in his inaugural lecture at Cambridge in 1981, it is important to remember that trends are powered by people; history is concerned with trends as they affect people; and individuals' reactions to trends constitute the historians' prime material (25). Few would want the past to become "history without a human face" (Coleman 641).

Looking back to the recent past, the historian can see a resurgence of biography in the same way that figurative art has also become more popular. "I don't think one has to explain why it's popular now," remarked the director of the (British) National Portrait Gallery, "but, [rather,] why it was relatively unpopular in the Sixties and Seventies, when it went right out of fashion because people weren't interested in the life of the individual" (Rose).

Recent books dealing with two of the most significant political developments of the twentieth century, the Russian Revolution and Germany under Hitler, each meld the analysis of major social forces with the life stories of individuals. The Russian Revolution was not "a march of abstract social forces and ideologies but [. . .] a human event of complicated individual tragedies." Orlando Figes's text "weaves between the private and the public spheres," emphasizing the "human aspect of its great events by listening to the voices of individual people whose lives became caught up in the storm" (xvi–xvii). Regarding Nazism, the Holocaust, and World War II, Ian Kershaw declares that we all have "the continuing duty to seek understanding of how Hitler was possible" (xii–xiv). Biography becomes not only useful but necessary.

"Marx and Freud are not in fashion," observed Brian Harrison, editor of the *New (British) Dictionary of National Biography*. Along with Lenin and Hitler, "in De Gaulle and Thatcher we have [instances] of individuals whose determination and vision have undoubtedly helped to mould their age" (15).

There are some figures whose power has been so pivotal that there is no question that a historical biography is important. Clearly, there are fewer women than men in this situation because, until recently, women have had less access to formal power, and most women led domestic lives. Historians, however, are arguing that the boundaries between private and public were permeable, and a reconsideration of the value of unpaid as well as paid work has led to the discovery of many women whose achievements and influence were not limited to their families. Consequently, biography can recall Johnson's predilection for less famous subjects and take as its topic the lives of hitherto unknown people, as long as there is enough evidence to sustain a study. Scholars are discovering the lives of women who broke the conventional mould and of those who conformed in their various ways. Would such biographies be considered history? My answer is: yes, under certain conditions.

I suggest that there are two criteria for considering if the biography of an unknown figure can have historical value. One is when a woman's—or a man's—achievements tell us about others' lives, or institutions, or attitudes. Does her life illuminate the wider society? Can we find out more about her world as well about her life?

The other criterion is method. A historical biography follows standard rules of historical research. The core of a biography is a body of primary sources: archival documents and the testimony of people who knew the subject. The historian uses such evidence to investigate the influences that form the person's character: family circumstances, education, the ideas that gave rise to the adult world view. Tracking the career, both paid and unpaid, over a lifetime, the historian places the subject into context, and the contexts are multiple.

The biography of any woman has to come to terms with historically specific expectations of gender. Whereas the story of a man's life deals with the impress of the protagonist's character on events, "each woman's story is moulded by a pattern" (Quilligan 261). Early-twentieth-century gender conventions assumed that a woman would live with her family until adulthood, and, after working in one of a narrow range of paid occupations, normally of low responsibility, she would marry, retire from the labour force, and for the rest of her life do unpaid work in a domestic context. She would raise the children while her husband was the breadwinner. She might do volunteer work, but her priority for the rest of her life would be not her own career, or her own life, but her family.

One of the major issues must be the extent to which the particular woman conformed to the dominant expectations of gender. Whether she obeyed or defied expectations, and how, needs explanation. Beyond this fundamental theme, a biographer must explain the particular political, economic, and social circumstances operating during the woman's life and reach a balance between the story of the woman herself and the environments in which she found herself. Simultaneously with the evolving analysis of her achievements is a study of her personality. What were her motivations? What were the important relationships of her life? What were her emotional commitments? Again, the biographer must negotiate the tension between the treatment of achievement and subjectivity.

Let me illustrate my argument by reference to the historical biography I am currently preparing of Mary Agnes McGeachy.

In October 1942, Clementine Churchill, wife of the wartime leader, wrote a note:

> My dear Miss McGeachy,
>
> I have been thrilled to read in all the newspapers that you have been given diplomatic status, and that you are the first woman to receive this distinction.
>   Please accept my warm congratulations. I feel this is a milestone in the history of British women and that we should all be grateful to you for it, and still more for the work you are doing for the Empire.
>
> Yours very sincerely,
> Clementine S. Churchill (Janet Holmes)

The letter raised questions. Who was Miss McGeachy? How had she achieved a milestone for British women? What work was she doing "for the Empire"?

I became interested in writing McGeachy's life. Would others be interested in reading it? I believe: Yes, because her life has historical relevance. McGeachy's story shows the interplay of twentieth-century gender and politics in the life of an ambitious woman born without advantages of wealth or family. It shows how dominant conventions of gender gave opportunities, and frustrations, for a woman that were different from those that affected men. Her career exemplifies some of the major social trends of the last century.

What information do the sources contain that helps us reflect on the work Mary McGeachy was doing for the British Empire?

McGeachy (1901–1991) had an international career. She served in the League of Nations Secretariat in Geneva during the 1930s, then in the British Ministry of Economic Warfare after 1940. She was sent to Washington and toured the United States describing life in the Blitz and in occupied Europe. She was a Canadian and was the first woman to be given British diplomatic rank: Clementine Churchill's "milestone." After the Americans entered the war, her work shifted to include post-war planning.

In 1944, the first worldwide relief agency was established—UNRRA (the United Nations Relief and Rehabilitation Administration). McGeachy was made Director of Welfare, responsible for the needs of women, children, and old people in the Displaced Persons camps of Europe. "Foster-Mother of Europe," the headlines said. She was the only woman in an executive position.

In her mid-forties, she married Erwin Schuller, a Viennese-born banker. Her life changed. She now became a corporate wife and as well a public-spirited woman doing volunteer work. After the war, she lived in Johannesburg, then Toronto, and finally New York, and she became involved with the International Council of Women, an organization promoting women's rights and welfare. For ten years, between 1963 and 1973, she served as president. She experienced first-hand the difficulties of navigating the politics of the Cold War at the level of a non-governmental organization in its liaison with the United Nations.

McGeachy's career was described in the contemporary media. A woman in a man's world was newsworthy. It was a considerable achievement for the daughter of a Gospel Hall preacher from a small city on the Ontario–United States border in Canada.

McGeachy was Ontario-Scots on both sides of her family. She had a brother and two sisters. As adults, all three McGeachy women led unconventional lives. Jessie became a physician and married a widower with two small children. Donalda was an actress then a speech therapist, and lived with a cousin, a woman doctor. Beyond the nuclear family, the McGeachy relatives were enterprising skilled craftsmen and labourers. They included an unmarried uncle who ran a candy store and had a mistress. His financial help augmented the scholarships that Mary McGeachy won to underwrite her University of Toronto career.

McGeachy's intellectual formation was most influenced at university by the Student Christian Movement. Its members were questioning Christians; they were Canadian nationalists, enthusiastic for the new League of Nations, and they acknowledged an obligation for university students to contribute to society. At its meetings, and those of student debating societies, McGeachy found herself among "world-minded" friends for whom Europe was their cultural "source," as she put it later (Archive for Women's History).

Besides earning a degree in history and English literature, McGeachy served on the editorial staff of *Varsity*, the student newspaper, and *The Canadian Student*, the first Canada-wide student journal. So far, she had made her way without any explicit restraint due to gender. But, when she applied to study for a graduate degree in history, she was advised to apply instead to the United States, on the grounds that she would not later get an academic position in her own country. "In Canada there are very few colleges for women," said her advisor, "and in co-educational institutions it is very hard to secure the appointment of a woman to the staff. [. . .] Hitherto, the authorities have preferred to appoint a man" (Prentice 212). McGeachy instead took a year's teacher training and then taught for two years at a high school in Hamilton, an industrial city near Toronto.

In 1927, she went on leave in order to attend conferences in Switzerland. Travelling around Europe, she decided she wanted to stay. She found a temporary job as editor of an international student newspaper, *Vox Studentium*, based in Geneva. In the summer of 1928, she succeeded in getting a position in the League of Nations.

McGeachy was thrilled. "Every serious young person wanted to work for the League in those days." For the next twelve years of her life, she said, "everything in my life was connected. There was no separation of work and life. Every waking moment went to the League. [. . .] It was an experiment. There were no precedents. Who wouldn't have been inspired!" (Moorhouse). She was an officer in the Information Section of the League, where, amongst other responsibilities, she interacted with the volunteer groups who lobbied the League in Geneva.

After the virtual collapse of the League in 1940, McGeachy went to work for the British Ministry of Economic Warfare and was sent to the United States as part of the propaganda machine to persuade the Americans to support the British side during the war. She was appointed First Secretary at the Embassy in Washington and in 1942 she was given diplomatic status.

McGeachy was in charge of liaison with volunteer agencies that were expecting to help with post-war relief. When UNRRA was established at the end of 1943, McGeachy, as a protegée of its deputy director-general, was appointed welfare director, the only woman in a top executive position.

It was half way through her tenure there that she married Schuller. After the termination of the UNRRA position, she retired from the labour force and took up volunteer work and concentrated on being the corporate wife in Johannesburg, Toronto, and finally New York. Obeying the prevailing gender conventions, she adopted two children, thus fulfilling "normality" by embracing motherhood.

What the primary documents show is that this smooth progression from one accomplishment to another, unusual for a woman, was not because of a recognition of her outstanding talents. Rather, her positions were achieved by persistence, hard work, and deliberate effort on her part, which can only be described as ambition. Without this supposedly masculine attribute, she would have been nowhere.

In 1928, her initial attempt to join the League was unsuccessful, so she lobbied the Personnel Department and offered to take only temporary employment until she was given a probationary term. After getting the job, she was not satisfied: she wanted promotion. For ten of her years in the Information Section of the League, she was resentful of having to remain at the same level. She let off steam in her correspondence with a Canadian newspaper editor, J.W. Dafoe, of the *Winnipeg Free Press*.

During the war, in the Ministry of Economic Warfare, her antics of self-promotion were mocked by her colleague, British intellectual historian Isaiah Berlin, who in private letters called her a "bare-faced equestrienne," and a "beautiful trapeze artist" (Wolfson College, Oxford).

In UNRRA, she found herself in charge of a head-office split between Washington and London and staff of primarily two nationalities. It was divided also by different approaches to the task in hand. The Americans, who considered themselves modern professional social workers, were dismissive toward the British, who to some extent celebrated volunteers in relief work. Her American subordinates caricatured her as the champion of the British way of bureaucracy as well as of relief work, and, throughout her time as director of Welfare, McGeachy had to withstand efforts to displace her. In the event, she outlasted most of her detractors, and her term as Welfare director lasted twice as long as that of most UNRRA officials in executive positions.

Twenty years later, as president of the International Council of Women, McGeachy found herself on the receiving end of what were described as "dirty tricks" during her own election. When there were candidates ready to succeed her two-term stint as president, she in turn manoeuvred to be offered a third term herself. Her ten-year presidency was not handed to her on a platter: she lobbied for it discreetly but effectively.

These signs of ambition were not evident from the interviews McGeachy gave during the war or in the short biography she prepared for her colleagues in the International Council of Women. Evidence for her appetite for power is to be found in archives, in the archives of the League, the correspondence of editor J.W. Dafoe, the personal papers of Isaiah Berlin, and the archives of UNRRA and the International Council of Women.

163

A more complete impression emerges of McGeachy the politician, fighting for her personal turf as well as for the ideas and the policies in which she believed. In no way does this portrait detract from her overall achievement. That can be said now, at the beginning of the twenty-first century, because of a change in cultural climate. As Carolyn Heilbrun noted, for most of the twentieth century it was impossible for women to admit the claim of achievement and ambition and the recognition that "accomplishment was neither luck nor the result of the efforts or generosity of others" (24). Times have changed. Ambition in a woman is no longer taboo. A public life, under certain circumstances, is acceptable, even praiseworthy, for a woman (*Times*).

Documents in the archives give clues that McGeachy's family life was not as bland as she liked to suggest. I was able to corroborate her personal life in correspondence and interviews with family members, developing an oral history archive that substantially augmented the written record and extended it in different directions. This information showed that the Schuller children suffered an unhappy childhood, and in 1967 her husband, Erwin, took his own life. Such tragedies beg explanations, but the historical method does not readily yield them.

As a historical biography, McGeachy's story tells us about differing gender conventions for men and women. Her own career and her husband's were miles apart, for instance, in the options available, the accommodation of ambition, and in their respective remuneration.

Her life also illuminates at the individual level different aspects of twentieth-century politics. McGeachy engaged in the struggles to substitute collective security and international co-operation for aggression and war. She was a part of the allied war effort. She contributed to the resumption of an ordered society after the colossal dislocation and brutality of World War II. She knew from her husband's experience what it meant to be defined as a Jew in Central Europe and to be treated as an enemy alien in Britain. In South Africa she saw apartheid at close quarters. During her time with the International Council of Women, she became drawn into Cold War politics. Her biography shows how all these trends were translated at a personal level. As French historian Jo Burr Margadant has written, "politics are most easily examined as well as empathetically imagined in the individual life" (7).

The surviving archives, both documentary and oral, cannot see into McGeachy's soul, although they do give a remarkable glimpse into her religious ideas throughout her life. Mysteries remain. There is a limit to the historian's speculation as to why she seemed unable to love her children and why her husband at the age of fifty-eight could not bear to live any longer. What the archives are able to do is document her accomplishments, achievements that contribute to our understanding of twentieth-century society and conventions. Through the picture of a complex personality who both defied and conformed to the dominant gender conventions of her time, we learn more about the assumptions of appropriate behaviour for men and women.

Is Biography History?

Biography as a genre is set to introduce new areas for academic discourse. As Richard Holmes, the first professor of biographical studies in a British university, writes, biography can serve as a link between the contemporary theoretical remoteness of university arts faculties and their wider communities. Biography, he argues, is a "bridge back: back into the living community, back into the collective memory, back into contention" (*Sunday Times*). As befits the editor of the multi-volume *New Dictionary of National Biography*, Brian Harrison sees no sign of decline for biography as a genre of historical writing (16).

In conclusion, I return to the subject of Dr. Johnson's gaze. I trust that my own biography of McGeachy will prove to be, in his words, "of the various kinds of narrative writing, that which is most eagerly read, and most easily applied to the purposes of Life" ("Idler").

WORKS CITED

Archival Collections

Archive for Women's History (AVG), Brussels. International Council of Women Collection.

National Archives of Canada. Mary Agnes Craig McGeachy and Erwin Schuller Collection.

United Nations Archives, Geneva. League of Nations Collection.

United Nations Archives, New York. United Nations Relief and Rehabilitation Administration Collection.

University of Manitoba Archives. J.W. Dafoe Collection.

Wolfson College, Oxford. Isaiah Berlin Archive.

Published Sources

Ankersmit, F.R. "Historiography and Postmodernism." *History and Theory*. Ed. Brian Fay et al. Oxford: Blackwell, 1998. 175–92.

_____ ."Reply to Professor Zagorin." *History and Theory*. Ed. Brian Fay et al. Oxford: Blackwell, 1998. 206–22.

Beales, Derek. *History and Biography: An Inaugural Lecture*. Cambridge: Cambridge University Press, 1981.

Boswell, James. *Life of Johnson*. Ed. R.W. Chapman [a new edition corrected by J.D. Fleeman]. London: Oxford University Presss, 1970.

Braudel, Ferdinand. *The Mediterranean in the Age of Philip II*. Trans. Sian Reynolds. London: HarperCollins, 1992.

Cameron, Elspeth. "Biography and Feminism." *Language in Her Eye: Views on Writing and Gender by Canadian Women Writing in English.* Ed. Libby Scheier et al. Toronto: Coach House Press, 1990. 72–82.

Caplan, Jane. "Postmodernism, Poststructuralism, and Deconstruction: Notes for Historians." *Central European History* 22.3/4 (1989): 260–78.

Carlyle, Thomas. "Biography." *English and Other Critical Miscellanies in Six Volumes.* London: Chapman and Hall, 1869. 3–22.

____ . "On History." *English and Other Critical Miscellanies in Six Volumes.* London: Chapman and Hall, 1869. 345–59.

____ . *On Heroes, Hero-Worship and the Heroic in History.* Intr. Michael K. Goldberg. Berkeley: University of California Press, 1993.

Carr, E.H. *What Is History?* 2nd ed. Ed. R.W. Davies. London: Macmillan, 1986.

Coleman, D.C. "History, Economic History and the Numbers Game." *Historical Journal* 38.3 (1995): 635–46.

Eddy, Donald D., ed. *Samuel Johnson and Periodical Literature.* New York: Garland, 1978.

____ . *Samuel Johnson and Periodical Literature. The Universal Chronicle.* New York: Garland, 1979, II.

Evans, Mary. *Missing Persons.* London: Routledge, 1999.

Evans, Richard J. *In Defence of History.* 2nd ed. London: Granta, 2000.

Figes, Orlando. *A People's Tragedy: The Russian Revolution, 1891–1924.* London: Jonathan Cape, 1996.

Gaffield, Chad. "Word from the President." *Bulletin of the Canadian Historical Association* 27.1 (2001): 2.

Glendinning, Victoria. "Lies and Silences." *The Troubled Face of Biography.* Ed. Eric Homberger and John Charmley. London: Macmillan, 1988. 49–62.

Harrison, Brian. "National Biography for a Computer Age." *History Today* 51.8 (August 2001): 16–18.

Haslam, Jonathan. *The Vices of Integrity: E.H. Carr, 1892–1982.* London: Verso, 1999.

Heilbrun, Carolyn G. *Writing a Woman's Life.* London: The Women's Press, 1989.

Holmes, Richard. "It's a Real Life Opportunity for Everyone." *Sunday Times* (London) 13 May 2001.

Huppert, George. "The 'Annales' Experiment." *Companion to Historiography.* Ed. Michael Bentley. London: Routledge, 1997. 873–88.

Hutcheon, Linda. "The Particular Meets the Universal." *Language in Her Eye: Views on Writing and Gender by Canadian Women Writing in English.* Ed. Libby Scheier et al. Toronto: Coach House Press, 1990. 148–51.

Johnson, Samuel. "The Idler," Number 85. *Samuel Johnson and Periodical Literature. The Universal Chronicle.* Ed. Donald D. Eddy. New York: Garland, 1978.

_____ . *Johnson's Lives of the British Poets*. Completed by William Hazlitt. London: Nathaniel Cooke, 1854.

_____ . *Life of Savage*. Ed. Clarence Tracy. Oxford: Clarendon Press, 1971.

_____ . "The Rambler," Number 60. *Samuel Johnson and Periodical Literature*. Ed. Donald D. Eddy. New York: Garland, 1978.

Kershaw, Ian. *Hitler, 1889–1936: Hubris*. London: Allen Lane, The Penguin Press, 1998.

Lipstadt, Deborah E. *Denying the Holocaust: The Growing Assault on Truth and Memory*. New York: Macmillan, 1993.

Margadant, Jo Burr. *The New Biography: Performing Femininity in Nineteenth-Century France*. Berkeley: University of California Press, 2000.

McKillop, Brian. "Storytellers in the Archives?" Presentation to a panel discussion, "The Return of the Narrator," at the Canadian Historical Association, Quebec City, 26 May 2001, 8, 20.

Moorhouse, Frank. "A League of Her Own." *Sydney Morning Herald* 4 September 1993.

Nadel, Ira Bruce. *Biography: Fiction, Fact and Form*. London: Macmillan, 1984.

Nelles, H.V. "Rewriting History." *Saturday Night* February 1981.

Novick, Peter. *That Noble Dream: The "Objectivity Question" and the American Historical Profession*. Cambridge: Cambridge University Press, 1988.

Perry, Adele. "The Historian and the Theorist Revisited." *Histoire Sociale / Social History* 33.65 (May 2000): 145–51.

Plutarch. *Lives of the Noble Greeks and Romans*. Trans. John Dryden, rev. Arthur Hugh Clough. New York: The Modern Library, 1932.

Prentice, Alison. "Laying Siege to the History Professoriate." *Creating Historical Memory*: *English-Canadian Women and the Work of History*. Ed. Beverly Boutilier and Alison Prentice. Vancouver: University of British Columbia Press, 1997. 197–232.

Quilligan, Maureen. "Rewriting History: The Difference of Feminist Biography." *The Yale Review* 77 (1988): 2, 259–86.

Rigby, H. "Marxist Historiography." *Companion to Historiography*. Ed. Michael Bentley. London: Routledge, 1997. 889–928.

Rose, Hilary. "The New Face of Painting." *The Times Saturday Magazine (London)* 23 June 2001, 36–38.

Shelston, Alan. *Biography*. London: Methuen, 1977.

Skidelsky, Robert. "Only Connect: Biography and Truth." *The Troubled Face of Biography*. Ed. Eric Homberger and John Charmley. London: Macmillan, 1988. 1–16.

Strachey, Lytton. *Eminent Victorians*. London: Chatto and Windus, 1918.

"This is Women's Work" *The Times (London)*. 8 May 2001.

White, Hayden. "The Historical Text as Literary Artifact." *History and Theory: Contemporary Readings*. Ed. Brian Fay et al. Oxford: Blackwell, 1998.

Woolf, Virginia. *A Room of One's Own*. London: Chatto and Windus, The Hogarth Press, 1984.

Zagorin, Perez. "Historiography and Postmodernism: Reconsiderations." *History and Theory: Contemporary Readings*. Ed. Brian Fay et al. Oxford: Blackwell, 1998. 193–205.

Did Paley Ignore Hume
on the Argument from Design?

Murdith McLean

Bernard Williams spoke for many professional philosophers when he thus concluded a study of David Hume's *Dialogues Concerning Natural Religion*: "After all this, little seems to be left of the Argument from Design, or indeed of the Christian conception of God" (87). A puzzle begins to emerge with the fact that what is often appealed to as a standard statement of this discredited argument is the version put forward by William Paley. Paley's *Natural Theology,* in which the famous analogy between watch and world was expounded, first appeared in 1802, twenty-three years after Hume's withering criticisms were published (posthumously) in *Dialogues.*

Commentators have not been slow to note this curiosity and have tended to assume that Paley was ignorant of Hume's accomplishment, or at least that he paid no attention to it. "Ironically, Paley's argument was attacked even before Paley set it down," writes Louis Pojman, "for David Hume [. . .] had long before written his famous *Dialogues Concerning Natural Religion,* [. . .] the classical critique of the teleological argument." Pojman observes, "Paley seems to have been unaware of it" (48). Paley scholar D.L. LeMahieu stops short of asserting that Paley was ignorant of Hume's demolition work but suggests at least that he chose to disregard it. "William Paley," he observes, "repeated virtually every one of Cleanthes's arguments, while at the same time adding an enormous amount of fresh empirical verification." But, he concludes, "in essence, Paley utterly ignored Hume's objections" (129). John Hick shares the sense of irony at what he, too, takes to be Paley's disregard of Hume. "The classic critique of the design argument occurs in David Hume's *Dialogues Concerning Natural Religion.* [. . .] Paley took no apparent account of Hume's criticisms—by no means the only example of lack of communication between theologians and their philosophical critics!" (24).

Faith, Reason, and Economics: Essays in Honour of Anthony Waterman. Ed. Derek Hum. Winnipeg: St. John's College Press, 2003.

The sense of incongruity deepens when one notices the remarkable durability of Paley's argument. For close to 100 years after its publication, Paley's justification of theism—apparently undermined before it was even set down—was a staple not only of theological education for ordinands but also of the general curriculum for students in the English-speaking world. Charles Darwin, speaking of his studies at Cambridge in the late 1820s, testifies: "In order to pass the B.A. examination, it was, also, necessary to get up Paley's *Evidences of Christianity*, and his *Moral Philosophy*. [. . .] The logic of this book and, as I may add, of his *Natural Theology*, gave me as much delight as did Euclid. The careful study of these works, without attempting to learn any part by rote, was the only part of the Academical Course which, as I then felt, and as I still believe, was of the least use to me in the education of my mind" (22).

Can it be that Paley's readers and their descendants for at least a couple of generations were as ignorant or neglectful of Hume as Paley himself is said to be? That is certainly LeMahieu's view. "The tremendous popularity of [Paley's] work," he says, "offers further testimony to the common-place but often forgotten assertion that Hume was an isolated figure in his own time" (129f).

My main argument in this paper is directed against the suggestion that Paley's case is simply an unwitting restatement of the argument which Hume is said to have demolished nearly a quarter-century earlier. I shall argue that it is difficult to suppose that Paley was unaware of Hume's arguments. But more importantly, I shall argue that Paley's case is constructed in such a way that many of Hume's principal criticisms are avoided or resisted. A close look at the relevant text invites the hypothesis that Paley's argument was formed in part by an exposure to Hume's discussion, whether or not the Archdeacon had *Dialogues* before him as he composed his treatise, or had Hume in the forefront of his mind as author of the case he was attempting to answer. My argument to this effect may also have the result of undermining a second notion: that Paley's following can be explained only by a shared ignorance of Hume on the part of Paley's readers, for I shall argue in passing that not only does Paley's argument show signs of having been formulated in part as a result of contact with Hume's objections but it should also be granted a measure of success in dealing with them.

The most telling evidence that Paley was not ignorant of Hume's strictures lies in an explicit mention in *Natural Theology*. "Mr. Hume, in his posthumous dialogues, asserts indeed of *idleness*, or aversion to labour, (which he states to lie at the root of a considerable part of the evils which mankind must suffer,) that it is simply and merely bad" (qtd. in Paxton 416, emph. Paley's). It must be admitted that this appears as little more than an aside. Why is it that we find no mention of Hume in the body of Paley's argument? Paley's own account of his scholarly practice suggests an answer. "I have scarcely ever referred to any other book; or mentioned the name of the author whose thoughts, and sometimes, possibly, whose very expressions, I have adopted. My method of writing has constantly been this; to extract what I could from my own stores and my own reflections in the first place; to put down that, and afterwards to consult upon each subject such readings as fell my way; which order, I am convinced, is the only one whereby any person can keep his thoughts from sliding into other men's trains" (E. Paley xiv–xv).

Paley speaks here, of course, about authors and writings the general drift of which he shares; but it is safe to assume that he worked just as informally, by today's standards, with authors whose ideas he was countering. Paley, in company with many of his contemporaries, simply did not generally work by focussing on particular texts of particular authors with whom he agreed or disagreed. The reading of those texts added to the general store of views which he then drew upon in expressing his own outlook, whether by agreement or disagreement, without the names of their authors necessarily being mentioned or even recalled (see E. Paley 136ff).

Did Paley, then, simply ignore Hume's objections? My estimate is that he did not, in at least this sense: Paley's argument is developed in such a way that it eludes a number of Hume's principle objections and entails a more or less explicit response to others. It is unlikely that Paley had *Dialogues* in front of him as he wrote. And I do not believe that he had Hume vividly in mind as he composed his case. But, given the structure of Paley's argument, and the near certainty that he was well aware of *Dialogues,* it is difficult to resist the impression that Paley's argument was formed, in part, by its author's absorbing Hume's critique in the course of some earlier exposure to it.

My general strategy here is simply to recall the criticisms advanced by Hume against teleological argument and show how Paley's argument is elaborated in such a way that it sidesteps or addresses many of them. Paley's case, I submit, is the sort of response to Hume that we might expect from one whose scholarly habits were as Paley describes his own.

Hume's elegant rendition of the argument from design is placed in the mouth of Cleanthes:

> Look round the world: contemplate the whole and every part of it: you will find it to be nothing but one great machine, subdivided into an infinite number of lesser machines, which again admit of subdivision, to a degree beyond what human sense and faculties can trace and explain. All these various machines, and even their most minute parts, are adjusted to each other with an accuracy, which ravishes into admiration all men, who have ever contemplated them. The curious adapting of means to ends, throughout all nature, resembles exactly, though it much exceeds, the productions of human contrivance; of human design, thought, wisdom, and intelligence. Since therefore the effects resemble each other, we are led to infer, by all the rules of analogy, that the causes also resemble; and that the Author of Nature is somewhat similar to the

mind of men; though possessed of much larger faculties, proportioned to the grandeur of the work, which he has executed. (Smith 143)

Notice two features of the argument as Hume frames it here, both arising from the analogy at its core. First, the argument is based, on the one hand, on an analogy between the whole world, regarded as a vast teleological system sub-dividable into component systems; and, on the other, on individual "produc-tions of human contrivance." Second, the analogy employed is a textbook example of "analogical reasoning." From the fact that two items are known to be alike in one or more specific respect(s), the inference is drawn that they are also alike in some further respect, which only one of them is known to possess (see, e.g., Salmon 117–18). Given that the world and machines are alike in displaying the "curious adapting of means to ends," the conclusion is drawn that they are alike in a further respect, which only machines are known to possess, that is, having an intelligent designer.

Hume's objections to this inference are, I shall presume, voiced largely by Philo. They emerge in the course of a dialogue embellished with rhetorical flourishes and with the interjections of theological hard-liner Demea, so it is not a straightforward undertaking to individuate and identify them. With that *proviso*, let me suggest that Hume offers, through Philo, something like eight criticisms of theistic argument from apparent design.

Hume's first complaint is that the analogy between world and machine is too weak to support the inference. "The dissimilitude is so striking," objects Philo, "that the utmost you can here pretend to is a guess, a conjecture, a presumption concerning a similar cause; and how that pretension will be received in the world, I leave you to consider" (Smith 144). The assumption is that an argu-ment to the similarity of two things in sharing some feature we know only one of them to have must rest on the two things being sufficiently similar overall. But, Philo insists, the universe is simply not enough like, say, a house, to support the reasoning. Given the enormous dissimilarities between the uni-verse and things known to have intelligent designers, the move to an intelli-gent designer for the universe is a gratuitous leap.

Second; Hume asks what reason we have to single out intelligent design as the origin of the world's order. It is true, Hume concedes in the words of Philo, that we observe thoughtful design as one of the origins of changes in material order; but it is only one. There is a general difficulty here, he contends, in generalizing from the way that outcomes are generated in one part of the uni-verse to a view about how the universe as a whole is produced. And, even were we to allow that, it seems arbitrary to seize upon deliberate design as the causal influence to generalize in this way. "But allowing that we were to take the *operations* of one part of nature upon another for the foundation of our judg-ment concerning the *origin* of the whole (which never can be admitted), yet why select so minute, so weak, so bounded a principle as the reason and design of animals is found to be upon this planet? What peculiar privilege has this little agitation of the [b]rain which we call thought, that we must thus make it the model of the whole universe?" (Smith 148).

Third; Hume suggests that the whole analogy-drawing enterprise founders on the fact that we have only one universe. What warrants our inferring that some entity, say a house, has some other entity, say a builder, associated with it, insists Philo/Hume, is that we have prior experience of an association between entities of those two kinds. "When two species of objects have always been observed to be conjoined together, I can infer, by custom, the existence of one wherever I see the existence of the other" (Smith 149). But, of course, we have no experience of the formation of universes to draw upon. Philo presses the point in a series of rhetorical questions. "Have you ever seen nature in any such situation as resembles the first arrangement of the elements? Have worlds ever been formed under your eye? and have you had leisure to observe the whole progress of the phenomenon, from the first appearance of order to its final consummation? If you have, then cite your experience, and deliver your theory" (Smith 151).

Fourth; Philo charges that Cleanthes's move to a designer does not really advance our understanding but only sets us off in a search for further explanations. In fact the problem with looking to a divine planner as an explanation of the world's order, asserts Philo, is that while it is offered as final and "conclusive," it actually sets in motion a search for explanation which cannot be brought to a close. The divine planner stands in as much need of explanation as the ordered world with which we began; and once we admit that, there seems no way we can avoid a flight to infinity in search of reasons. "A mental world, or universe of ideas, requires a cause as much, as does a material world, or universe of objects. [. . .] Have we not the same reason to trace that ideal world into another ideal world, or new intelligent principle: But if we stop, and go no farther; why go so far? Why not stop at the material world? How can we satisfy ourselves without going on *in infinitum*" (Smith 160–61).

Fifth; Hume argues that, if there *is* an analogy sufficient to support the argument, you cannot be sure of arriving at the god of traditional theism in the conclusion. Analogical reasoning, Hume/Philo reminds us once again, rests on the degree of "likeness" which holds between the things compared; the more alike they are with respect to known characteristics, the more they may be inferred to be alike in others they are not known to share. In an argument to causal agents, such as the one we have here, the resulting maxim is "the liker the effects are, which are seen, and the liker the causes, which are inferred, the stronger is the argument" (Smith 165).

The problem is that while the works of nature may be conceded to be far more complex and marvellous than the products of human invention, they are not so different as to support the differences the theist wishes to posit between God and humans. What gets the argument going, Philo suggests, is a degree of similarity alleged between human artefacts and objects in nature. How, then, can we infer the existence of a creator of the latter which is so categorically different from the human creator, in being infinite, perfect, and so on. Indeed, why should we suppose there is just one such divine creator?

> For as the cause ought only to be proportioned to the effect, and the effect, so far as it falls under our cognizance, is not infinite; what pretensions have we, upon your suppositions, to ascribe that attribute to the Divine Being? [. . .]
>
> You have no reason, on your theory, for ascribing perfection to the Deity, even in his finite capacity; or for supposing him free from every error, mistake, or incoherence in his undertakings. [. . .]
>
> And what shadow of an argument, continued Philo, can you produce, from your hypothesis, to prove the unity of the Deity? A great number of men join in building a house or ship, in rearing a city, in framing a commonwealth: why may not several deities combine in contriving and framing a world? (Smith 166–67)

Philo drives the point home with delicious irony. If all one has to go on is this slender fact of apparent resemblance between the world and human contrivance, imagination alone can supply any further suppositions as to the character of this entity. We may as well suppose that the world is the embarrassing product of an "infant Deity," the disparaged effort of an apprentice god, or perhaps the abandoned creation of a retired divinity.

Sixth; Hume raises the possibility that there are other and better analogies than the one at the heart of argument from apparent design. Philo has already complained that there is insufficient likeness between the universe and the products of human contrivance to support an inference to a contriver of the universe. He elaborates with the claim that, if comparisons are to be drawn, there are others more attractive than the one to which Cleanthes appeals. "I affirm that there are other parts of the universe (besides the machines of human invention) which bear still a greater resemblance to the fabric of the world, and which therefore afford a better conjecture concerning the universal origin of this system. These parts are animals and vegetables. The world plainly resembles more an animal or a vegetable, than it does a watch or a knitting-loom. Its cause, therefore, it is more probable, resembles the cause of the former. The cause of the former is generation or vegetation" (Smith 176).

In fact Hume/Philo employs this line of argument, in part, as a kind of *reductio* of the idea of attempting to infer the origin of the universe by appeal to analogy. When Demea complains that the comparison is far-fetched, with no "data" to support it, Philo replies that his whole contention is that there are no data to establish *any* comparison. If one insists that "similarity" is the proper ground for establishing suitable analogies, then Philo insists that his suggestion is at least as good as Cleanthes's (Smith 177).

Seventh; Hume suggests that if we're looking for an explanation of the world's orderliness we need look no farther than a simple appeal to chance variations over infinite time. Hume's critique, and Paley's advocacy, both took place before the intellectual revolution which many would say finished off teleological argument for theism: Darwin's theory of random variation and natural selection. One of the most striking, and impressive, features of Hume's argument is the way in which he anticipates the deflationary effect of a theory like Darwin's. He does this by inviting the reader to consider a series of alternative theories which, Philo claims, would account equally well for the phenomenon of order which gets the Design argument off the ground.

He begins with a variation of the "old Epicurean hypothesis." Assuming a finite number of particles of matter rearranging themselves over an infinite span of time, it follows that an arrangement like the one we now have is bound to occur; in fact will also have occurred both before this time and after it. This conjecture suggests another: that an order like the present one, once established in the course of random re-arrangements, will have the property of preserving itself for a considerable period. "The continual motion of matter, therefore, in less than infinite transpositions, must produce this economy or order; and by its very nature, that order when once established, supports itself, for many ages, if not eternity. But, wherever matter is so poised, arranged, and adjusted as to continue in perpetual motion, and yet preserve a constancy in the forms, its situation must, of necessity, have all the same appearance of art and contrivance, which we observe at present" (Smith 183).

Following this line, Hume arrives at a perfectly proto-Darwinian explanation of order in the world of living things. "It is vain, therefore, to insist upon the uses of the parts in animals or vegetables and their curious adjustment to each other. I would fain know how an animal could subsist, unless its parts were so adjusted? Do we not find, that it immediately perishes whenever this adjustment ceases, and that its matter corrupting tries some new form" (Smith 185).

Eighth and finally; I include an argument which may be regarded as an extension of Hume/Philo's contention that the conclusion of a design argument like Cleanthes's cannot be assumed to resemble in any significant way the god of traditional theism. This is the extensive discussion which takes place in *Dialogues* on the subject of evil.

Hume shrewdly has Demea and Cleanthes begin the catalogue of human misery, the contemplation of which is said by Demea to be the true ground of religious conviction. Philo joins with relish in elaborating the catalogue and extending it to the animal kingdom; but, predictably, he turns this inventory of misery to his own critical purposes.

> And is it possible, Cleanthes [. . .] that after all these reflections, and infinitely more, which might be suggested, you can still persevere in your anthropomorphism, and assert the moral attributes of the Deity, his justice, benevolence, mercy, and rectitude, to be of the same nature with these virtues in

human creature? His power we allow infinite: Whatever he wills is executed: But neither man nor any other animal are happy: Therefore he does not will their happiness. His wisdom is infinite: He is never mistaken in choosing the means to any end: But the course of nature tends not to human or animal felicity: Therefore it is not established for that purpose. (Smith 198)

Cleanthes attempts to reply by disdaining the concept of infinity in theological discourse, maintaining that terms such as "*admirable, excellent, superlatively great, wise, and holy*" (Smith 203, emph. Hume's) represent all that is required by right religion. But Philo swiftly counters the suggestion that the facts of worldly woes may be reconciled with an inference even to a being described with this comparative modesty. "Is the world considered in general, and as it appears to us in this life, different from what a man or such a limited being would, *beforehand,* expect from a very powerful, wise, and benevolent Deity?" (Smith 205, emph. Hume's). The question is rhetorical.

Hume makes it clear that his claim is not that worldly woes are inconsistent with the existence of a benevolent Deity. It is that an argument from the character of the world can never license an *inference to* such a being. "I conclude, that, however consistent the world may be, allowing certain suppositions and conjectures, with the idea of such a Deity, it can never afford us an inference concerning existence" (Smith 205).

I shall assume that the above provides a serviceable account of Hume's main objections to the argument from design, each of them developed in the flowing prose of a dialogue, with amendments, flourishes and variations worked on many of the proposals. Before turning to the question of whether Paley can fairly be accused of "utterly ignoring" them, or even of being "unaware" of them, it must be asked what impression a person in Paley's position might reasonably have had of their import. One may gain a sense of this by touching on the scholarly controversy surrounding the question as to what Hume himself considered the upshot of *Dialogues* to be.

There is considerable controversy, to begin with, on the subject of which figure(s) associated with *Dialogues* should be considered spokesman(men) for their author (Smith 57–59; Penelhum, *Hume* 180–81). Even if we accept the majority view (as I have done above) that Philo is Hume's chief (though not his only) representative, we would still be some distance from establishing what Hume's views were. For it is far from clear what Philo's are. Philo is, of course, the persistent and penetrating critic of Cleanthes's attempts to argue from experience of the world's character to a god that matters. His frequent gestures in the direction of some form of belief are dismissed by many (notably Smith 57–75) as part of their view that he really represents the stark agnosticism expressed in the final paragraph of Hume's *The Natural History of Religion.* By no means everybody agrees, though, that this is Hume's conclusion in *Dialogues.* Even among those who agree that Philo's protestations of faith are not to be taken at face value, there are those who argue (e.g., Penelhum, *Hume* 191–96; *Themes* 206–21; Pike 206–21) that his astonishing *volte-face* in Part 12 of *Dialogues*— where he goes so far as to suggest that the argument to a designing agent is so irresistible that the atheist is really pursuing a semantic quibble in declining to call this agent "god"—requires a more nuanced reading.

The only conclusion that can be drawn is that determining what Hume himself took to be the outcome of his arguments is now, as it must have when they were published, what Terence Penelhum has described as "akin to water-divining" (personal conversation, 20 Feb. 2002). If, therefore, we suppose—as I have argued we should—that William Paley was acquainted with Hume's arguments, it does not follow that he would have regarded them as so utterly destructive of the case from apparent design that they must be met with the explicit and detailed rebuttal later commentators have expected of him.

Paley's case for the existence of God is developed over the course of sixteen chapters: 441 pages in the edition of 1838. He makes no attempt to supply a capsule statement of the argument, so any "in-a-nutshell" rendition of it necessarily omits the astonishing wealth of detail and development which helped make the original a textbook for generations of university students and an inspiration to Darwin. The essential structure of the argument, however, is revealed in the opening of Chapter 1 of *Natural Theology*, though we must fast-forward to the beginning of Chapter 3 to get an explicit conclusion.

> In crossing a heath, suppose I pitched my foot against a *stone* and were asked how the stone came to be there: I might possibly answer that for anything I knew to the contrary it had lain there forever; nor would it, perhaps, be very easy to show the absurdity of this answer. But suppose I had found a *watch* upon the ground, and it should be inquired how the watch happened to be in that place; I should hardly think of the answer which I had before given—that for anything I knew the watch might have always been there. Yet why should not this answer serve for the watch as well as for the stone? Why is it not as admissible in the second case as in the first? For this reason, and for no other, viz. that, when we come to inspect the watch, we perceive (what we could not discover in the stone) that its several parts are framed and put together for a purpose, e.g. that they are so formed and adjusted as to produce motion, and that motion so regulated as to point out the hour of the day. [. . .] This mechanism being observed (it required indeed an examination of the instrument, and perhaps some previous knowledge of the subject, to perceive and understand it; but being once, as we have said, observed and understood), the inference we think is inevitable, that the watch must have had a maker: that there must have existed, at some time and at some place or other, an artificer or artificers who formed it for the purpose which we find it actually to answer; who comprehended its construction and designed its use.
>
> Every indication of contrivance, every manifestation of design, which existed in the watch, exists in the works of nature; with the difference, on the

side of nature, of being greater and more, and that in a degree which exceeds
all computation. (Paxton 1–3, 13)

The conclusion is fully spelled out at the closing of Chapter 23: "Design must
have had a designer. That designer must have been a person. That person is
God" (Paxton 366).

It is insufficiently noticed how different this is from the argument Hume sets
out and attacks. I drew attention above to two central features of Hume's target,
both of them concerning the analogy at its heart: (1) an analogy is drawn
between the world considered as a whole, as well as distinguishable parts of it,
and machines known to be the product of human craft; and (2) the analogy is
the framework for a standard-form argument from analogy. The first of these is
not true of the argument offered by Paley, and the second is only in a qualified
sense.

First, Paley's case involves a parallel between an obviously ordered object,
a watch, and particular *items in* the world, such as the eye of an animal. Paley's
argument does not involve the world considered as a whole; only distinguishable elements of it with parts ordered in such a way that they bring about some
end. Paley took himself to be developing a *cumulative* case, each of a very
large number of instances of teleological order in the natural world contributing to a case in which each instance supports an argument of its own. Chapter 6,
entitled "The Argument Cumulative," concludes with the emphatic assertion
that "the argument is cumulative, in the fullest sense of that term. The eye
proves it without the ear; the ear without the eye. The proof in each example is
complete; for when the design of the part, and the conduciveness of its structure to that design is shown, the mind may set itself at rest" (Paxton 62).

Second, it is crucial to notice that these individual items are compared, in
the first instance, not with machines known to have been designed and created
but with objects simply displaying a striking teleological order. This should
alert us to the fact that Paley's piece of reasoning is not, like Hume's, a straightforward argument from analogy. Paley does not begin with the claim that parts
of the world resemble machines in at least one crucial respect, that is, in being
teleologically organized, and infer from that that those world-parts are therefore likely to resemble machines in another respect known to be possessed by
machines, in having an intelligent designer. In fact Paley goes out of his way to
stress that his argument does not depend in any way on our knowing that
watches have designers. "Nor would it," he insists, "weaken the conclusion,
that we had never seen a watch made; that we had never known an artist capable
of making one; that we were altogether incapable of executing such a piece of
workmanship ourselves; or of understanding in what manner it was performed"
(Paxton 3). What Paley argues is that, in the case of something like a watch, as
in the case of something like an eye, the fact of teleological order cries out for
an explanation. "In the watch which we are examining are seen contrivance,

design, an end, a purpose, means for the end, adaptation to the purpose. And the question which irresistibly presses upon our thoughts is, whence this contrivance and design?" (Paxton 11) He concludes that only an appeal to an intelligent designer will answer the cry. Paley's argument is first of all an argument to a best explanation, combining a case for the claim that an explanation is needed with the claim that God alone provides it.

I shall note below a passage toward the end of *Natural Theology* where Paley does employ analogical reasoning in support of his choice of explanation. And it is clear that more than one of Hume's complaints apply to a designer posited as best explanation. The moral, no doubt, is that there is no great gulf fixed between analogical considerations and inferences to a best explanation. But Paley's argument brings out, in a way that Hume's does not, the sense of something's crying out for explanation. In this connection, one is reminded of the suggestion made by Nelson Pike (204–38) that a distinct and more direct argument may be discerned in Part 3 of *Dialogues,* to which no rebuttal is offered, and which is the ground of Philo's reversal in Part 12. Pike's suggestion is that in this line of reasoning the notion of a designer is said to be evoked immediately by thoughtful consideration of such a thing as the eye. Arguably, Paley's argument is of just this kind.

Already, therefore, we have grounds to be wary of claims to the effect that "William Paley [. . .] repeated virtually every one of Cleanthes's arguments," or that "Paley's argument was attacked even before Paley set it down." Paley's argument is, to begin with, significantly different from the one which Hume attacked.

One consequence of this is that the first of Hume's complaints—a critique of the analogy upon which Hume's (first?) version of the argument is based—must be at least rephrased to have any grip on Paley's case. Hume's objection that "the dissimilitude" between world and machine "is so striking, that the utmost you can here pretend to is a guess, a conjecture," may be a relevant reply to an argument based fundamentally on an inference-licensing analogy between world and machine; but Paley's case is not of this sort. First of all, it rests not on a claim about the whole world but on a series of claims about individual structures within it. There is therefore no need to establish a relevant similarity between the entire cosmos and a mechanism known to be the result of design. Second, Paley's initial appeal is not to an analogy at all but to the mystery presented to us by teleological structures in nature.

Much later (Ch. 23) in *Natural Theology,* Paley does resort to a form of analogical reasoning as backing for his claim that intelligent design alone solves the mystery. It is as though, having relied on the immediate-evocation style of argument for twenty-two chapters, in which examples from the detailed anatomy of fauna and flora are piled one on another, Paley feels obliged to make explicit something underlying the instinctive move from observing these structures to the conviction that a designer is responsible for them.

> Whenever we see marks of contrivance, we are led for its cause to an *intelligent* author. And this transition of the understanding is founded upon uniform experience. We see intelligence constantly contriving; that is, we see intelligence constantly producing effects, marked and distinguished by certain properties; not certain particular properties, but by a kind and class of properties, such as relation to an end, relation of parts to one another, and to a common purpose. We see, wherever we are witnesses to the actual formation of things, nothing except intelligence producing effects so marked and distinguished. Furnished with this experience, we view the productions of nature. We observe *them* also marked and distinguished in the same manner. We wish to account for their origin. Our experience suggests a cause perfectly adequate to this account. No experience, no single instance or example, can be offered in favour of any other. (Paxton 346)

So Hume's worry about the aptness of analogy cannot be ignored, though once again it must be re-expressed to apply to Paley's argument. The multitude of individual items to which Paley draws attention—Hume/Philo might say—simply do not, individually, have enough in common with known contrivances to support a conclusion about common origins. Eyes and seeds and gastric juices and duck mandibles are not sufficiently like lathes or looms or watches for us to infer anything about the origins of natural objects.

It is not difficult to assemble a reply to Hume from the passage just cited. Paley may be understood as stating that what makes a comparison between ordered natural objects and human contrivances useful is not just the sharing of "certain particular properties." Rather, it is the joint ownership of a "*kind and class* of properties, such as relation to an end" (emph. mine), and so on. In the jargon of modern logic, what makes an analogy between two items a satisfactory basis for inference is not the sharing of many properties; they may share quite few. What matters is that they have in common *positively relevant* properties—ones that make the sharing of the additional feature mentioned in the conclusion more likely—and lack negatively relevant properties. Where the positive relevance of shared properties is high, few will suffice. What Paley spends page after page hammering home is the claim that teleological arrangement is so striking, and so relevant, that it supports the instinctive movement in thought (perhaps rooted in a buried analogy) from teleological structure to designer.

Whether Paley wrote as he did with Hume specifically in mind may be doubted. But that his comments here imply a reply to Hume cannot. Hume's criticism seems based on the idea that in drawing conclusions about what a thing is like on the basis of comparing that thing with some other, when it comes to shared characteristics the more the merrier and the fewer the sadder. The response implied by Paley's way of proceeding is that it is entirely appropriate to rest the analogical case on a slender base of highly relevant properties; in this case, the ones he returns to again and again in his examples from nature.

And surely on this point, Paley is correct. It is not (contra Hume) the length of the list of resemblances that counts; it is the relevance of its contents. Teleological organization is highly relevant to the additional property of intelligent design. It should not be surprising that Paley's nineteenth-century readers were impressed by his catalogue of teleological structures.

Hume's second (in my list) criticism must also be transposed to apply to Paley. Hume's complaint is that we have no business generalizing from one way ordered things are produced in one corner of the cosmos to a supposition as to how the entire cosmos came to be. Again, though Paley does conclude to a creator of all, his case does not rest on the universe considered as whole. Hume's objection must be applied to Paley's argument by rephrasing it as a complaint about the arbitrariness of selecting the agency of thinking beings as a model to explain the origins of teleological systems in nature. Why pick out intelligent activity as the putative explanation of eyes and all the rest?

For the most part, it appears that Paley is bent on arousing his reader's sense of wonder at the apparent design of natural objects, on the assumption that, once aroused, it will find satisfaction only in the theistic explanation. Nevertheless, Paley is driven by something like the question Hume raises here to set out the analogical thinking cited above. Having observed teleologically structured natural objects, Paley observes, "we wish to account for their origin. Our experience suggests a cause perfectly adequate to this account. No experience, no single instance or example, can be offered in favour of any other." Why single out intelligent agency as the explanation for the order we observe in nature? Because, Paley avers, it is our uniform experience that this, and this alone, is what produces order in things.

One can imagine Hume reminding us, in the spirit of Philo's criticism listed sixth above, that in fact we *do* observe other things bringing about order in nature. We observe animal and vegetable generation leading to many of those instances of order that move Paley to talk about the necessity of a designer. Why wouldn't those things do as well to relieve any sense of mystery we may have concerning the origin of origins of teleological order in nature?

Paley meets this proposal head-on. He imagines that the discoverer of the watch learns that "it possessed the unexpected property of producing, in the course of its movements, another watch like itself" and asks what effect this should have on his inclination to suppose the watch to have a creator. His answer is that "he would perceive, in this new observation, nothing but an additional reason for doing what he had already done—for referring the construction of the watch to design, and to supreme art." He goes on to insist that, although "the watch before him were, *in some sense*, the maker of the watch which was fabricated in the course of its movements" (emph. Paley's), it cannot be regarded as the originator of its "constitution and order" (Paxton 7).

Later, Paley considers specifically the claim that "the air, the light, the elements, the world itself, is *generated*" (Paxton 354, emph. Paley's). Paley professes

181

incomprehension at the suggestion. "I am at a loss to conceive, how the formation of the world can be compared to the generation of an animal. If the term generation signify something quite different from what it signifies on ordinary occasions, it may, by the same latitude, signify any thing. In which case, a word or phrase taken from the language of Otaheite would convey as much theory concerning the origin of the universe, as it does to talk of its being generated" (Paxton 354f).

Beyond this, however, it is plain that in Paley's encyclopaedic treatment of examples from nature, the processes of plant and animal generation are believed to call out for an explanation, not to provide one. It is not difficult to suppose that Paley's readers shared his intuition on this matter. Indeed, as pointed out above, it is easy to think that in the last analysis Philo and Hume align themselves with Paley on this point. It may well be that the question of which processes and events demand further explanation, and which ones provide a satisfactory resting place, can be answered only in terms that take context into account. Nevertheless, Paley's assumption that "generation" falls into the former class, and not the latter, chimes well with the instincts of many. This second of Hume's criticisms hardly seems devastating when placed up against Paley's case.

Consider now Hume's objection (third in my list) that no analogy can be employed here because we have not observed a number of universes coming into being through intelligent agency. This protest surely rests on a confusion. Hume is considering an argument from analogy, but his complaint treats it as though it is an induction by enumeration. When we appeal to an analogy as the basis for inferring some property of a U, we look to things we believe are relevantly similar to, but not identical with, U's as the basis for our reasoning precisely because we lack the right sort of access to U's themselves. Hume's complaint that we have not observed universes being fashioned misses the point. Paley's argument is similarly untouched by Hume's criticism. If Paley even considered it, he could be excused for ignoring it.

Consider now Hume's objection (fourth in my list) that explaining the universe by reference to a designer merely invites a further and unstoppable quest for explanations. In Chapter 23 of *Natural Theology,* Paley pursues a line of argument relevant to this complaint.

> The *not* having that in his nature which requires the exertion of another prior being, (which property is sometimes called self-sufficiency, and sometimes self-comprehension) appertains to the Deity, as his essential distinction, and removes his nature from that of all things which we see. Which consideration contains the answer to a question that has sometimes been asked, namely, Why, since something or other must have existed from eternity, may not the present universe be that something? The contrivance perceived in it proves that to be impossible. Nothing contrived can, in a strict and proper sense, be eternal, forasmuch as the contriver must have existed before the contrivance. (Paxton 346, emph. Paley's)

It must be admitted that this combination of flat assertion concerning a face-saving attribute of God, and question-begging on the matter of "contrivance," does not constitute an impressive reply to a complaint like Hume's. Indeed the response framed by Cleanthes is considerably more satisfying. He refers again to that immediate impression of order requiring an orderer and maintains there is no reason to feel embarrassed at stopping there. "You ask me, what is the cause of this cause? I know not; I care not; that concerns not me. I have found a Deity; and here I stop my enquiry. Let those go farther, who are wiser or more enterprising" (Smith 163). Paley's implied response, though less apposite than Cleanthes's, is relevant nevertheless. It should further undermine the idea that Paley simply and uncritically reproduced the argument attacked by Hume in *Dialogues,* though in this case it must be acknowledged that Paley does little to turn the edge of Hume's critical weapon.

This brings me to the fifth in my list of Hume's criticisms: the objection that an argument from design does not necessarily yield the god of traditional theism. Hume's point is that the very analogy which grounds the inference leads to the anthropomorphism Philo delights in ridiculing. Once again, one finds material in Paley's argument which relates directly to this challenge. Chapter 24 of *Natural Theology* is entitled "The Natural Attributes of the Deity," and in it Paley employs three strategies to connect the conclusion of his argument with the deity worshipped in the Christian tradition.

To begin with, Paley takes quite a different view from Philo as to the sort of attributes one is warranted in ascribing to a creator of the cosmos. Philo insists that we have no more reason to ascribe the standard list of perfections to God on the basis of what we observe than an observer would be in postulating an ingenious boat builder on the basis of viewing an impressive vessel. In the latter case, it may actually be the product of a dim-witted and imitative crafts-man at the end of a string of failed attempts. A similar possibility must be allowed in the case of the universe. Paley's makes the case for quite a different conclusion. "The *attributes* of [God], suppose his reality to be proved, must be adequate to the magnitude, extent, and multiplicity of his operations: which are not only vast beyond comparison with those performed by any other power, but, so far as respects our conceptions of them, infinite, because they are unlim-ited on all sides" (Paxton 366f, emph. Paley's). Of course Paley is here elaborat-ing the reasoning exhibited by Cleanthes in his original statement of the argu-ment. Interestingly, a similar move is also voiced by Philo, but with a different purpose. At the outset of Part 5, Philo argues that the comparative scope and grandeur of the cosmos, and our increasing awareness of its complex structures, make it hard to infer anything very like a human designer. Cleanthes is then made to insist that the mind of the designer must be like a human mind. "The liker the better, insisted Philo. To be sure, said Cleanthes" (Smith 166). It is not at all clear why Cleanthes feels driven to this crude anthropomorphism. His original position, that "the Author of nature is somewhat similar to the mind of man; though possessed of much larger faculties, proportioned to the grandeur of the work, which he has executed," seems orthodox enough. In any case, Paley adopts something like the position originally occupied by Cleanthes, and repeated by Philo, but maintains—as does Philo—that the comparison of nature with human artefacts points *away* from anthropomorphism.

The second element in Paley's strategy emerges from this same line of reasoning. Paley interprets the traditional attributes—omnipotence, omniscience, and the rest—as essentially superlatives born of our lacking the grounds to assign any limit to the quality in question. His explication of omnipotence serves as an example. "We ascribe power to the Deity under the name of 'omnipotence,' the strict and correct conclusion being, that a power which could create such a world as this is, must be, beyond all comparison, greater than any which we experience in ourselves, than any which we observe in other visible agents; greater also than any which we can want, for our individual protection and preservation, in the Being upon whom we depend. It is a power, likewise, to which we are not authorized, by our observation or knowledge, to assign any limits of space or duration" (Paxton 368). Paley uses this approach to explicate a sense for "infinite" in this context; a concept notably attacked by Philo and repudiated by Cleanthes. "The degree of knowledge and power requisite for the formation of created nature cannot, with respect to us, be distinguished from infinite" (369). This construal of the attributes is hardly the full-blooded interpretation descended from neo-Platonism which orthodox theology has traditionally employed. But it is considerably richer and closer to the tradition that the raw anthropomorphism to which Cleanthes somehow feels impelled.

Paley's third step is to appeal to revelation, the revelation for which Philo is represented as expressing a "longing desire" at the conclusion of *Dialogues* (Smith 227). Paley concludes, "These points being assured to us by Natural Theology, we may well leave to Revelation the disclosure of many particulars, which our researches cannot reach, respecting either the nature of this Being as the original cause of all things, or his character and designs as a moral governor; and not only so, but the more full confirmation of other particulars, of which, though they do not lie altogether beyond our reasonings, and our probabilities, the certainty is by no means equal to the importance" (Paxton 437).

There is more (Paley, for instance, devotes a chapter to establishing the unity of God in what could be taken as a reply to Philo's contention that a multiplicity of designers is more legitimate inference than a single being), but perhaps enough has been said to reinforce the notion that Paley does not ignore the issues raised in what I have identified as the fifth of Hume's objections to argument from design.

Since Hume's seventh criticism—the complaint that the beneficent character of any designer cannot be inferred—is a near-relative, let me comment on that now. Philo's negative case is, of course, built out of the familiar data of the problem of evil, particularly natural evil. His claim is not that this evil is inconsistent with the goodness of a designer, but that goodness cannot be inferred from the character of the alleged creation. In Chapter 26, "The Goodness of the Deity," Paley argues precisely that it can.

Paley bases his claim on two propositions, each of which he argues can be supported by attending to nature: (1) the workings of nature where design is apparent are, on the whole, beneficial to creatures in the sense that they serve their interests; and (2) nature provides pleasure to sentient creatures beyond what is needed to serve their needs. Space does not permit even a summary of his arguments to these effects. Suffice it to say that, in attempting to support the first proposal, he recognizes that that which is "serviceable" to one creature (e.g., the equipment for successful predation) may be harmful to another and offers responses of varying plausibility. As backing for the second proposition, Paley draws attention to a vast range of behaviour which suggests gratuitous experiences of pleasure on the part of an array of sentient beings, from swarms of new-born flies through shoals of leaping fish, to humankind. (Paley is marvellously non-anthropocentric!) One might think that in all this the Archdeacon takes an overly optimistic view of the balance of goods over evils—a charge which he anticipates and attempts to rebut. Some of his examples offered in support of this balance display ingenuity, while others may strike us as quaint. Paley's defence of the *infinite* goodness of the creator is of a piece with his earlier apology for limitless divine attributes. "What is benevolence at all, must in him be *infinite* benevolence, by reason of the infinite, that is to say, the incalculably great, number of objects upon which it is exercised" (Paxton 402).

This impressionistic account of Paley's arguments concerning the inference to divine benevolence cannot support a balanced consideration of their cogency. I submit that Paley's case is not implausible, but the reader will need to weigh Paley's detailed arguments to form a grounded opinion on that score. What is clear even from this summary, however, is that it cannot be said that Paley disregards the claim that one cannot infer a *benevolent* designer from the data of nature.

There remains to be considered one powerful criticism voiced by Philo of design arguments: the one in which Hume anticipates Darwin. Although I have argued that Paley's argument is materially different from the one considered by Hume in ways that affect relevance of Philo's case, this objection is a direct challenge to Paley. Paley's argument is to a best explanation, and Hume/Philo proposes that another explanation, in terms of random variation over time, is as good as or better than Paley's.

Interestingly, Paley considers precisely this proposal. "There is another answer, which has the same effect as the resolving of things into chance; which answer would persuade us to believe, that the eye, the animal to which it belongs, every other animal, every plant, indeed every organized body which we see, are only so many out of the possible varieties and combinations of being, which the lapse of infinite ages has brought into existence; that the present world is the relic of that variety; millions of other bodily forms and other species having perished, being by the defect of their constitution incapable of preservation, or of continuance by generation." Paley greets the suggestion with scorn. "Now there is no foundation whatever for this conjecture in any thing which we observe in the works of nature; no such experiments are going on at present; no such energy operates, as that which is here supposed, and which should be constantly pushing into existence new varieties of beings. Nor are there any appearances to support an opinion, that every possible combination of vegetable or animal structure has formerly been tried" (Paxton 52).

From this side of Lyell and Darwin, Paley's rejoinder seems woefully inadequate. Even someone of Paley's time who had an acquaintance with animal husbandry might have had some qualms. But it is easy to imagine that, prior to the revolution occasioned by that thinking of which Darwin's *The Origin of Species* was a culmination, Paley's explanation cohered perfectly with assumptions widely shared and easy to make. Hume's proposal would appear entirely speculative, all at odds with what most people took for granted about the fixity of the species and the age of the universe. It is not difficult to account for the durable appeal which Paley's argument exercised, nor is it hard to see why Darwin's earth-shattering proposal put a decisive end to all that. The argument from apparent design had to await re-casting as an argument based not on teleological structures in the world, but on the regularities that produce or permit those structures (Tennant 86ff; Swinburne), to recover a measure of credibility. But, once again, the claim that Paley simply ignores Hume's criticism does not stand up to closer scrutiny.

I hope to have shown that Paley's extended argument in *Natural Theology* is not the product of a time warp but a case developed with full awareness of objections like Hume's. I believe Paley so thoroughly digested his acquaintance with *Dialogues* that he no longer identified it specifically but incorporated its contents into his response without identifying individual antagonists. Whether that is correct or not, it cannot be denied that his argument is framed partly as a response to criticisms strikingly like those raised in *Dialogues*.

It would be a mistake to represent Paley's treatise as a crushing refutation of the objections put forward in Hume's, though I have argued that a number of Paley's arguments should be accorded a measure of success as rejoinders. My main contention, however, is that it is a graver mistake to disregard the elements in Paley's case which attach directly to Hume's complaints. The appropriate response to William Paley's *Natural Theology* is to identify and deal with the parts of his argument that bear on Hume's strictures, not to dismiss Paley's case as though it contains nothing relevant to them.

WORKS CITED

Darwin, Charles. *Autobiography of Charles Darwin: With Two Appendices, Comprising a Chapter of Reminiscences and a Statement of Charles Darwin's Religious Views*. Ed. Francis Darwin. London: Watts, 1929.

Hick, John. *Philosophy of Religion*. 4th ed. Englewood Cliffs, NJ: Prentice-Hall, 1990.

Hume, David. 1757. *The Natural History of Religion*. Ed. James Fieser. New York: Macmillan, 1992.

LeMahieu, D.L. *The Mind of William Paley: A Philosopher and His Age*. Lincoln: University of Nebraska Press, 1976.

Paley, Edmund, ed. *The Works of William Paley, D.D.: With Additional Sermons . . . and a Corrected Account of the Life and Writings of the Author*. Vol. IV. 7 vols. London: C. and J. Rivington, 1825.

Payley, William. *Natural Theology*. London: Wilks and Taylor, 1802.

Paxton, James, ed. *The Works of William Paley*. Vol. IV. 5 vols. Oxford: Printed by J. Vincent, 1838.

Penelhum, Terence. *Hume*. Philosophers in Perspective. London: Macmillan, 1975.

_____ . *Themes in Hume: The Self, the Will, Religion*. Oxford; New York: Oxford University Press, 2000.

Pike, Nelson, ed. *Dialogues Concerning Natural Religion*. 1779. By David Hume. Indianapolis: Bobbs-Merrill, 1970.

Pojman, Louis P. "The Teleological Argument for the Existence of God." *Philosophy of Religion: An Anthology*. Ed. Louis P. Pojman. 3rd ed. Belmont, CA: Wadsworth Publishing Company, 1998.

Salmon, Merrilee H. *Introduction to Logic and Critical Thinking*. 3rd ed. Fort Worth: Harcourt Brace College Publishers, 1995.

Smith, Norman Kemp, ed. *Dialogues Concerning Natural Religion*. By David Hume. 1779. 2nd ed. London, New York: T. Nelson, 1947.

Swinburne, Richard. *The Existence of God*. Oxford: Clarendon Press, 1979.

Tennant, F.R. *Philosophical Theology*. Vol II. 2 vols. Cambridge: Cambridge University Press, 1928.

Williams, B.A.O. "Hume on Religion." *David Hume: A Symposium*. Ed. D.F. Pears. New York: St. Martin's Press, 1966. 77–88.

Isaiah Berlin and the Preconceptions of Economics with Regard to Liberty

Warren J. Samuels

Isaiah Berlin: A Life is a biography, both personal and intellectual, of one of the most remarked-about intellects of the twentieth century, written by an admirer and friend of his, who, in my personal estimate, is himself a great intellect of the succeeding generation (Ignatieff; all otherwise unspecified page references are to this book).

Isaiah Berlin (1909–1997) was both one of the foremost historians of ideas and one of the leading philosophers of liberalism of his time. In addition to essays and books on historiographical and technical philosophical subjects, Berlin published books on the Enlightenment, Romanticism, Chaim Weitzman, J.L. Austin, John Stuart Mill, Giambatista Vico, Johann Gottfried Herder, and many others, as well as a biography of Karl Marx. He taught at Oxford University and at numerous U.S. universities.

Michael Ignatieff (1947–) is known amongst historians of economic thought for the collection, edited with Istvan Hunt, *Wealth and Virtue: The Shaping of Political Economy in the Scottish Enlightenment*. His other published books include studies on the penitentiary and punishment, and on ethnic nationalism and war both in general and in Kosovo, as well as two novels. He is an accomplished essayist, having appeared, for example, in *The New York Review of Books*. He has also been a broadcaster for BBC and CBC. He is professor of the practice of human rights policy and director of the Carr Center of Human Rights Policy in the John F. Kennedy School of Government at Harvard University. He is a member of the International Commission on Sovereignty and Intervention, charged with recommending to the secretary-general of the United Nations possible norms for human intervention. He was the Tanner Lecturer at Princeton University in 2000. And he has given us his biography of Berlin.

Faith, Reason, and Economics: Essays in Honour of Anthony Waterman. Ed. Derek Hum. Winnipeg: St. John's College Press, 2003.

Isaiah Berlin was well known, by historians of economics and by many others, for at least two conceptual dichotomies. The first is his distinction between those whose mentality is like a fox, who knows many things, and those whose mentality is like a hedgehog, who knows one big thing, which Berlin acquired from the Greek poet Archilochus through Lord Oxford (173). The second is his distinction between negative and positive liberty, his stress on the former resonant with one of the presuppositions, that of liberty (= freedom), that form the philosophical foundation of economic theory in particular and much economics in general. It is the second distinction with which my essay is primarily concerned.

Berlin was born in Riga, Latvia, then a part of Imperial Russia, to a well-to-do Jewish family. The tragic events of the inter-war period drove his family from Riga to Petrograd and finally to London. He went to Oxford and, after serving the British government in Washington, DC, reporting and advising on United States public opinion during World War II, returned to Oxford, where he left technical philosophy (he was an early critic of logical positivism and later of "the positivist pedantry of American social science" [190]) for intellectual history—the history of ideas—and his work on the philosophy of liberalism. He "had a lucky and privileged life" (7); he met more or less intimately many of the great intellectual and political figures of his day. He developed an extraordinary reputation as a conversationalist, though he himself feared that it represented shallowness, being a "chatterbox" (174), "a minor Oxford personality" (176), or "an intellectual entertainer for the rich" (176). A few others thought he was a poseur (he was often attacked for his frivolity and worldliness [173]); but most people seemed to have found him impressive. He wrote a great deal and presented several notable lectures and lecture series but lamented that he never produced a large major work.

He was at the centre of a famous story by virtue of his absence. Winston Churchill had admired Isaiah's reports and, on learning in early February 1943 from his wife that Irving Berlin was in London, mistook Irving for Isaiah and invited him for lunch. Churchill asked numerous questions, including, when did Berlin think the war would end, to which Berlin responded, "Mr Prime Minister, I shall tell my children and grandchildren that Winston Churchill asked *me* that question," and, what was the most important thing Mr. Berlin had written, to which the reply was "White Christmas" (126). Ignatieff recounts the story, which became well known, in detail (125–26). As Ignatieff put it in his interview with Brian Lamb, aired 24 January 1998, Churchill was amused and told the story on himself, and "suddenly a very obscure intellectual laboring in the basement of the British Embassy in Washington finds himself famous for having been the man who didn't meet the prime minister."

A recurring theme in the biography is Berlin's extreme sensitivity to criticism. Self-denigration, we are told, was "a pre-emptive strike against criticism" (7), "self-doubt, [. . .] however real it sometimes was, [. . .] was also part of a carefully cultivated strategy of self-deprecation, intended to deflect and disarm criticism" (19). The self-denigration may well have been part of his character, perhaps reinforced by his appreciation that, as well as he might master a subject, there was always more that he had not mastered. One of his teachers had thought him "superficial," and Berlin thought, "There is a certain truth in it" (31); the idea may never have left him. Ignatieff suggests that Berlin repeatedly had "the uneasy feeling that his peers were asking themselves whether his reputation was deserved" (205). In any event, his status as an exile reinforced a "need to belong" and "a slight touchiness, a hyper-sensitivity to small slights, to any gesture that treated him as an outsider" (34). In time, however, he became a distinguished public intellectual, and the foregoing seems to have been part of the genesis of his success—notwithstanding the criticism he faced, writes Ignatieff, because "in convictions he was a liberal social democrat, but he was more comfortable socially among Conservatives" (197).

Berlin was secular and sceptical. He retained his Jewish identity and observance but was an agnostic or atheist, a Humean sceptic (41; see also 65, 81, 279, 293); observance did not mean affirmation of belief in a theological creed (42, 293). He was intimate with Chaim Weitzman and David Ben Gurion, an opponent of Jewish terrorism (177), an early supporter of a two-state solution for the problem of Palestine Arabs and Israelis (293, "two rights of self-determination of equal validity"), and a Zionist who did not identify with the people of Zion (179). He was "troubled by the Zionist myth of Palestine as a land without people given to a people without land. There *was* a people on the land and a reckoning with their claims was inevitable" (80). Zionism—in the sense of the obligation of Jews to live in Israel—meant that Jews could not "have the same right to fashion their own lives as any other people [. . .] a self-chosen life. Berlin's Zionism was a defence of Israel as the necessary condition not for Jewish belonging but for Jewish freedom" (183–84), and he wished the same freedom for the Palestinian Arabs.

Berlin's moral philosophy was moral pluralism. Although he apparently knew no technical economic theory, I am inclined to express his moral pluralism as follows: Scarcity (in the sense that values are incompatible and therefore cannot all be fully effectuated) leads to the necessity of choice and thence to conflict and inevitable tragedy in the realization of opportunity cost. Berlin's solution to this predicament is liberalism in the form of moral and political pluralism, that is, tolerance, forbearance, sympathy (in Adam Smith's sense), and compromise. A witness to Nazi and Soviet practices, he had a horror of physical violence and the extremes of political experimentation, thus a deep "lifelong preference for all the temporizing compromises that keep a political order safely this side of terror" (24), though this did not mean appeasement. Modernism aligned with revolution, he thought, too easily turned into tyranny (147). Berlin was a sceptic regarding the claims of both religion-theology and secular ideology. Furthermore, while liberty was a value for Berlin pre-eminent to justice, still justice—questions of structure—could not be ignored.

A correlative position was his antagonism to determinism (44, 84, 93), though he is Humean, too, in his emphasis upon, indeed defense of, convention (44–45). Ignatieff importantly writes that, for Berlin, "the function of historical understanding was to identify the precise range within which historical actors enjoyed room for manoeuvre; to understand how and why they used their freedom; and to evaluate their actions by the standard of what real alternatives were possible to them at that time" (206).

Ignatieff quotes the following from Berlin as the quintessence of Berlin's liberalism, and of what Berlin found in England (apropos of which Ignatieff both remarks that "if the English took to him, it was because he offered them back their most self-approving myths" [36] and cites Perry Anderson for the criticism that Berlin served up "to the English a self-congratulatory picture of their own supposedly liberal virtues" [234]): "That decent respect for others and the toleration of dissent is better than pride and a sense of national mission; that liberty may be incompatible with, and better than, too much efficiency; that pluralism and untidiness are, to those who value freedom, better than the rigorous imposition of all-embracing systems, no matter how rational and disinterested, better than the rule of majorities against which there is no appeal" (36).

This brings me to what Ignatieff considers "the central focus" (188) of Berlin's later work, though it might also be called one of the predicaments confronted by his liberalism, or, better, one of the predicaments for which his liberalism was a solution. Berlin, says Ignatieff, believed that "individuals must have secure cultural belonging if they are to be genuinely free." While apparently neither insensitive to nor emphatic that culture (or society, in the sense of John Stuart Mill's *On Liberty*) could be a threat to freedom, his main concern was that "individuals in modern societies were incorrigibly divided about the nature of the good and that the faiths men professed were in irremediable contention. In place of cultural unity there was now an irreducible conflict between competing human goods." For Berlin, this was "an unchangeable fact about the modern world" (188).

For Ignatieff, the notion of Berlin having a "central focus" is a major theme. Ignatieff writes that, while the range of Berlin's work "may make him seem like a fox, who knows many things; in reality, he was a hedgehog, who knew one big thing." His purpose in "this book is to elaborate what this one big thing was" (7). Ignatieff also writes that most of Berlin's friends "saw him as an archfox—nimble, cunning, quick-witted, darting from subject to subject, eluding pursuit. Yet he was also the type of fox who longs to be a hedgehog—to know one thing, to feel one thing more truly than anything else" (173; see also 197). The "one big thing," says Ignatieff, was "the theme of freedom and its betrayal" (201), also rendered as dissociating "the defence of liberty from liberation, personal or social" (230), and its genesis resided in the foregoing model of scarcity, necessity of choice, conflict, and tragedy. Another rendering of Berlin's "central focus" identifies his "whole project" as "held together by an overarching commitment to defend the validity of liberal principles in the face of their apparent historical relativity" (244; see also 285–86), apropos of which Ignatieff concludes that at bottom one finds "obvious circularity" and no adequate solution (286).

In any event, the place to start is with the theme of conflict. Conflict is due to the fact of competing, often incompatible and incommensurable, goals (89, 188, 228, 229, 246, 286, 291, and passim). Such conflict has existed from time immemorial and is truly a fundamental characteristic of the human situation. One implication is that "life's essential problems might not always be soluble" (190). Another is that there is no necessary "one right way for human beings to live" and no "one answer for all questions" (192). Still another is that because of conflicts of values and the necessity of choice, tragedy and tragic loss is unavoidable (228, 245, 291, and passim). These goals are important, in part, because they become the basis of social control and public policy.

In Berlin's own case, a major example of conflict involved "his pro-Israeli convictions" pulling in one direction and "his anti-colonialist inclinations" pulling in the other (237; see also 293, and passim).

In certain respects, Berlin's position resembles that of Friedrich A. von Hayek, particularly his emphasis on individualism and spontaneity and his critique of rational constructivism (e.g., 198). And Berlin confronted the same difficulty as did Hayek: how to promote individual freedom to choose without, in the name of doing so, superimposing one's own choices, for example, by proposing an absolutist counter faith (199), thereby foreclosing the liberal process. Indeed, the basis of Berlin's rationale for pluralism and a liberal policy was the fact of fundamental conflict itself (203, 229, and passim). Twice Ignatieff uses the same phraseology to emphasize a key Berlinian point. Instead of catering to "the human desire to be relieved of the burden of choice" (198), Berlin lauded "the necessity of politics." Because human goals were in conflict, "politics was not an emancipatory activity, merely a necessary one" (227); thus, "this least political of men mounted a defence of the necessity of politics" (285). As I have been wont to put it, politics, in being a mode of self-government, is a mode of working things out. This may be what Hayek's system actually boils down to (Samuels, "Hayek"), but it is far from the sentiments that denigrate government and rational constructivism and laud "spontaneous order."

The problem in interpreting and assessing Berlin's (or any other) philosophy of liberalism is its character as an ideology or sentiment in relation to what I will call certain fundamentals of the economic role of government. It would appear that, however attractive Berlin's philosophy of negative liberty as sentiment is, it is an incomplete treatment of liberty, an incomplete understanding of the Enlightenment in the history of dangers to liberty, and an incomplete and deeply misleading view of the importance of government within any status quo. Indeed, Berlin has to be understood as emphasizing *both* negative and positive liberty.

One aspect of Berlin's analysis with which I disagree is the relation of the Enlightenment to the question of whether "for any one genuine question there must be one true answer" (244–45). In my view, the Enlightenment thinkers in general wanted to enlarge the range of those whose values, perceptions, and interests formed public policy, no longer restricted to the elite, a view that did not preclude contrary tendencies. Absolutism, it seems to me, can derive from all modes of thought, did not arise for the first time with the Enlightenment, and was not all there was to the Enlightenment.

What *is* comprehensible is Berlin's emphases on toleration, on avoiding extreme suffering (250), and on empathy (256–57). But, like so many others, Berlin was uncomfortable with any implication that empathy meant relativism. Ignatieff says that for Berlin empathy "meant coolly establishing what could be negotiated across the frontiers between convictions and what could not." "The result," he says, "was a moral psychology of liberal life which, while unsystematic, was as deep as anything within the liberal canon since Adam Smith's *Theory of Moral Sentiments*" (257). If this is not, descriptively, prag-matic relativism, I do not know what it is, however much it conflicts with the absolutist legitimation and psychic balm needs of humans in society.

At one point, Ignatieff writes that Berlin's "liberal theory was intransigent in its emphasis on the necessity of tragic choice and in its commitment to negative rather than positive liberty" (257), thus tying the two themes together. I now turn to Berlin's "two concepts of liberty," first elaborated in his inaugural lecture as Chichele Professor of Social and Political Theory at Oxford on 31 October 1958.

Berlin, as is now well known, distinguished between negative liberty and positive liberty. Negative liberty meant "leaving individuals alone to do what they want, provided that their actions did not interfere with the liberty of others," the curbing of "authority as such." Positive liberty was "emancipa-tory," enabling the use of authority, political power, "to free human beings to realize some [hitherto] hidden, blocked or repressed potential." The former signified that "men should be free to choose," whereas the latter signified that "they should only be free to choose what it would be rational to desire" (226). One is freedom to do what one wants; the other is freedom to do the right thing. One is to act by one's own lights, independent of the interference of others; the other is to act by the lights of others, as one is compelled by the interference of others, say, either because of some idea of what is right and good for both oneself and others, or because some notion of order requires limitation and direction. These ideas need to be deconstructed, or unpacked. What does the distinction between positive and negative liberty involve?

(1) The place to begin is with the qualification built into Berlin's definition of negative liberty as "leaving individuals alone to do what they want, *provided*

that their actions did not interfere with the liberty of others" (226, emph. mine). Negative liberty does not, therefore, mean that there is no social control of, no interference with, no limitations on one's doing what one wants. The very fact of the existence of others means interference. One cannot have negative liberty without limitations on others' negative liberty. Berlin famously wrote that "freedom for the pike is death for the minnow." The paradox of freedom is that liberty must be constrained in order to promote liberty. The question is always whose or which liberty is to be constrained in favour of someone else's liberty. The question is: Which liberty, which individuals, which structure? The exercise of liberty by Alpha may well interfere with the liberty of Beta. Definitions of "interfere" and of evidence of "interference," coupled with normative distinctions between different modes of interference, help instantiate both particular dimensions and conceptions of liberty and therefore of structure. *Some* notion of public good is necessary to deal with actions that interfere with the liberty of others; indeed, it is, in part, such notions that help determine which actions are specifically *perceived* to interfere and thus require collective action.

(2) Take any society. It has a culture and a system of social control. It has a structure of power. Those so motivated and with the power to act do what they want; they are free to choose, given the value system of their society. They do what they want, within the constraints of social control. Since all societies are hierarchical, let us divide the society into giants and pygmies. They are giants and pygmies, respectively, because of their control or lack of control of the value and social control systems of society, manifesting, for example, the Lockean-Smithian dictum that government exists to protect the property of the rich from the poor, which implicitly involves the proposition that that which is protected as property is dependent on the interests of those who control government. So, if the giants are purple people and the pygmies are orange people, the giants are giants because the purple people control government and property involves the protected interests of purple people.

Inter alia, the foregoing means that not only do the giants have negative liberty but they also control positive liberty, insofar as they determine the restrictions—non-rights—inherent in the system of property; it is *their* conception of the right and the good that becomes the basis of social control, that constitutes the domain of negative liberty. The foregoing also means that every society has to work out three aspects of the division of power: First, the division of power within the nominally private sector; second, the division of power between the nominally private and nominally public sectors; and third, the division of power within the nominally public sector. I say "nominally" here for three reasons. First, everything tends to be simultaneously both private and public in nature, and our perception of them as "private" or "public" is selective. Second, because these divisions of power are worked out in and through what I call the legal-economic nexus (Samuels, "Legal-Economic"). Third, because official or public government coexists with unofficial or private government in a total system of governance.

(3) Define "socialism" as the movement to extend what hitherto has been the privileges (property rights) of the giants (= rich = purple people) into the rights of all people, including the pygmies (= poor = orange people). Berlin's dichotomy boils down to this: Negative liberty is that under the old system. Positive liberty involves the transformation of social structure. The orange people want pretty much what the purple people have had, namely, to be property owners.

Or it may turn out that the orange people want to change not only the property system of society but also its value system and culture. From a system of nominally private ownership they want to change it to a system of nominally public ownership. The rich no longer have property and the poor continue to have no property. This is "socialism." Negative liberty is that under the old system. Positive liberty involves the transformation of social structure, culture, and value system.

From Berlin's point of view, negative liberty prevents others from preventing the individual from doing what he or she wants to do. (Notice that purple and orange can be identified in terms of men and women.) Positive liberty for him involves the imposition of some, or someone else's, notion of social control and social change, whether (say) one form of socialism or the other. Negative liberty includes all the accumulated deliberative and non-deliberative restraints on the individual's freedom to choose. Positive liberty involves the deliberative imposition of new restraints, that is, the use of political power to realize new potential. Constraints under a regime of negative liberty are not designated by the pejorative use of the term *coercion*. The constraints newly imposed are so designated.

The irony is obvious. Once new constraints are imposed, they become part of the bundle of negative liberty's accumulated deliberative and non-deliberative restraints on the individual's freedom to choose, seemingly part of the natural order of things.

In other words, Berlin's dichotomy is closely aligned with that of Hayek in his model of spontaneous order in the manner of Carl Menger (Samuels, "Hayek"). They distinguish between institutions that have grown up spontaneously and non-deliberatively and those that are imposed through rational constructivism. The problem is that both men contemplate the rational critique of received institutions, such that after the initial stage all institutions are blends of non-deliberative and deliberative action (= non-legal and legal action). The Hayekian system tends to define coercion as legal change (change through law), but his system encompasses coercion by this definition as well as by other definitions (Samuels, "Concept").

196

(4) The foregoing turns in part on Berlin's interpretation of the Enlightenment (relating to Hayek's distinction between the French and Scottish Enlightenments). Writes Ignatieff: "The European Enlightenment, he argued, was divided by a central contradiction: between maintaining that men should be free to choose and insisting that they should be free to choose what it would be rational to desire" (226), meaning by free-to-choose choice within the pre-existing system and by free-to-choose-what-it-would-be-rational-to-desire choice of and choice within the new system. This both obfuscates and conflates several separable things, including: The system of restraints within the pre-existing system; indeed, the system of restraints that define it, and the difference between deliberative change along the lines of socialism. Furthermore, granted the condemnation of fascism and communism (Hitler Germany and the Soviet Union) as systems of coercion in the pejorative sense, Berlin both conflates the coercion of all systems of social control, that of the pre-existing system and that of the new system, and obfuscates the totalitarian and authoritarian nature of the ancient dynastic (in Thorstein Veblen's usage) regimes. Berlin is said by Ignatieff to affirm that "the revealed preferences of ordinary men and women must be the limit and also the arbiter of all practical politics" (226). Did Berlin really believe that the revealed preferences of ordinary men and women were the limit and also the arbiter of all practical politics in the ancient regimes and in modern plutocratic capitalist/ market regimes? Did Berlin really believe that the Enlightenment represented only faith in moral universals—as opposed, say, to seeking as the rights of all what hitherto had been the privileges of the elite few—and/or that such a faith had been "transformed into the Romantic exaltation of all that was irrational in human nature" (249; see also 201–04)? And what about his own belief in "moral universals" (250)? I think not.

As Ignatieff notes, Berlin's "pursuit of the distinction between Enlightenment and Romantic modes of thought drastically over-simplified the antithesis" (204), as does the naïve Hayekian who thinks that some institutions are non-deliberative and others deliberative and defines coercion as the exercise of deliberative legal change.

(5) Perhaps the game is given away when Ignatieff writes that "'Two Concepts' was consciously crafted for an era of de-colonisation, and its message towards colonial people demanding their liberty was highly skeptical. [. . .] To call national liberation a fight for liberty was to mistake the motives behind such colonial revolts, and hence to guarantee disillusion when they fail to deliver the emancipation they promised" (227). If this is Berlin's message, then he was not descriptively wrong. But he was erecting one aspect of liberty into a general theory of liberty. If the ruling purple people face an orange liberation movement, it is certainly likely true that (1) the liberation movement will tend to advance the interests and perceptions of one group of orange people, and (2) a successful orange liberation movement will bring about liberty from the

purple but perhaps no necessary other elements of liberty. Berlin may have had British India in mind; he surely did not have Britain's eighteenth-century American colonies in mind, and yet both points apply to both movements.

Ignatieff also writes that "'Two Concepts' was an attack on the faith common to classical republicanism, to Marxism and to utopian socialism, that politics could liberate men from [. . .] inner and outer conflicts" (227). I do not deny that some people have made such claims—puffery and absolutist legitimation—but surely it is a gross exaggeration to so identify the operatively meaningful faiths of those systems. As for classical republicanism, that faith is hardly present, if effectively present at all, in the Federalist papers. Republicanism is a mode of dealing with, of working out, conflicts of values, not a way of substituting for them.

(6) Ignatieff also writes that many of Berlin's "listeners on the left took the lecture to be a defence of *laissez-faire* individualism. But the robust after-life of 'Two Concepts' would be inexplicable if it had been only a defence of the status quo; instead, it was its psychology—its view of human beings choosing between often incompatible and incommensurable goals, which gave it such influence" (227–28). "The original aspect of his political philosophy lay in his psychology of the divided human self and his insight into the human susceptibility to utopias promising release from the burden of moral choice" (231). But, if this is so, how does one square the argument emphasizing negative liberty with that underscoring the necessity of politics? It is precisely because of conflicting goals and the necessity of choice, says Berlin, that politics is both inevitable and necessary.

I am inclined, therefore, to say the following: The position on negative liberty almost inevitably tends to reinforce the status quo, whatever status quo (and however specified) is in place. Coercion in the pejorative sense is ubiquitous. Some system of positive liberty generates, is ensconced within, and undergirds every system of negative liberty. The question of structure is ineluctable—including the division of power nominally between private and public spheres and that within the nominally private sphere (i.e., the problem of private versus public government in a total system of governance). What is there in the nature of things that privileges the received hierarchical structure, of British colonial rule in North America or India, or of the *ancien régime*?

No wonder, therefore, that one difficulty with Berlin's argument was that it failed to deal with the question of "how much social justice was compatible with negative liberty" (229). This is true even if one ignores another difficulty, his failure to "explain why negative liberty should have priority over other political values" (229). The question of structure—which individuals?—is indeed ineluctable. It is at bottom a question of dealing with Berlin's qualification, "provided that their actions did not interfere with the liberty of others." What/whose preconceptions of justice, indeed, what/whose preconception of negative liberty, are ensconced within the definitions of "interfere" and of evidence of "interference," and what/whose normative distinctions between different modes of interference, help instantiate both particular elements and conceptions of liberty and therefore of structure?

Berlin's theory, therefore, is a complete theory of neither positive liberty nor the relationship of negative and positive liberty. In an exchange of e-mails, I asked Ignatieff, "Does his [Berlin's] criticism of positive liberty apply only to socialism/communism/fascism/utopian absolutism?" Ignatieff replied that he "always felt [that] the critique of positive liberty was directed at all forms of coercive good intentions, including liberal democratic ones" (April 5 and April 8, 2001). This is quite different from government efforts to restrain nominally private coercion, to deal with conflicts arising from the actions of individuals that "interfere with the liberty of others," and to make a power structure more pluralistic by extending as rights for all what hitherto had been the privileges of a relative few (socialism).

(7) What can one say about liberty? I suggest the following:

(a) Liberty exists within systems of social control. All societies have liberty specific to their respective systems of social control.

(b) Liberty is multifaceted, comprising many possible dimensions.

(c) Liberty must be comprehended in terms of structure, in terms of who enjoys and who does not enjoy particular dimensions of liberty.

(d) Liberty derives its meaning in part, perhaps in large part, from a process of conflict. Liberty in practice or perceptions is largely the conception of liberty maintained by the winners.

(e) Socialization involves, in part, the inculcation of particular concepts and structures of liberty. In this process, concept influences structure and structure influences concept, and selective perception and attribution are ubiquitous.

(f) The foregoing means that liberty is relative in several ways. So, far from implying that all elements or concepts of liberty are equal, the foregoing underscores both the fact and necessity of choice between different elements and concepts of liberty; this is another, deeper, level of Berlin's fundamental notion of conflict, the necessity to choose, and tragedy. To take liberty as an absolute is to privilege one element and/or one conception of liberty over against all others.

(g) One can envision a model of social theory and practice in which liberty and justice are alternatives. But just as the invocation of considerations of liberty in matters of justice is important, so too is the invocation of considerations of justice in matters of liberty. For liberty not being an absolute, the questions of structure, of power, of whose interests are to count become important. Both invocations are rendered complex because considerations of liberty and of justice, respectively, are multiple and contradictory yet are necessary in working out the domain of negative liberty with regard to actions that are perceived to "interfere with the liberty of others."

(h) In the real world in which we live, the meaning and structure of liberty must be worked out. Particular theories of liberty, and of justice, may appear to be defining some natural or transcendental or absolute notion of each, but in practice—and always subject to selective perception—each theory is but a hypothesis or proposal thence to make its way in the process of working things out. Solutions to problems—even the nature and existence of problems—have to be worked out; they cannot be prescribed without endangering liberty for many, if not all, people.

(i) In the real world, too, the structure of power undergoes both deliberative and non-deliberative change.

(j) In particular, Berlin's negative liberty does not, cannot, exist independently of his positive liberty, and he did not think they did. In certain respects important to both him and me, they are mutually exclusive. But in other respects also important to both him and me, they are complementary. The meaning of each derives from its position in a total system. One's negative liberty, or freedom from, depends on how much positive liberty one has and how much positive liberty others have. For the Alpha to have freedom from Beta, Beta must be restrained in his or her freedom to, and vice versa. Without resources and the opportunities that ensue from them, without freedom to, freedom from is potentially hollow and formal. Without freedom from, resources and opportunities are useless. In actuality, one's freedom from is derived in part on restrictions placed on others' freedom to. One's liberty is part of a total structure of negative and positive liberties, of freedom from and to, of opportunities and constraints, of immunities and exposures.

In his interview with Brian Lamb, Ignatieff makes clearer than he does in the book Berlin's complete liberal position, one apparently parallel to that of John Rawls. Ignatieff says that Berlin believed that "you can't have individual private freedom unless you create the common conditions for all on which that individual liberty can stand." With a state that protects the individual, you also need protection of "the individual against the state." In other words, Berlin chose a politically pluralist rather than oligarchic interpretation of negative freedom. And answers to the question Which individual? need to be worked out. Neither Berlin nor anyone else has provided an unequivocal formula for that, and did not try to do so.

I am not sure that Berlin would entirely agree with the foregoing. But the foregoing is what I think is involved in the combination of his famous dichotomy combined with this theme of the necessity of choice, conflict, and tragedy. Berlin's program was different from mine, however much I agree with his overall normative position. Berlin sought to provide a viable philosophy of a free society, or what Frank H. Knight once called an effective propaganda for a free society. My program has been to identify the objective fundamentals of the economic role of government, indeed, of the total system of governance, power, and social control, like it or not. Without the latter analysis, the former can readily become matters of wishful thinking, grandiose utopianism, and abuse, the last in the service of particular interests as they seek to legitimize certain interferences with the liberty of others (or one set of elements, or one conception of liberty). Without the former analysis, the latter offers no reasoned basis for decision making. Knight, for example, wished that freedom be discussed independently of power; but doing so ignores the inequality, however achieved, governing which individuals and whose interests count. The ultimate difficulty is that choice must be made, results must be worked out.

The necessity for decision making is Berlin's message. But part of that message, too, in one of Ignatieff's best lines, is Berlin's "strong sense that politics led people to make fools of themselves" (72).

Finally, Ignatieff remarks that Berlin was "more curious about the varieties of human self-deception than *realpolitik*" (5). Berlin on varieties of human self-deception is probably more important for historians of economic thought than Berlin on *realpolitik*. But Ignatieff's statement should not be taken to be dismissive of Berlin on *realpolitik*, especially in light of the importance he placed on the necessity of politics in a world of fundamental conflicts. Ignatieff himself is enlightening. He tells of Berlin's appreciation that certain things could be stated publicly but others were not for public consumption (104). The theme of inevitable tragedy is certainly relevant; for example, "[Berlin's work in] Washington taught him that even great political figures rarely understood the history they were trying to shape to their own design, and that politics always had a potential for tragedy, because the forces it sought to master were never fully within human grasp" (124). We are told of Berlin's consideration of lesser and less activist positions in Paris or at Whitehall to be "a vegetarian diet after the satisfactions of a carnivore's feast at the centers of power" (130) and that he was, like Arthur Schlesinger Jr., "fascinated with power and influence" (191). He "once said, with memorable bite: 'whenever you hear a man speak of "realism," you may always be sure that this is the prelude to some bloody deed'" (225). And we read of Berlin having "reserves of political acumen" (264, apropos of the founding of Wolfson College). Though we are told that "he was not drawn towards the flame of power" (243), we are also told that "he rejoiced in worldliness, in having some grasp of the inner workings of the world of power and influence" (63); the latter rings truer than the former.

At bottom, however, Ignatieff is correct insofar as his account interprets Berlin to have been both a fox and a hedgehog. He was a great intellectual, even though he did not unequivocally solve the enormous problems that he took up. No one else has; he is not alone.

WORKS CITED

Hunt, Istvan, and Michael Ignatieff, eds. *Wealth and Virtue: The Shaping of Political Economy in the Scottish Enlightenment.* New York: Cambridge University Press, 1983.

Ignatieff, Michael. *Isaiah Berlin: A Life.* New York: Henry Holt, 1998.

_____. Interview with Brian Lamb. <www.booknotes.org/transcripts/50499.htm>

Samuels, Warren J. "The Legal-Economic Nexus." *George Washington Law Review* 57 (August 1989): 1,556–78.

_____. "The Concept of 'Coercion' in Economics." *The Economy as a Process of Valuation.* By Warren J. Samuels, Steven G. Medema, and A. Allan Schmid. Lyme, NH: Edward Elgar, 1997. 129–207.

_____. "Hayek from the Perspective of an Institutionalist Historian of Economic Thought: An Interpretive Essay." *Journal des Economistes et des Etudes Humaines* 9 (June–September 1999): 279–90.

What Ricardo et al. Didn't Quite Understand about Their Own System

Paul A. Samuelson

Classical economics was pessimistic about how fixity of land *cum* superfecundity of humans would in the absence of new technological discovery limit the gains in human well-being. (This is why Carlyle dubbed economics "the dismal science.") But the classicals were, on the whole, optimistic about how technological inventions would enhance welfare in defiance of the law of diminishing returns, at least in the intermediate run.

Belatedly, in Ricardo's third edition, he came to realize that, alternatively, technical change could hurt labour's wage. Unfortunately, his exposition of this genuine truth was so flawed that later commentators—notably Wicksell, Kaldor, Schumpeter, Stigler, Blaug, and Samuel Hollander—seemed to have inferred that Ricardo's third-edition recantation had to commit the heresy of denying both Say's Law and competition's invisible-hand achievement of Pareto Optimality. Samuelson ("Mathematical"; "Ricardo") demonstrated that those modern commentators misunderstood Ricardo's correct perception of the following banality, that some inventions can harm the wage return of a subset of the labour-land-capital factor inputs even under the purest of competition.

What is not a banality and what Ricardo seems never to have explicitly affirmed is that any invention viable under pure competition must (if anything) bring gain to the winning factors bigger than the loss to the losing factors. In other words, viable inventions under perfect competition must, if anything, improve what is today called total-factor productivity properly measured.

In this essay, I advance clearer understanding by showing how Ricardo's kernel of truth need have zero dependence on his palaver about (1) "circulating" capital versus "fixed" capital, or about (2) "*gross*" aggregate product versus "*net*" aggregate product, or about (3) his Malthusian stipulations that

Faith, Reason, and Economics: Essays in Honour of Anthony Waterman. Ed. Derek Hum. Winnipeg: St. John's College Press, 2003.

there will be a mandatory reduction of labour supply when the real wage falls. As a bonus, the present 1820 kind of analysis dramatizes how (what might seem to be an *unbiased) invention can accentuate economic inequality*.

This paper can be regarded as a second instalment to the Samuelson (2003) critique of P. Sraffa's unfinished proposed critique of modern economic theory (Samuelson, "Brief"). A later instalment must grapple properly with the special complications of the intertemporal capital-theoretic problems.

A DRAMATIC ARCHETYPICAL EXAMPLE

Eschewing post-1870 neoclassical marginal productivities of the Clark-Douglas-Solow type, I contemplate a Ricardo scenario where corn output is produced timelessly by (homogeneous) labour input and (homogeneous) land input. Initially independent competitors all can know only two discrete alternative productive techniques: α technique uses little labour and much land; β uses little land and much labour:

(α : each 1 of corn needs 4 of land and 1 of labour)

(β: each 1 of corn needs 1 of land and 4 of labour). (1)

Pre-Smithians like Cantillon and post-Smithians like Ricardo and the Mills could handle the resulting equilibria. When one of the factor endowments exceeds four times the other's endowment, it will be a redundantly free factor; and all of the corn product will be competitively distributed to the other factor. In each of the extreme alternatives, we would face a Labour Theory of Value; or we would face a Land Theory of Value.

Economics becomes more interesting when the endowment ratio of labour/Land, $\equiv L/A$, falls in the wide interval of (1/4, 4). In so simple a one-good model, technology and cost turn out to alone determine a unique competitive relative factor price ratio $\equiv$ wage/rent of land $\equiv (w/R)^*$. Because of the artfully contrived symmetry of my α and β example, necessarily $(w/R)^*$ will be exactly one.

It is not only *relative* factor returns that get determined by society's L/A endowment ratio, but also the *real corn wage rate* is determined at a unique market-clearing level:

real corn rate* = w* = 1/5 corn per worker, 1/4 < L/A < 4. (2)

Obviously, in this symmetric scenario, the real *rent* rate is also uniquely and constantly set at *any* (intermediate) L/A endowment ratio:

R* = 1/5 corn per acre of land, 1/4 < L/A < 4. (3)

No magic is required here, only supply-demand market clearing along with competitive self-interest arbitrage. Elsewhere (Samuelson, "Brief"), I have spelled out (in a first critique of Sraffa's never-completed critique of mainstream economic theory) what was called "Sraffa-Samuelson marginalism." This has some *qualitative* resemblance to post-1880 J.B. Clark marginalism. But the two marginalisms are logically and empirically distinguishable. With a stretch, 1820 Ricardo—who had invented the arithmetic analysis of Portugal-England comparative advantage—could follow the present discrete-technology numerical example(s), which require no differential calculus at all.

My α and β scenario has an ultra-simple comparative statics: in it a fall or rise for L/A, toward 1/4 or toward 4, has *no effect at all* on the (w/R^*) terms of trade! These are classical "natural prices" with a vengeance. However, when it comes to ultra *redundancy* of a factor, its real price does fall just as the earliest economists' intuition would have suggested.

HOW INVENTION CAN DEPRESS ONE OF EITHER WAGE OR RENT

Now I use 1820 arithmetic to explore what a new γ invention can do to lower either the competitive real wage rate or the rent rate. Add to α and β a newly discovered intermediate-intensity technique that is not particularly biased to be labour-saving or land-saving:

$$(\gamma\text{: each 1 of corn needs 2 of land and 2 of labour}). \tag{4}$$

What must be the new equilibrium distribution of income between wages of workers or rent of land? For isolation of an invention's effect, keep total factor endowments exogenously constant at, say,

$$L = 60, A = 40. \tag{5}$$

The new proto-Schumpeter dynamic innovation must, so to speak, rupture the previous competitive equilibrium with its $(1/5\ 1/5) = (w^*\ R^*)$ of Equations (2) and (3). Why and how? Knowledge spreads gradually: those who first learn of the new γ technique will be tempted to use it because primitive calculation shows that it lowers their unit cost of corn production by 20 percent when $(1/5\ 1/5)$ still prevails. They draw some L and some A from either or both of the α and the β techniques. However, if Ricardo's new full employment is to be reached and maintained, it will have been labour that is made relatively superabundant until market clearing changes in (w R) are effectuated. The same arithmetic (not previously explained by me) that mandated the ante-invention status quo will mandate that only at

$$(w^{**} \ R^{**}) = (1/6 \ 1/3) \tag{6}$$

will there result the post-invention new status quo.

Remorseless Darwinian self-serving competition must work to eliminate completely the old α technique as no longer competitively viable. Why, readers should ask themselves, must the β technique avoid α's fate of extinction? The reason is that if γ *alone* prevailed, some of the 60 of labour could not find jobs cooperating with the 40 of land. The same way that the ante-invention (1/5 1/5) had previously cleared the competition ("auction") market will now mandate that labour wage must lose and land rent must gain—and must do so in the new exact (1/6 1/3) way. Remark: (1/5 1/5) came so that the α and β techniques shared total production in that way which maximized pre-invention corn output at 20 bushels of corn. (That was Smith's Invisible Hand working teleologically in a way that you cannot expect Smith or Ricardo to have understood in those pre-Pareto days. However, unthinking competition still works out in a way that requires no understanding on the part of its actors or its unseen observers.) After the γ invention $Q^* = 20$ gets increased to $Q^{**} = 23 \ 1/3$, a 16 2/3 percent jump in output.

The rules of the game prevailing *after* the last historical invention require no sophisticated understanding by anyone. All that is required is dog-eat-dog myopic selfishness. Follow the money trail. (In my appendix, I explicate the petty arithmetic, not of Ricardo's Portuguese wine exports and his English cloth exports, but rather of Darwinian least-cost survivability in the present corn-labour-land scenario.)

SUMMARY

Was Ricardo right when late in life he admitted that invention could hurt the real wage rate of labour? Yes:

$$w^{**} = 1/6 \text{ corn per workers} < 1/5 \text{ corn per worker} = w^*. \tag{7a}$$

What about land rent? If w^{**} falls, then necessarily R^{**} must rise. And it does:

$$R^{**} = 1/3 \text{ corn per acre} > 1/5 \text{ corn per acre} = R^*. \tag{7b}$$

Readers will note that 1/3 exceeds 1/5 by more than 1/5 exceeds 1/6. More conclusive proof that inventions viable under competition do raise "total-factor-productivity" comes from the calculations that post-invention corn output, Q^{**}, does exceed pre-invention Q^*, namely:

$$Q^{**} = 23 \ 1/3 \text{ corn output} > 20 \text{ corn output} = Q^*. \tag{7c}$$

So, despite Wicksell's and Kaldor's accusation that Ricardo's recantation violated Pareto-optimality, here it is demonstrated that the same (60 labour 40 land) do now produce an extra 3 1/3 of corn. Yes, Virginia, there is such a thing as a "free lunch." It comes every time post-Newtonian know-how increases efficiency of useful production (and does so without violating Nature's Law of Constancy of Total Energy).

What about a possible Ricardo innuendo (Ricardo 380) that the harm that can come to labour might not be able to happen to a non-labour factor like land or "Kapital?" A zealous reader should also redo my appendix arithmetic when (60 labour 40 land) is replaced by (40 labour 60 land). My artful contrived symmetry in numerical examples will show that then (1/5 1/5) changes to (1/6 per acre 1/3 per worker). Ergo. *Any* subset of factors can be hurt, but never can that hurt exceed the gain elsewhere.[1]

In concluding, I want to emphasize that the present exercise does not convict any pre-1821 scholar of ignorance, incompetence, or imperfection. We gain better understanding of earlier heroes in science when we uncover just what they did know and what they only imperfectly knew. If that be Whiggery, then by whatever name it mandates scholars doing it as well as imperfect human beings can.

APPENDIX

Before Invention

When the L/A endowment is between the L_α/A_α ratio of 1/4 and the L_β/A_β ratio of 4, full employment of (60L 40A) necessitates that *both* techniques must competitively coexist. For this to happen, α's and β's unit costs of corn production must be brought into equality by the one and only w/R ratio that ensures this.

Here then are the implied relations for factor prices:

$$\text{Corn } P_\alpha = w.(1/4)+R.4$$
$$= \text{corn } P_\beta = w.4+R.1. \tag{A-1a}$$

Equation (A-1a) implies arithmetically, when $P_\alpha = P_\beta$ = corn price as *numeraire*

$$1 = w.(1/4)+R.4, \quad 1 = w.4+R.1 \tag{A-1b}$$

or

$$w^* = R^* = 1/5. \tag{A-1c}$$

To calculate out how much Q_α^* and Q_β^* will then have to be, the following arithmetic relations must hold:

$$60 = L = L_\alpha{}^* + L_\beta{}^* = Q_\alpha{}^* .1 + Q_\beta{}^* .4$$
$$40 = A = A_\alpha{}^* + A_\beta{}^* = Q_\alpha{}^* .4 + Q_\beta{}^* .1. \tag{A-2a}$$

Only the following equilibria can satisfy Equations (A-2a):

$$Q_\alpha{}^* = 20/3 \text{ corn}, Q_\beta{}^* = 40/3 \text{ corn; total } Q_\beta{}^* = 20/3 + 40/3 = 20. \tag{A-2b}$$

After Invention

With the (γ: 2L 2A) technique newly available and viable, if Say's Law is to be relied on to fully employ 60L and 40A, more than one of the three (α β γ) techniques must be in positive use. Exploration of arithmetic will reveal that *all three* of the following least-cost relations can *never coexist*:

$$\alpha: \quad 1 = w1 + R4$$
$$\beta: \quad 1 = w4 + R1$$
$$\gamma: \quad 1 = w2 + R2. \tag{A-3a}$$

Since use of only one of the α, β, γ techniques cannot use up 60L and 40A, the final competitive equilibrium for (w** R**) must come from one and only one of the following two-techniques-in-use cases:

$$\alpha\&\beta, \text{ or } \alpha\&\gamma, \text{ or } \beta\&\gamma \tag{A-3b}$$

We know already that (1/5 1/5) is the (w* R*) that prevails when γ gets no use at all. Here are the alternative results when $\beta\&\gamma$ and $\alpha\&\gamma$ are tried out:

$$\beta\&\gamma: 1 = w4+R1, 1= w2+R2; w** = 1/6, R** = 1/3 \tag{A-3c}$$

$$\alpha\&\gamma: 1 = w1+R4, 1= w2+R2; w*** = 1/3, R*** = 1/6 \tag{A-3d}$$

Which of these last pairs can survive as definitely better than the pre-invention $\alpha\&\beta$? Superficially, it can be said that in some respect either of these new pairs might be better than $\alpha\&\beta$. Why? Because one of (1/5 1/5) is exceeded in each alternative new case. However, do remember that Say's Law dictates fulfillment of full employments of both 60L and of 40A. Both α and β do use L/A in lower ratio than the 60/40 endowment ratio. Ergo, out of $\beta\&\gamma$ and $\alpha\&\gamma$, only the mixture $\beta\&\gamma$ can keep employment full.

$$L_\alpha/A_\alpha = 1/4 < 60/40, L_\gamma/A_\gamma = 2/2 = 1 < 60/40 \tag{A-4}$$

Theorem: When the γ option is added to the α and β options, the new post-invention equilibrium must cause α to drop out Darwinianly as unnecessarily expensive. Ergo, what was (1/5 wage 1/5 rent) must newly become (1/6 wage 1/3 rent), and *wage earners will be the losers from the remorseless new invention.* QED.

There remains the task of explicating what must be the post-invention allocation of resources between the old-retained β technique and the new viable γ technique.

The following relations are defining

$$\beta\&\gamma: 60 = L_\beta{}^{**}+L_\gamma{}^{**} = Q_\beta{}^{**}4+Q_\gamma{}^{**}2$$
$$40 = A_\beta{}^{**}+A_\gamma{}^{**} = Q_\beta{}^{**}1+Q_\gamma{}^{**}2 \tag{A-5a}$$

Equation (A-5a)'s implied unique solution must be as follows:

$$Q_\beta{}^{**} = 20/3, \; Q_\gamma{}^{**} = 50/3 \tag{A-5b}$$
$$Q^{**} = 20/3 + 50/3 = 23 \; 1/3 > Q^* = 20. \tag{A-5c}$$

Note that the new γ invention does indeed raise total-factor productivity by 16 2/3 percent!

One confirms (A-5c)'s output approach from the ("duality") income side by

$$w^{**}L+R^{**}A = 1/6 \; (60)+1/3 \; (40) = 23 \; 1/3 \tag{A-5d}$$

$$= 1 \; 1/6 \; [w^*L+R^*A] = 1 \; 1/6 \; [1/5 \; (60) + 1/5 \; (40)]. \tag{A-5e}$$

Remark: If the endowments had been held constant at (50L 50A), the new γ option would then have instead Darwinianly singularly driven *both* old α and old β out of use. Only γ could then survive competitively, and total corn would rise from 20 bushels to 25 bushels, a 25-percent increase. But, in this singular razor's-edge endowment ratio case, the new w/R ratio could be indeterminately anything from zero to infinity!

Linear Programming Summary

In an MIT graduate seminar, when treating elementary economics from an advanced viewpoint, I could summarize all the many present pages by solving the following standard parametric linear programming problem, *primal* and its *dual* L.P. problem:

Subject to

$$1Q_\alpha +4Q_\beta +2Q_\gamma \le L = 60, \; (Q_\alpha \; Q_\beta \; Q_\gamma) \ge 0$$

$$4Q_\alpha+1Q_\beta+2Q_\gamma \le A = 40, \tag{A-6a}$$

$$\text{Max}_{Q's} \; [Q_\alpha+ Q_\beta + Q_\gamma] \tag{A-6b}$$

$$= Q_\alpha^+ + Q_\beta^+ + Q_\gamma^+ = q(A,L)$$
$$\equiv q(40,60) = 23 \ 1/3 \ bu., \ q(\lambda A, \lambda L) \equiv \lambda q(A,L) \qquad (A\text{-}6c)$$

$$= Min_{w,R} \ [Lw + AR]$$
$$= Min_{w,R} \ (60w+40R)= 60w + 40R = 60/6 = 40/3 = 23 \ 1/3 (A\text{-}7a)$$

$$\text{s.t.} \quad 1w+4R \geq 1, \ (w \ R) \geq 0$$
$$4w+1R \geq 1$$
$$2w+2R \geq 1. \qquad (A7b)$$

The production function q(L,A) is not smoothly differentiable as with Clarkian neoclassicism. But it is first-degree-homogeneous, monotone-non-increasing in its arguments, concave in them, and does consist of Sraffa-Samuelson *cornered line segments* for q(L/A, 1), with comparative statics

$$(\Delta Q/\Delta L)_A \geq 0, \ (\Delta Q/\Delta A)_L \geq 0; \ [(\Delta L/\Delta w)]_R \leq 0, \ [(\Delta L/\Delta R)]_w \geq 0 . \qquad (A8)$$

The standard George Dantzig simplex method will converge to $(Q_\alpha^+ \ Q_\beta^+ \ Q_\gamma^+ ;$ $w^+, R^+)$ in a finite number of ascending steps. See Dorfman, Samuelson, and Solow for details and G.B. Dantzig for fuller treatment

NOTE

1. Joan Robinson's excellent primer on Marx's economics fails to comprehend this subtlety. Marx's Law of Worker Impoverishment and his Law of the Falling Rate of Profit cannot *both* obtain in her scenario of his system. But in neither of Robinson's two editions does she state or seem to realize this logical truth.

WORKS CITED

Blaug, M. *Economic Theory in Retrospect*. 3rd ed. Cambridge: Cambridge University Press, 1978.

Dantzig, G.B. *Linear Programming and Extensions*. Princeton: Princeton University Press, 1963.

Dorfman, R., P.A. Samuelson, and R.M. Solow. *Linear Programming and Economic Analysis*. New York: Dover Publications, 1958.

Hollander, S. "The Development of Ricardo's Position on Machinery." *History of Political Economy* 3 (1971): 105–35.

Kaldor, N. "A Case against Technical Progress?" *Economica* 12 (May 1932): 180–96.

Ricardo, D. *On the Principles of Political Economy and Taxation*, 3rd ed. 1821. Vol. 1 of *The Works and Correspondence of David Ricardo*. Ed. Piero Sraffa, with the assistance of M.H. Dobb. Cambridge: Cambridge University Press (for the Royal Economic Society), 1953.

Robinson, J. *An Essay on Marxian Economics*. London: Macmillan, 1942.

Samuelson, P.A. "Mathematical Vindication of Ricardo on Machinery." *Journal of Political Economy* 96 (1988): 274–82.

_____ . "Ricardo was Right!" *Scandinavian Journal of Economics* 91 (1989): 47–62.

_____ . "A Brief First Critique of Sraffa's Unfinished Critique of Marginalism." *Festschrift* for C.-C. von Weizsäcker, forthcoming January 2003.

Schumpeter, J.A. *History of Economic Analysis*. New York: Oxford University Press, 1954.

Sraffa, P. *Production of Commodities by Means of Commodities, Prelude to a Critique of Economic Theory*. Cambridge: Cambridge University Press, 1960.

Stigler, G.J. "The Ricardian Theory of Value and Distribution." *Journal of Political Economy* 60 (1952): 187–207. [Also ch. 6 of Stigler, *Essays in the History of Economics*, 156&97. Chicago: University of Chicago Press, 1965.]

Wicksell, K. *Lectures on Political Economy*. English translation. London: Routledge and Kegan Paul, 1934.

_____ . "Ricardo on Machinery and the Present Unemployment, 1923." *Economic Journal* 91 (1981): 202&05.

Aristotle on the Aged: A Re-Assessment

John Wortley

Urban myths may be something of a fantasy, but academic myths certainly are not. They are those statements that one author takes from another and that pass down the generations, unchallenged and unsuspected of being anything other than valid. In many cases, such statements are perfectly valid; but every so often a familiar *datum* turns out to be false, to have been an academic myth. All disciplines have them lurking unsuspected deep within their heritage of traditional learning, newer disciplines probably more often than the older ones. The study of the aging process is a relatively new discipline; hence it is hardly surprising to discover that one of its cherished tenets is false.

This is how it came about: In 1995, there appeared in Italy, in Italian, a work of considerable importance for all who are in any way interested in the classical aspects of the debate about aging. Under the editorship of Umberto Mattioli (who supplies a fine introductory essay) it is a collection of essays by various people, a first volume dealing with the ancient Greeks, a second with the Roman epoch. My remarks in this essay are concerned wholly with the Greek volume.

Because most of the evidence surviving from classical antiquity is textual, it is hardly surprising that the studies in this collection work almost exclusively from literary bases. On the whole, they are studies made by philologists for philologists and therefore may not be easily accessible to the informed reader whose skills lie in a different field. Yet what they have to say is far too important to remain the exclusive possession of classicists. Hence, in this essay I attempt to open up these studies to a wider audience by taking one aspect (only one, but a very important one) of one article in the collection. By translating key passages and supplying some supplementary material, I endeavour to

Faith, Reason, and Economics: Essays in Honour of Anthony Waterman. Ed. Derek Hum. Winnipeg: St. John's College Press, 2003.

make its message easily accessible; it is a message that seriously questions a statement generally endorsed by writers heretofore.

Each of the fourteen essays in Volume 1 deals with some compartment of Greek literature: heroic poetry, for instance, tragedy, historical writing. Each writer attempts to provide the sort of analysis that has long been needed and without which a task that has too often been vainly attempted remained impossible: the formulation of some solidly based judgements on what the Greeks really did think (or said they thought) about becoming and being old. For far too long, we have had to rely on general works that, taking a little bit from here, a little bit from there and, often relying on the misconceptions of earlier writers, purport to provide an informed and complete picture of Greek thought about aging. Many of those with experience of Greek literature have long felt uneasy about some of the conclusions of those books; some have already attempted a number of case analyses showing the inadequacy of one or more of their more widely disseminated general opinions. I had already completed some such studies before the appearance of Mattioli's collection; happily, these are not doubted by any of the Italian studies (apart from some slight over-lapping in the study in Vol. 2), while on the whole those do come to conclusions remarkably similar to my own (Wortley: "Desert"; "Aesopic"; "His"; *"Greek"*; "Four-Age").

One of the most widespread misapprehensions concerning the Greeks' attitude to old age is largely due to one of the best-known of modern works on aging, that of Simone de Beauvoir. It is she who speaks of "l'attitude morose des Grecs à l'égard de la vieillesse" (122). In this, she has been followed more or less unquestioningly by other popular writers, for instance by Georges Minois, who entitles his chapter on the Greeks "La triste vieillesse." To be sure, these conclusions are not completely mistaken; it would be misleading to suggest that, for the Greeks, aging was all skittles and roses. But, as usual, the truth is to be found neither at the north pole nor at the south. Indeed, as one should expect of a people who in so many ways pioneered what we have come to know as the western intellectual tradition, Greek thought about aging (as about many things) was highly *nuancé*. It is like a picture with great variation of shade, colour depth and intensity: a picture that can by no means be described in single words, or even paragraphs. This becomes increasingly clear as one reads the studies brought together by Mattioli and follows the scholars that he treats. As the sources are made to reveal their variegated responses to the inevitability of advancing time and the toll it takes on the individual, one is yet again overwhelmed by the richness and the freshness of Greek thought. Indeed, there is a certain irony in questioning those writers who seem never to grow old about the matter of growing old. Even on that topic, their thought has an evergreen youthfulness that renders it often optimistic and always attractive.

In some ways, for gerontologists the most interesting of the articles in Volume 1 will be the last one, "La medicina graeca antica," in which Giodano Pisi examines what ancient medicine had to say about geriatrics (a term unknown until recent times). Inevitably, unlike most of the others in Volume 1, this article takes us well into the Roman era as most of the medical men continued to write in Greek rather than Latin (Celsus was the exception, hence his great popularity at the time of the Renaissance). Pisi goes a long way to correcting many of the misapprehensions to be found in general works about ancient medicine by taking a complete overview of the entire classical medical tradition, a *tour de force* of no mean order. Predictably, here too, although a general consensus did eventually emerge on the pathology and therapy of old age, it was not before a complicated debate between the various medical "schools" of antiquity had run its course. Even so, there were those (most significantly, the great Galen) who gave their consent reluctantly to what we might call "the numbers game" (see Wortley: "His"; "Four-Age").

It is, however, primarily to the article of Renzo Tossi on Greek thought from the Presocratics to the Peripatetics (Tossi) that I wish to direct attention, more particularly to Section 4 of his article, the one that deals with Aristotle (218–25.) I select this section for particular examination because here Tossi takes issue with something Aristotle wrote, something that has been used more than any other passage of Greek literature to *darken* the prevailing view of what the Greeks thought about the elderly. It has been referred to and quoted with relentless monotony, sometimes as "the last word" (as if there could ever be such a thing!) on Greek attitudes to the elderly (witness Charles, following Haynes). It may not be exaggerating to say that no piece of writing has ever been so misused to produce a more distorting effect than this one. It was high time for this celebrated passage to be evaluated in its own context and its effects reconsidered. This Tossi has done.

Neither Beauvoir (121–22) nor Minois (93–96, section entitled "Aristote contre les vieillards"), who follows Beauvoir unquestioningly in this matter, nor Tossi himself, nor any other author as far as I can discover, does more than refer obliquely to or, at best, cite snippets from the passage in question. Beauvoir had certainly read it (in a recognizable translation), but Tossi has obviously studied it in depth. The problem is that he rather assumes that his reader is equally familiar with the text. Since this might not always be the case and, since the text is unlikely to be easily to hand in an accessible language for everybody, I include here a version of it more or less in English. But *caveat lector:* Greek is a notoriously difficult language to translate and Aristotle's Greek even more difficult that most authors', mainly because what he left behind is not much more than lecture notes rather than finished pieces. Hence, this is very far from a perfect translation (even if such a thing could ever exist). I take full responsibility for its shortcomings; it is from Aristotle's *Rhetoric* 2.12, 1388b–1389a, a work generally thought to have been composed around 330 BC. Aristotle was probably born around 384; hence, he was in his upper-fifties when he wrote *Rhetoric*. One assumes that he would have considered himself "an old man" by that time, but not very old. This is what he jotted down:

Let us proceed to [consider] the nature of men's characters in terms of their emotions, their habits, their ages and their fortunes. By "emotions" I mean such things as rage and desire, of which we have just been speaking; by "habits" I mean their customary vices and virtues. Of these too we have already spoken; [it is a question] of what kind of choices men exercise and what sort of deeds they might perform. The "ages" are: youth, maturity and old age. By "fortune" I mean being well-born, rich and powerful and their opposites, or good and bad fortune in general.

It is the nature of young people to have strong desires and to do what they desire to do. Of the corporal desires, they are most attached to their sexual instincts and least able to master them. They easily tire of one desire and change to another one. The stronger a desire, the sooner they desist from it, for their desires are sharp but short, like the hunger and thirst of an invalid. They are passionate, boiling within, swept away by rage, slaves to their hot temper. Their self-esteem will brook no slight; indeed, they are moved to anger if they think they have been slighted. They love to receive honours, but even more so to be winners, for youth loves to dominate and winning is a kind of domination. Winning and dominating they crave even more than wealth. Wealth they do not much care for because they have not yet experienced the lack of it, as Pittaeus said to Amphiaraus. The characters of youths are not bad, but good, because they have not yet experienced much affliction. They are trusting because they have not been greatly deceived. And they are full of hope, for the young are by nature as hot-blooded as men in their cups. Theirs is a time of life at which they have encountered few obstacles; so, for the most part, they live in hope. Now hope looks to the future, whereas memory is concerned with the past. For young people the future is very, very long while the past is quite short. In the morning of life there is nothing to remember and everything to hope for. So, for the reason just mentioned, youths are easily led astray: hope comes easily to them. They are braver too, prone to be carried away and hopeful. The one makes them fearless, the other bold, for no man is afraid when he is angry; and confidence is inspired by the hope of some benefit to come. [Youths] are modest too, for they can conceive of no other good [than that which they know,] having been raised under no other law [than that of conventional morality.] And they are high-minded, since they have not yet been humbled by life. Not to have been seared by necessity and to count oneself worthy of greatness, that is high-mindedness and this all comes from hope. They choose to do what is right rather than what is expedient; they live to build character rather than to calculate what is advantageous for themselves, for calculation smacks of expediency whereas virtue is noble. Youths are more devoted to their friends and companions than are people of other ages. This is because they delight in the company of others and, as they judge nothing by expediency, nor do they so choose their friends. [1389b] All their faults are offences against the maxim of Chilon ["nothing too much"]. They do everything inordinately; they love inordinately, hate inordinately and everything else likewise. They think they know everything and stubbornly cling to that belief; that is why they do everything inordinately. When they offend, it is by acting inordinately, not out of malice. They are compassionate in that they believe all men to be kind and better [than they really are.] They measure their neighbours by their own innocence, to the point of believing that those people suffer undeservedly. They love laughter and therefore repartee too, for repartee is a disciplined excess [temperée par la bonne éducation / cultured insolence].

Such then is the character of the young; elders [*presbyteroi*] and those who have passed their florescence have for the most part characteristics which are just the opposite of these. Because they have lived many years; because they have many times both been led astray and have gone astray; because human affairs often turn out for the worse—on no account will they [ever] commit themselves to anything, always stopping short of what is called for. They "think" but "know" nothing. Being of two minds, they always add "perhaps" or "maybe"—they always talk like that, never affirmatively. Their characters are bad, for it is the nature of a bad character always to look on the black side. Their pessimism also arises from their distrust: experience has made them suspicious. That is why they neither love nor hate very much, but rather follow the precept of Bias [of Priene] to love as those who are going to hate and to hate like men who will love. They are mean-spirited because they have been humbled by life. They have no desire for anything grand or extraordinary, only for the necessities of life. They are not free with their possessions for these they number among the necessities of life and, in any case, they know from experience that possessions are much easier to dispose of than to acquire. They are fearful and apprehensive of everything, just the opposite of the young; cold, where youth is hot. Old age ushers in timidity, for fear is a kind of refrigeration. They cling to life, more especially towards the end, because desire focuses on that which is absent; hence, we desire more fervently that which we lack. They are excessively self-loving, far more so than is called for; in this too they are mean-spirited. And because they are excessively self-loving, they live by the rule of expediency, not of goodness, *i.e.* of the beautiful as an absolute good. They are shameless rather than modest and, since they have no more regard for the beautiful than for what is expedient, they care not what people think of them. Experience has taught them not to hope, for most things turn out badly and many for the worst. This accounts for their timidity. Rather than live in hope, they live with their memories. Only a small portion of life is left for them while there is a great deal of it already in the past. Hope pertains to the future, memory to the past. This explains their garrulity: they go on and on about the things that happened in the past, for they enjoy recalling them. Their transports of anger are intense, but feeble; and of their desires, some no longer function at all and others are weakened. They neither feel desire nor are they prompted by it to action in order to satisfy it, but only for gain. Thus they appear to be abstemious, their desires lying dormant, but they are in fact enslaved to acquisition. They live by calculation [*logismos*] for calculation has to do with expediency: character with virtue. When they do wrong, it is out of malice, not excess. The elderly can be moved to pity, but not in the same way as the young. In their case it is out of love of one's neighbour: in the elderly it is a weakness. For the elderly think that everything is closing in on them to make them suffer, which inclines them to [self]-pity, whence they take to complaining. They have no love of repartee and laughter; complaining is the opposite of love of laughter. Such then are the characteristics of the young and of the old. (*Rhetoric* 2.12–13, 1388b–1389a).

As Tossi observes, there is no denying that this picture (of the elderly) is completely negative. Its pejorative effect is greatly intensified by the antithetical effect of the foregoing portrait of an idealized *jeunesse dorée*, so unreal that it should already be sending out a warning signal that the writer is not here in the business of reflecting life "as it really is," but of something other than that. Inevitably the contrast with Plato's very different portrayal of the aged in the first book of the *Republic* comes to mind. Some authors (Beauvoir and Minois among them) have tried to play the one off against the other by characterizing Plato and Aristotle as optimist and pessimist respectively as far as old age is concerned. This is understandable, for Plato sings loudly and clearly a message that recurs often enough elsewhere in his own work and in subsequent literature: there is a sense in which becoming elderly is not so much a deterioration as an amelioration. A certain decline is inevitable as far as the physical constitution is concerned but, from an intellectual point of view, he sees the aging process in a very different light. In *Symposium,* for instance, he makes Socrates tell Alcibiades: "The sight of the intellect begins to see clearly when the eyesight begins to decline" (Plato, *Symposium* 219a.) Elsewhere he writes: "A man's grasp of [political] affairs is at its dullest when he is young but at its keenest when he is old" (Plato, *Laws* 4, 715d-e. See also *Republic* 6, 498b.) Philo of Alexandria expresses the same thought in a noble aphorism: "The soul blossoms in scholarship and/or understanding [*episteemee*] when the excellence of the body is dilapidated by old age (Philo of Alexandria, *de Somniis* 1.11) while in Christian literature Athanasius may have a similar thought in mind when he makes Antony say: "The intelligence of the soul is strengthened when the pleasures of the body weaken" (Athanasius 7.9).

In a word, Plato looks like the apostle of a determined effort to search out and state some *good* thing about being old, while Aristotle appears equally determined to say the worst he can of it. Renzo Tossi rightly protests that this comparison of the two philosophers' pictures of the elderly can only be misleading. He insists that Plato's "portrait" is no more realistic than Aristotle's; it is an idealization that probably had very little to do with life as it really was. In the ancient and mediaeval world, such idealizations were not considered irrelevant or irreverent in the way they might well be considered today. We have innumerable biographies of philosophers, famous men, and saints, that probably have far less to do with the lives those people actually led than they have to do with how their authors thought their readers *ought* to live. Such writings (created long before the invention of the press prompted a sharper distinction between "truth" and fiction) were accepted as goals to aim for or as examples against which to measure oneself. They had their part to play at one time, but they are of limited value in telling future generations "how it really was," other than in a rather oblique way.

This said, there is still no comparing the two philosophers' "portraits" of the aged, for, in the case of Aristotle, far from trying to create a model or ideal *ut supra* when he describes the elderly, he is doing something completely different; Tossi reminds us what it is. He points out that the book in which Aristotle's "portrait" of the elderly is found is a treatise on rhetoric: a teaching book for the would-be orator, neither more nor less. (We can add that the complete title of *Rhetoric, The Technique of Oratory,* makes this quite clear.) You have to imagine that Aristotle is addressing a young neophyte, telling him how he might best succeed in the profession of orator, which (in the ancient world) was lawyer, journalist, publicity-maker, "PR man," politician and a host of other things all rolled up into one. The orator's job was to persuade people to believe whatever he was being paid to promote (or denigrate.) In order to succeed, just like our publicity men and mind-benders of today, he had to be able to get inside the mentality of his hearers and be able to understand how they might think and react. Tossi says: "To alert the orator to the "negative" attitude in his audience, Aristotle has no choice but to emphasise the dangerous elements, the psychological under-currents which might prejudice a favourable response to his discourse." In other words, far from painting a "realistic" or even an optimistic picture of the elderly, Aristotle is deliberately stating the worst that might be said of the worst of them—in fact, of the most resistant to the skills of the orator. He as good as says as much in the words at the end of *Rhetoric* 2.13 following his disastrous picture of old age: "Wherefore, since all men are willing to listen to speeches which harmonise with their own character and to speakers who resemble them [or "speeches which resemble (or reflect) it (their character")] it is easy to see what language we must employ so that both ourselves and our speeches may appear to be of such and such a character" (Aristotle, *Rhetoric* 1390a 17–21, trans. J.F. Freese). This is probably the nearest thing there is to be found in ancient literature to preaching the advantages of what today we would call "market research," that is, suiting the message to the mentality of the audience. No doubt, a very similar lesson is given to today's would-be masters of business administration in their customer-manipulation courses.

It is worth noting in passing Tossi's suspicion that Aristotle might have succeeded to such a degree in his caricature of the aged (for a caricature it most surely is) that he unwittingly gave rise to a recurrent literary type, the "cross old man" found in Theophrastus and the New Comedy. If he is correct in this, then neither can those characters (any more than Aristotle's caricature) be entered as evidence of Greek attitudes to the elderly. They, too, are mere "cardboard cutouts" so to speak, created to serve another's purpose (there, to entertain).

Tossi next makes this telling point: he observes that, by the very hyperbole with which he states his case to the young orator, Aristotle places himself in a paradoxical situation. Of this he could not have been unaware: further indication that (for didactic purposes) he has assumed an attitude with which his real self does not identify. The paradox is this: by downgrading experience to a succession of knocks and bruises that merely brutalize and deform the aging person, he depreciates the very thing (experience) that, elsewhere, he exalts very highly and holds in great esteem. Thus Tossi: "In *Nichomachean Ethics* 6.1142a 10–15 (for example) he remarks that a youth can be competent in geometry and mathematics, but cannot be wise without a good dose of experience." To say that experience makes a man *wise* is a very different thing from saying it renders him bitter, timid, indecisive, and all those other things itemized in the instruction to the young orator.

The heart of Tossi's criticism comes, however, when, following Dryoff, he relates what is said to the young orator to the wider pattern of Aristotle's psychoethical theory. This, briefly comprehended under the heading of "the golden (or just) mean" (*aurea mediocritas*) turns upon the conviction that every good thing is a mean; a judicious balance or centre-point between two extremes. The example most often given is that of bravery, which Aristotle saw as a "mean" between cowardice on the one hand (a deficiency of courage) and foolhardiness on the other (an excess of courage). This theory is fully worked out as far as morality is concerned: virtue is in every case a "mean" between a deficiency and an excess of some quality. The virtuous man is the one who has learnt to strike the balance correctly in every situation. But this "Aristotelian" principle was applied far more widely than to merely ethical questions. It gained a firm foot-hold in medical theory; all disease came to be seen as a deficiency or excess of one of the four "humours" or as an improper balance between (say) wet and dry, and so forth. Well into the last century, patients were routinely deprived of blood in an attempt to lower the heat of the body, in which, alas, the process was all too often extremely successful. The *theory* was that the removal of some blood would restore the right balance between two extremes of hot and cold. One encounters the notion that excellence is a "golden mean" between two poles throughout the length and breadth of western literature, for instance: "Chantez; l'ardent refrain flamboie; / Jurez même, noble ou vilain! Le chant est un verre de joie / dont le juron est le trop plein" (Hugo 249).

Turning back now to Aristotle's two "caricatures," that is, of youth and old age respectively, it becomes clear that he is setting the stage for what comes after. First, he shows two extremes that, on closer examination, are easily seen as an excess (youth) and a deficiency (old age) of various qualities: hope, trust, optimism, and so forth. In every case, the youth has too much of them, the oldster too little (or none at all). But, Aristotle argues, between all pairs of extremes there is a "golden mean." He has already warned the reader: "The 'ages' are [three]: youth, maturity and old age" (xxx). This is curious. Some

220

Greeks believed there were many more "ages of man"; ten, even twelve, are known; seven was more common, but in Aristotle's time (and for long after) the prevailing belief was that there were *four* ages of man, roughly corresponding to the four seasons (starting with spring.) But Aristotle opts for three precisely because it fits his "ternary" view of things: the best is always *tertium quid*, a third factor, like the point of balance between the two extremities of a beam. "This [three-age system] provides for a 'just mean' between two negative poles" (youth and old age), Tossi remarks, "one of deficiency, the other of excess," a mean that he calls a "robust maturity"—"a description of which and of its precise limits will be provided in 1390 a28–b12 [2.14]—on either side of which stand respectively old age and youth."

This is how Aristotle works it out:

> It is evident that the character of those in the prime of life [*hoi akmazontes*— those who are at their *acmê* or zenith] will be the mean of that of the other two, if the excess in each case be removed. At this age, men are neither over-confident, which would show rashness, nor too fearful, but preserving a right attitude in regard to both, neither trusting nor distrusting all, but judging rather in accordance with actual facts. Their rule of conduct is neither the noble nor the useful alone, but both at once. They are neither parsimonious nor prodigal, but preserve the due mean. It is the same in regard to passion and desire. Their self-control is combined with courage and their courage with self-control, whereas in the young and the old these qualities are found separately; for the young are courageous without self-control, the old are self-controlled but cowardly. Speaking generally, all the advantages which youth and old age possess separately, those in the prime of life possess combined; and all cases of excess or defect in the other two are replaced by moderation and fitness. The body is most fully developed from thirty to thirty-five years of age, the mind at about forty-nine. (Aristotle, *Rhetoric* 2.14, 1390 a 28–b 12, translated by J.H. Freese)

Straight away it begins to look as though Aristotle has even led himself somewhat astray when he speaks of "all the advantages of [. . .] old age." From the reading of *Rhetoric* 2.13, it would be very hard indeed to imagine what (if there are any) such advantages might be, which is as clear an indication as one could wish for that the picture in 2.13 is purely imaginary, a mere caricature detached from reality; a teaching model useful perhaps for neophyte orators, but of little use for anything else. And, when he seems to relent a little at the end of 2.14 (where he concedes that the mind attains maturity only at about age forty-nine, seven times seven), not only is he falling in line with traditional Greek "heptadic" thinking about aging, but he actually seems to be echoing the belief of that very Plato whom some would hold up as the antithesis of Aristotle as far as the aged are concerned: advancing years bring intellectual maturity. We are reminded of a question posed by the same philosopher else-where: "Why have we more sense when we grow older?" (Aristotle, *Problems*

30.5, 955b 22). This sounds like a *very* different Aristotle from the one who so stigmatized the same *presbyteroi* in *Rhetoric* 2.13. But maybe there is an explanation.

To be sure, all teachers exaggerate somewhat in order to make a point sufficiently clear; clearly, Aristotle has exaggerated the foibles of the elderly in order to impress his student-orator. Thus, Tossi:

> Seeing that the orator cannot at the beginning of his discourse openly take into account the actual psychological shades of each of his hearers, he has to base himself on an abstract generalisation, inevitably a pessimistic one by virtue of the ambient circumstances. So Aristotle presents the orator with two pictures: an audience of old people and one of young. They are opposites, both far removed from that balance of common sense which ought to characterise a mature audience. The three-fold Aristotelian criterion applied *sic et simpliciter* to the ages of life cannot fail to be excessively schematic and, as such, merciless in its approach to old people as they really are. Nevertheless, it represents a valid attempt to furnish the orator with the necessary parameters for his oratory.

It may be a foolhardy (rather than a courageous) undertaking to criticize him whom generations knew as *the* Philosopher and whom Dante even calls *lo maestro di nostra vita* (4.23.8), but might it not be that, on this one occasion, Aristotle has allowed his commitment to the doctrine of the mean as a point between two opposites to go a little too far? It is one thing to say that a coward and a fool have too little and too much courage respectively; but these are matters over which one has at least a little control. One can school oneself to be less impulsive or timid. In another dimension, one can even exert industry or generosity to correct a defect or an excess of wealth. Generations of doctors believed measures could be taken to restore a right balance between the "humours" in the body, and so forth. The point is that in most of the situations in which Aristotle asserts a mean, choices are possible and effective measures can be taken (at least to a certain extent) to correct an apprehended imbalance. But who, by taking thought, can add one day to his age or subtract anything from it? The march of time is inexorable, therefore its ravages can certainly have no moral dimension, any more than can have the transit of the seasons or the setting of the sun. So, while we may applaud the judicious balance of "robust maturity" and even, in many cases, admit the undesirable nature of the extremes between which it is the mean, we have to bear in mind that no choices are involved. "Time with its ever rolling stream bears all her sons away," whether they want it or not. Hence, we simply cannot accept the attachment of blame to persons whose only "crime" is to be too few or too many years of age. To be sure, aging has many dimensions; few people were more aware of it than the Greeks. But a moral dimension it does not have, and, if Aristotle were trying to inject one, then in this respect he had no takers, no philosopher to follow in his train. But, then, it is hard to believe that he was trying to do that. The object of his exercise was to instruct a neophyte orator, that was all; and to do so he made a caricature. The sad thing is that the caricature has so often been taken for a model of universal Greek attitudes to the elderly. Tossi has done us all a great service in demonstrating conclusively that this should never have happened. In a word, he has cleared the stage of some old débris so that reconstruction can begin. I think that in due course it will emerge that, with the rest of his own article and most of the others in this collection, reconstruction is already well on the way.

WORKS CITED

Athanasius. *Vita Antonii*. Ed. and trans. G.J.M. Bartelink. *Athanase d'Alexandrie, Vie d'Antoine*. Paris 1994, *Sources Chrétiennes* 400.

Beauvoir, Simone de. *La Vieillesse*. Paris: Gallimard, 1970.

Charles, D.C. "Literary Old Age: A Browse through History." *Educational Gerontology* 2 (1977): 237–57

Dante Alighierie, *Il Convivio*. Ed. G. Busnelli and G. Vandelli, 2 vols. Florence: Felice Le Monnier, 1964.

Dryoff, A. *Der Peripatos über das Greisenalter*. Paderborn: n.p., 1939.

Haynes, M.F. "The Supposedly Golden Age for the Aged in Ancient Greece." *The Gerontologist* (1962): 193–98.

Hugo, Victor. "Hilaritas." *Les Chansons des rues et des bois*.

Mattioli, Umberto. *SENECTUS: La vecchiaia nel mondo classico*. 2 vols. Bologna: Pàtron Editore, 1995.

Minois, Georges. *Histoire de la Vieillesse en Occident de l'Antiquité à la Renaissance*. Paris: 1987.

Pisi, Giordano. "La Medicina Greca Antiqua." *SENECTUS: La vecchiaia nel mondo classico*. Ed. Umberto Mattioli. Bologna: Pàtron Editore, 1995. 1.44–87.

Tossi, Renzo. "Il pensiero greco dai Presocratici al Peripato." *SENECTUS: La vecchiaia nel mondo classico*. Ed. Umberto Mattioli. Bologna: Pàtron Editore, 1995. 193–229.

Wortley, John. "Aging and the Desert Fathers: The Process Reversed." *Aging and the Aged in Medieval Europe*. Ed. Michael Sheehan. Toronto: Pontifical Institute for Medieval Studies, 1990. 63–74.

_____ . "Aging and the Aged in Aesopic Fables." *International Journal of Aging and Human Development*.

_____ . "His Acts Being Seven Ages": Greek and Roman Theories of Aging by Sevens." *Journal of Aging and Identity* 2.2 (June 1997): 101–16.

_____ . "Aging and the Aged in *The Greek Anthology*." *International Journal of Aging and Human Development* (1998)

_____ . "Four-Age Systems of Human Development." *Journal of Aging and Identity* 3.4 (1998): 213–30.

Concerning Madrigals

Lawrence Ritchey

In his informative and entertaining treatise, *A Plaine and Easie Introduction to Practicall Musicke*, Thomas Morley has this to say of the madrigal:

> The light music hath been of late more deeply dived into so that there is no vanity which in it hath not been followed to the full; but the best kind of it is termed Madrigal, a word for the etymology of which I can give no reason; yet use showeth that it is a kind of music made upon songs and sonnets such as Petrarch and many poets of our time have excelled in. [. . .] As for the music, it is, next unto the Motet, the most artificial and, to men of understanding, most delightful. If therefore you will compose in this kind you must possess yourself with an amorous humour (for in no composition shall you prove admirable except you put on and possess yourself wholly with that vein wherein you compose), so that you must in your music be wavering like the wind, sometime wanton, sometime drooping, sometime grave and staid, otherwhile effeminate [. . .] the more variety you show the better shall you please. (294)

One of the great triumphs of the Italianate arts in the cinquecento, the madrigal was conceived by Florentine musicians (the first printed volume of *Madrigali* appeared in Florence in 1530) and brought to full flower by composers in Venice and Rome, most notably Cipriano de Rore and Luca Marenzio. Printers scrambled to meet the public's seemingly insatiable demand for this new music, and a steady stream of madrigal sets and collections spread throughout Italy and the continent. In England, the Elizabethan taste for Italian culture ensured a busy importation of madrigals—at first, in manuscript—and in the waning years of Elizabeth's reign, a number of these were "Englished" by Elizabethan poets. Though continental composers for the most part closely imitated the Italian style, the English madrigalists took the road less travelled and cultivated a distinct and uniquely English style and voice for their madrigals. The redoubtable

Faith, Reason, and Economics: Essays in Honour of Anthony Waterman. Ed. Derek Hum. Winnipeg: St. John's College Press, 2003.

Thomas Morley showed the way: his *Madrigalles to foure Voyces, the first Booke* appeared in 1594 and marks the first time that the title "madrigal" graced a printed music written in England by an Englishman to English words.

"There be another sort of lovers of music who do either learn the science as aforesaid, or to play and sound on musical instruments, or else to sing pricksong, for that they would therewith either set forth God's glory in the Church, or else use it for the same purpose in private houses, or else for their own recreation" (Osborn 205). Madrigals, whether of Italian or English crafting, are by design a chamber music intended for the entertainment of the singers themselves. They were sung "in private houses" by amateurs, with but one voice to a part. These intimate and informal musical evenings were not the sole preserve of noble households (where amateurs could rely on the supportive benefit of professional musical establishments and visiting minstrels) but were a feature of Elizabethan middle-class culture as well, where such family singing after dinner was a popular and widely practised pastime. In the words of his (imaginary) student, Philomathes, Morley refers to the practice: "But supper being ended and music books (according to the custom) being brought to the table, the mistress of the house presented me with a part earnestly requesting me to sing; but when, after many excuses, I protested unfeignedly that I could not, every one began to wonder; yea, some whispered to others demanding how I was brought up" (9). Though other types of vocal music (ballads and catches) were sung on these occasions, the madrigal was the clear favourite well into the Jacobean period.

The immense popularity of the English madrigal was due in no small part to the Elizabethans' heightened awareness of the vitality of their language, which they celebrated in both the theatre and the Church. The great William Byrd, Morley's teacher, noted on the title page of his *Psalms, Songs, and Sonnets* (1611) that vocal music should be "framed to the life of the words." Elizabethan musicians were literary and Elizabethan poets were musical. Thomas Campion, by profession a medical doctor, was both a celebrated poet and a respected composer. The development of the English madrigal demonstrates this close association and cross-fertilization of poetry and music. Word painting becomes ever more vivid, aided by a vocabulary of evocative melodic figures and a fuller exploitation of chromaticism within an unequivocally tonal harmony; musical rhythms respond sensitively to the stride of the poetic feet; and imitative counterpoint evokes the Elizabethans' love of metaphoric play, or "conceits." Above all, the English madrigalists sought to express the mood of the lyric as fully as was possible within the musical craft.

WORKS CITED

Morley, Thomas. *A Plaine and Easie Introduction to Practicall Musicke*. 1597. Ed. R.A. Harman. London: J.M. Dent and Sons, 1952.

Osborn, J.M., ed. *The Autobiography of Thomas Whythorne*. c. 1576. London: Oxford University Press, 1962.

There Is A Garden

Words: Thomas Campion (1567 - 1620)

Music: Lawrence Ritchey (Spring, 2002)

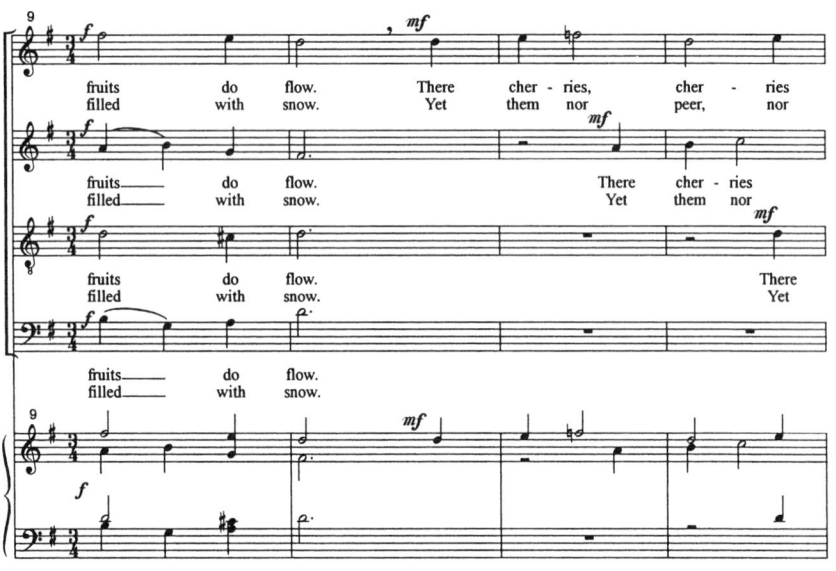

cher - ry, cher - ry - ripe them - selves do cry.

cher - ry, cher - ry - ripe them - selves do cry.

cher - ry, cher - ry - ripe____ them - selves do cry.

cher - ry, cher - ry - ripe them - selves do cry.

Her eyes like an - gels watch them still; her brows like bend - ed bows do

Her eyes like an - gels watch them still; her brows____ like bend - ed bows____ do

Her eyes like an - gels watch them still; her brows____ like bend - ed bows do

Her eyes like an - gels watch them still; her brows like bend - ed bows do

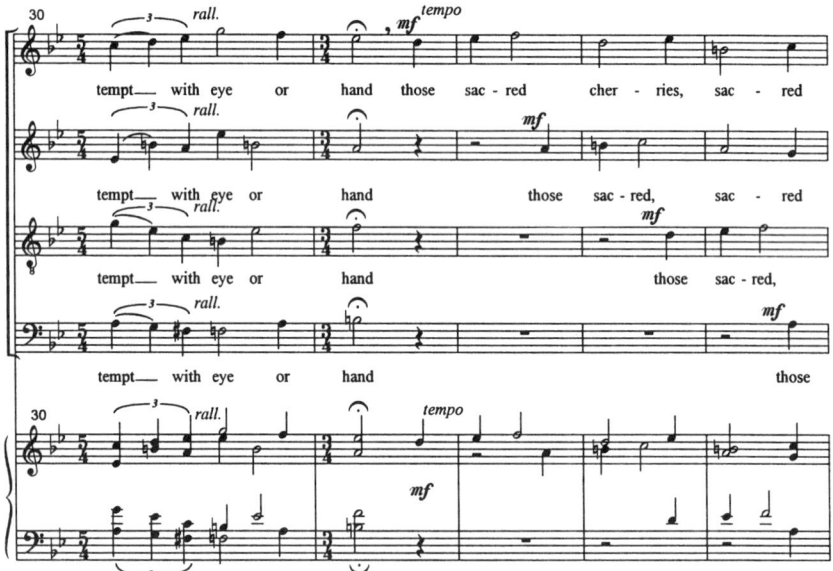

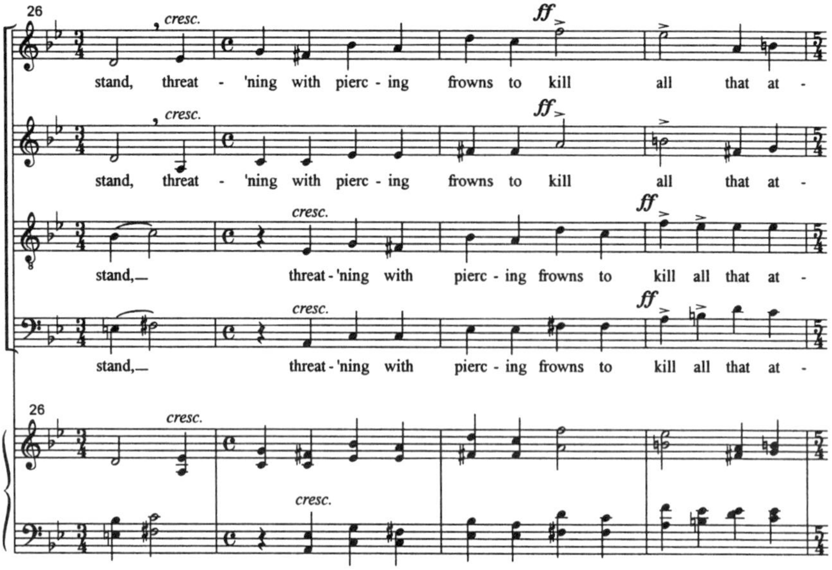
26
cresc.
ff
stand, threat - 'ning with pierc - ing frowns to kill all that at -
stand, threat - 'ning with pierc - ing frowns to kill all that at -
stand,— threat - 'ning with pierc - ing frowns to kill all that at -
stand,— threat - 'ning with pierc - ing frowns to kill all that at -

30
rall.
tempo
mf
tempt— with eye or hand those sac - red cher - ries, sac - red
tempt— with eye or hand those sac - red, sac - red
tempt— with eye or hand those sac - red,
tempt— with eye or hand those

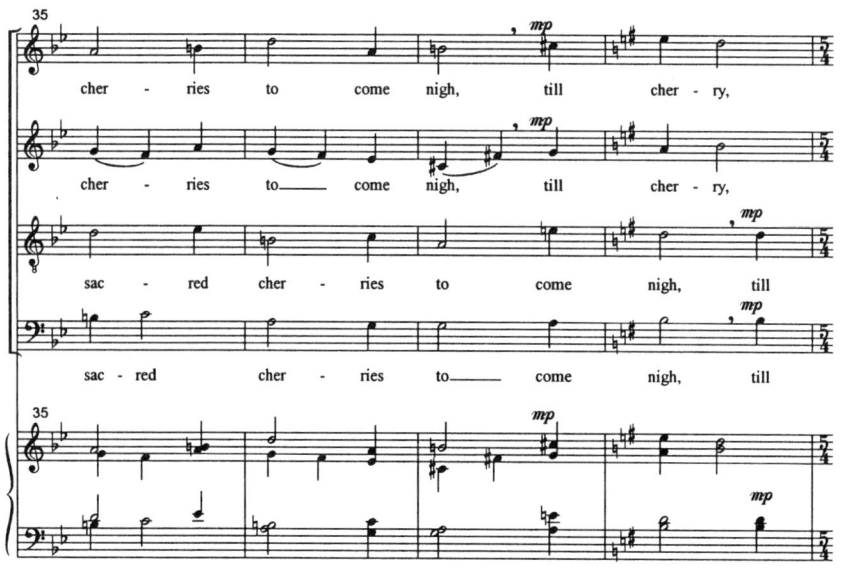

cher - ries to come nigh, till cher - ry,

cher - ries to come nigh, till cher - ry,

sac - red cher - ries to come nigh, till

sac - red cher - ries to come nigh, till

cher - ry, cher - ry - ripe them - selves do cry.

cher - ry, cher - ry - ripe them - selves do cry.

cher - ry, cher - ry - ripe them - selves do cry.

cher - ry, cher - ry - ripe them - selves do cry.

Contributors

GEOFFREY BRENNAN, Professor of Economics, Australian National University

JONATHAN CLARK, Professor of History, University of Kansas

ALEXANDER C. DOW, Professor of the Scottish Economy,
    Glasgow Caledonian University

SHEILA DOW, Professor in Economics, University of Sterling

SHELAGH M. ELTIS, Oxford, England

WALTER ELTIS, Exeter College, Oxford University

ROSS EMMETT, Professor of Economics, Augustana University College

NANCY FOLBRE, Professor of Economics, University of Massachusetts at Amherst

EVELYN FORGET, Professor of Economics, University of Manitoba

KNUD HAAKONSSEN, Professor of Philosophy, Boston University

ALAN HAMLIN, Professor of Economics, University of Southampton

SAMUEL HOLLANDER, Professor of Economics, Ben-Gurion University of the Negev

DEREK HUM, Professor of Economics, University of Manitoba

ALAN HUTTON, Senior Lecturer in Economics, Glasgow Caledonian University

MARY KINNEAR, FRSC, Professor of History, University of Manitoba

MURDITH McLEAN, Associate Professor of Philosophy, University of Manitoba

WARREN J. SAMUELS, Professor of Economics, Michigan State University

LAWRENCE RITCHEY, Associate Professor of Music, and University Organist,
    University of Manitoba

PAUL A. SAMUELSON, Nobel Laureate in Economics, 1970, Massachusetts
    Institute of Technology

JOHN WORTLEY, Professor of History, University of Manitoba